ARTHUR, PRINCE OF WALES

This book is dedicated to Gerard, whose love and encouragement gave me the space to write it.

And to the Royal History Geeks community, whose clicks, likes, shares and comments made it possible.

ARTHUR, PRINCE OF WALES

Henry VIII's Lost Brother

GARETH BENJAMIN STREETER

PEN & SWORD HISTORY

AN IMPRINT OF PEN & SWORD BOOKS LTD.
YORKSHIRE – PHILADELPHIA

First published in Great Britain in 2023 by
PEN AND SWORD HISTORY
An imprint of
Pen & Sword Books Ltd
Yorkshire – Philadelphia

Copyright © Gareth Benjamin Streeter, 2023

ISBN 978 1 39908 462 8

The right of Gareth Benjamin Streeter to be identified as Author of this work has been asserted by him in accordance with the Copyright, Designs and Patents Act 1988.

A CIP catalogue record for this book is available from the British Library.

All rights reserved. No part of this book may be reproduced or transmitted in any form or by any means, electronic or mechanical including photocopying, recording or by any information storage and retrieval system, without permission from the Publisher in writing.

Typeset in Times New Roman 10/13.5 by
SJmagic DESIGN SERVICES, India.
Printed and bound in the UK by CPI Group (UK) Ltd.

Pen & Sword Books Limited incorporates the imprints of Atlas, Archaeology, Aviation, Discovery, Family History, Fiction, History, Maritime, Military, Military Classics, Politics, Select, Transport, True Crime, Air World, Frontline Publishing, Leo Cooper, Remember When, Seaforth Publishing, The Praetorian Press, Wharncliffe Local History, Wharncliffe Transport, Wharncliffe True Crime and White Owl.

For a complete list of Pen & Sword titles please contact
PEN & SWORD BOOKS LIMITED
George House, Units 12 & 13, Beevor Street, Off Pontefract Road,
Barnsley, South Yorkshire, S71 1HN, England
E-mail: enquiries@pen-and-sword.co.uk
Website: www.pen-and-sword.co.uk

Or
PEN AND SWORD BOOKS
1950 Lawrence Rd, Havertown, PA 19083, USA
E-mail: Uspen-and-sword@casematepublishers.com
Website: www.penandswordbooks.com

Contents

Introduction		vi
Family tree: House of Lancaster		x
Family tree: House of York		xi
Family tree: Katherine of Aragon's descent from Edward III		xii
Chapter 1	Out of Avalon	1
Chapter 2	The Once and Future King	14
Chapter 3	A Christian Prince	21
Chapter 4	Diseased Minds	33
Chapter 5	The King's Most Dear Son	48
Chapter 6	The Prince of Wales	60
Chapter 7	The Maintenance of His State	68
Chapter 8	The Marcher Lord	75
Chapter 9	So Great the Abundance	85
Chapter 10	A Rose Between Thorns	94
Chapter 11	The Spanish Princess	105
Chapter 12	Secure in His Kingdom	115
Chapter 13	The Condition of Wedlock	125
Chapter 14	Portrait of a Prince	134
Chapter 15	A Night in Spain	145
Chapter 16	Righteous Order and Wisdom	154
Chapter 17	Le Morte d'Arthur	162
Chapter 18	King Arthur	172
Epilogue: The Shadow of a Prince		183
Notes		186
Selected Bibliography		195
Index		198

Introduction

The cathedral church of St Paul's had been adorned with beautiful tapestries and covered with precious jewels. At its centre stood two nervous young people, dressed in silk garments, and perched on a raised stage. The King of England was about to marry his son and heir to a daughter of the most powerful monarchs in Europe. For one fleeting moment, Henry Tudor may have finally felt safe on his throne.

St Paul's was the most public wedding venue that the early sixteenth century had to offer. The cathedral had been packed full of the nobility and gentry. Outside, the crowds had been encouraged to gather. After the solemnities were complete, the new bride and groom would emerge from the church and show themselves to the people. The Tudors, much like today's house of Windsor, knew that royalty must be seen to be believed. This was the greatest moment of the family's triumph. Everyone must be compelled to witness it.

Just as the ceremony reached its peak and Arthur, Prince of Wales, was solemnised to the Infanta Katherine of Aragon, the sounds of an old woman weeping filled the cathedral.

Margaret Beaufort, mother of the king and grandmother to the bridegroom, was one of the most seasoned survivors of the dynastic conflict known as the Wars of the Roses. She knew only too well how quickly fortune's wheel could spin. Defeat could easily follow triumph. Even when at the centre of great events, her thoughts of happiness were eclipsed by a quagmire of fear. Her family had risen higher than she could ever have imagined. How long would it be before destiny humbled them?

Margaret's weeping had become a common feature of great Tudor occasions. Happily, for her son, she was a better worrier than she was a prophet. While Henry VII had endured more than his share of challenges, he had always emerged victorious. Against all the odds, he had defeated the last Plantagenet king in battle. Despite the challenges of two well-resourced pretenders, he had kept hold of his throne. Though rebels had risen, they had quickly been defeated. The Tudor dynasty might have been an unlikely one. But they were proving to be a lucky one.

But, tragically for the Tudors, their matriarch's sense of foreboding was this time justified. Within five months of his triumphant marriage, Arthur Tudor was dead. It was a personal tragedy and a dynastic crisis. Margaret must have been the first to notice that her own son never truly recovered.

Introduction

Too often, the death of Arthur is where the Tudor story begins. Given our centuries-old fascination with the marital antics of Henry VIII, Arthur is reduced to little more than a footnote in his younger brother's origin story. The forgotten elder brother, whose untimely death paved the way for the reign of Henry VIII and the revolution that would take place across four decades, and six wives, of his reign.

Yet, during his short life, Arthur was at the centre of one of the most dramatic and gripping epochs of England's history. As this account will establish, as he grew older, he asserted himself more in his own affairs and came tantalisingly close to shaping his own destiny. Arthur's story is interesting in its own right, and it deserves to be told.

The sources for Arthur's life are monumentally mixed in terms of the detail they offer. Thanks to thorough accounts of great occasions written by heralds within Henry VII's court, some individual days of Arthur's life can be retold in vivid detail. Yet, there are entire periods of his existence where we know little of his activities and can't even be sure where he was residing.

As a result, this book seeks to provide detail where it exists and intelligent speculation where it does not. The herald accounts of his baptism, creation as Prince of Wales, marriage and funeral have been used to their fullest. Records of payments, grants and wider knowledge about the upbringing of noble boys have been used to paint a picture of what daily life for the prince may have looked like. As negotiations for Arthur's marriage to Katherine of Aragon developed and progressed, letters from the Spanish ambassadors provide another rich source of information on the growing boy and his prolific family. Albeit information that we must treat with a degree of caution.

But none of these alone are sufficient to place Arthur in his context. Despite the fact that he was often geographically far from the centre of political events, his administration along the Welsh border was a crucial part of early Tudor government. He and his household would have been impacted by the major events of his father's reign. As such, I have devoted significant time on the pages that follow to events that Arthur had no direct involvement with but would nevertheless have preoccupied his thoughts, hopes and fears.

This is most obvious in the Perkin Warbeck conspiracy, where for almost a decade, a young pretender threatened to take his father's throne and deprive Arthur of his inheritance. While we have no knowledge of what Arthur made of it, there is huge merit in placing the activities of his upbringing and crucially the negotiations toward his marriage against the backdrop of the grave threat to his future which can rarely have been far from his thoughts.

Many will understand my decision to chronicle the Warbeck episode across three chapters of this book. But they may be more puzzled by my decision to devote an entire chapter to the Simnel campaign, a threat to Arthur's father that the prince was too young to be aware of and was quickly dispelled. However, there is every reason to believe that the outcome of the campaign had a direct impact on the influences that the king would allow to shape Arthur's life. And, as we shall see, there is every reason to believe that Arthur's birth six months before the campaign was part of the reason for his father's success.

Other valuable sources for Arthur's life can be found in the activities of his council which was tasked with governing and policing the principality of Wales and its border with England. In accessing this information, I am in the debt of the masterful Dr Sean Cunningham, who in 2016 released a thematic study of Arthur's life titled *Prince Arthur: the Tudor King who never was*. This excellent work provides rich information about the politics of the Welsh marches and the key figures that helped shape it. While I have used Dr Cunningham's work to inform aspects of my account, I have not attempted to replicate his research into the prince's government. That's partly because the constraints of a project such as this don't truly afford the time and partly because there is little point in repeating work which has already been artfully undertaken. Where I have become aware of any new aspect of Arthur's story because of Dr Cunningham's research, I have ensured he is duly credited.

Another crucial secondary source has been the collection of articles edited by Steven Gunn and Linda Monckton and released as *Arthur Tudor, Prince of Wales: Life, Death and Commemoration*. Anyone interested in Arthur's story should ensure they read both Dr Cunningham's study and Gunn & Monckton's collection.

Over the last thirty years, the explosion of "popular" or "narrative" history has seen the Tudors placed under greater scrutiny than ever before. Many romantic, Victorian portrayals have been deconstructed. Arthur has been no exception. But because, as I have said earlier, the first Tudor prince is usually granted just a few pages in accounts attempting to tackle the reign of his brother, or the trials of his wife, Katherine of Aragon, such deconstructions have run the risk of repeating a series of over-simplifications.

While the Victorians assumed a weak and sickly prince, today's writers prefer a robust, athletic teenager. While previous generations had little interest in the boy's personality, twenty first century historians envisage a serious, studious boy, lonely and isolated from the rest of his family.

As I have delved more into Arthur, exploring his story just for the sake of his story, I found that many of these assumptions must be questioned. To my surprise, I have arrived at a different perspective on Arthur's health to the one I set out with. Yes, Arthur probably wasn't the ever-sickly child of Victorian imagination. Nor was he a perfectly healthy teen who just happened to succumb to an outbreak of the plague.

Introduction

As someone who writes and edits a royal history blog, I am well aware that, for at least some readers, the main questions associated with Arthur are simply this: did the prince ever consummate his marriage to Katherine of Aragon, and was her subsequent marriage to Arthur's brother Henry, valid as a result? The second is beyond the scope of this book. The first is covered in detail. And while I have arrived at a conclusion that must be taken lightly, it is increasingly my view that we can be surer of the answer than many have previously dared to be.

Throughout this project, I have been helped and guided by several more experienced and incredibly kind-hearted historians. I won't name them here, through fear that they could be inadvertently held accountable for any of my mistakes. But I will make a point of thanking them properly.

I am also grateful to the members of the "Arthur, Prince of Wales" Facebook group who have been on this journey with me since the beginning. Members of the group have continually fed back on copy, sense checked my ideas and provided inspiration for the topics to cover. While my name is on the cover, this book is a co-creation. I hope that they each see it as their own.

But my deepest thanks are reserved for my partner Gerard, for providing the space, love, and support for me to research and write this book during an incredibly busy chapter of our lives. Like all partners of Royal History Geeks, Gerard is used to sharing me with the Royals of the fifteenth and sixteenth centuries. But his constant love and support has shown once again that he is the only prince I need.

Gareth Benjamin Streeter
May 2022
Shirley, Croydon

Arthur, Prince of Wales

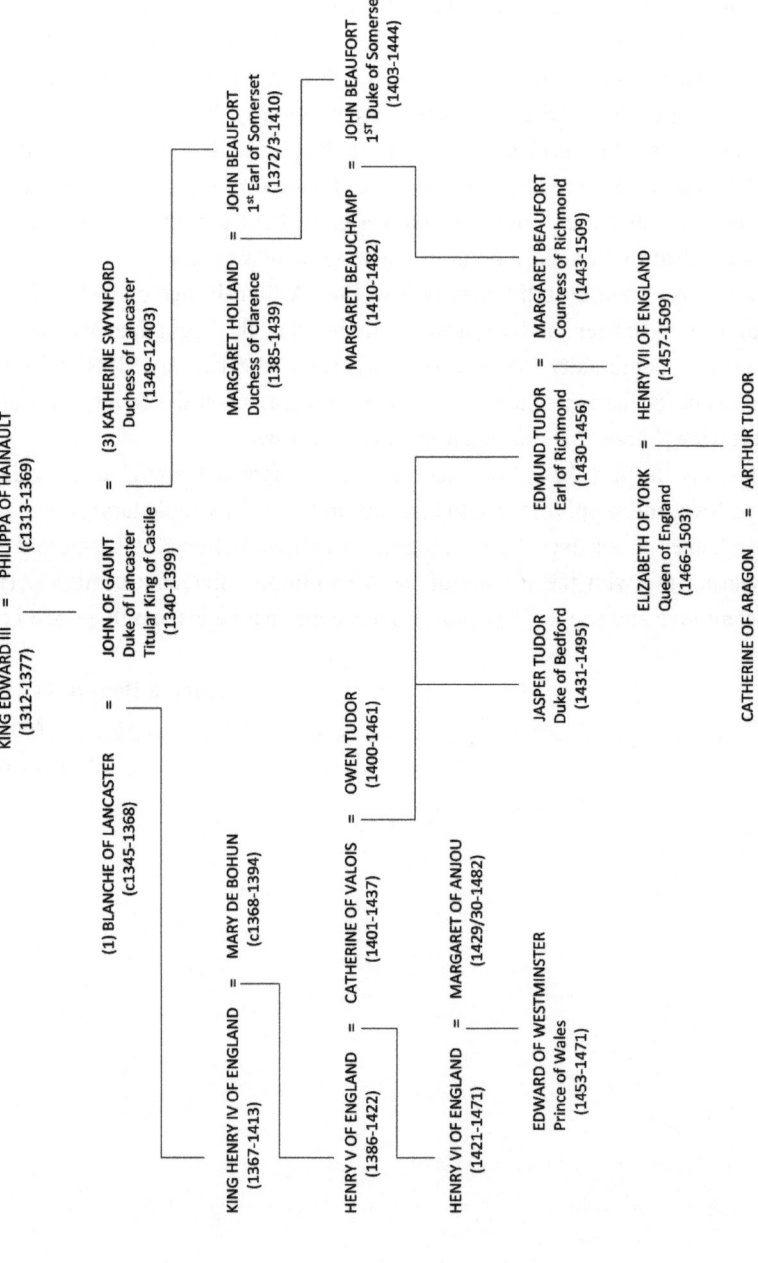

Introduction

ANCESTRY OF ARTHUR TUDOR, PRINCE OF WALES – YORKIST LINE

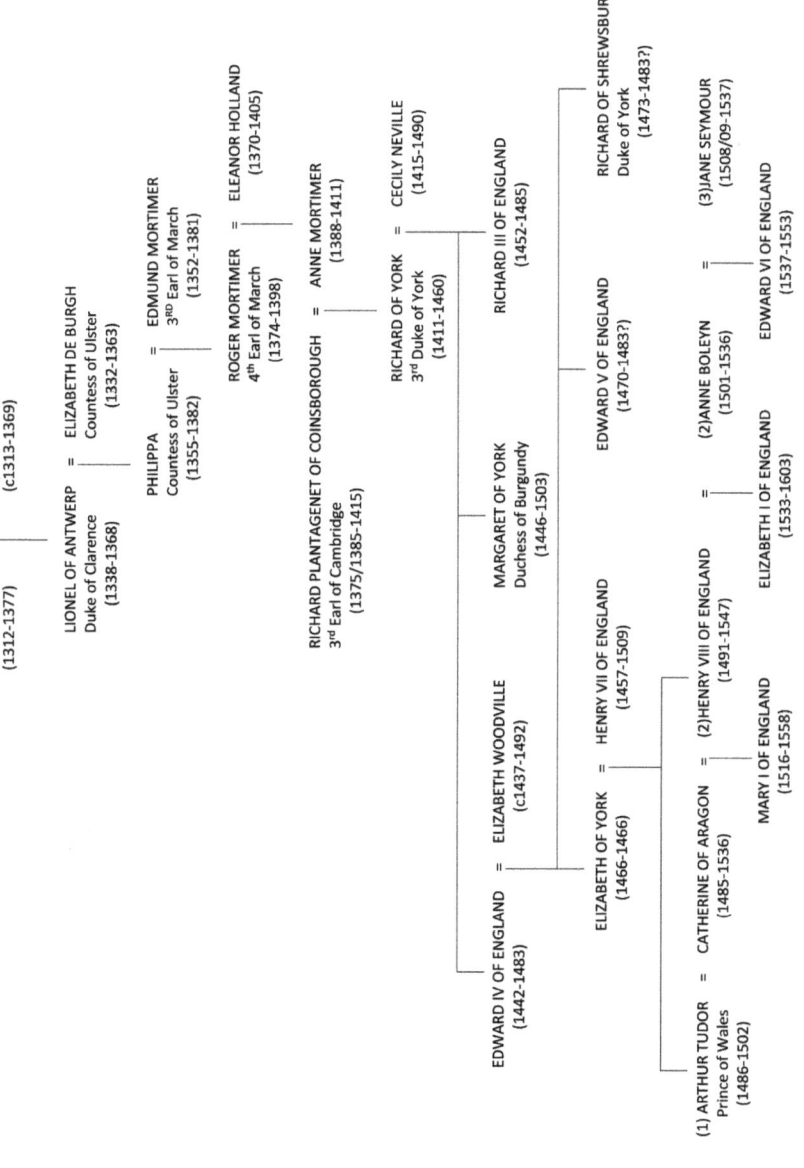

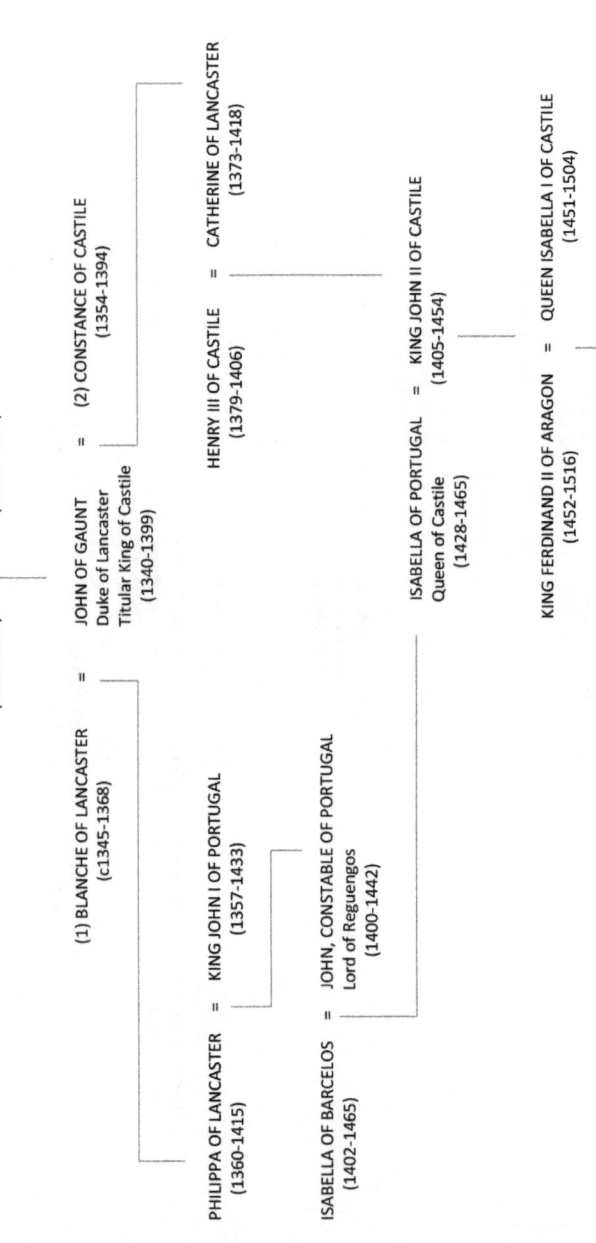

Chapter 1

Out of Avalon

For over three hundred years, and probably more besides, the fabled figure of King Arthur had set the standard for English kings to follow. The victorious son of Uther Pendragon was, in the words of Geoffrey of Monmouth, the conqueror that 'no country could resist.' Kings came "of their own free will to promise tribute and to do homage."[1]

Arthur held more than the hopes of heroism. His was a tale of caution. Camelot's king knew what it was to be betrayed and abandoned. He suffered defeat and humiliation. He had even been made a cuckold. Any king that made Arthur his example was one who would never let a crown rest too easily on his head. Defeat could follow even the most glorious of victories.

Toward the end of the fifteenth century, the tales of King Arthur, Camelot and his knights of the round table had acquired a new significance in England. The stories of a king who could triumph over his enemies, only to be betrayed by those nearest to him, found a new poignance in a half century where kings rose and fell with unprecedented pace.

Yet, just as Arthur's tales were flourishing in literature, a new wave of men were seeking to expunge him from the history books. These men fostered a new form of learning, which we today call "renaissance humanism". They were adamant that this treasured king of the Britons was nothing more than a myth.

But there was at least one humanist who disagreed sharply with this reassessment. His name was Henry Tudor, and thanks to his victory on the battlefield in 1485, he had emerged victorious in the dynastic battles which had raged in England for thirty years. To the newly crowned Henry VII, King Arthur was far from a fable. He was family.

The Tudors, like all newly enthroned dynasties, were on a quest for legitimacy. And it was in their Welsh ancestry that they searched for it. They descended, so they claimed and probably believed, 'from the ancient Briton kings' making them the true heirs of Brutus, Cadwaladr and most significantly, Arthur himself.[2] The Tudors were no new dynasty. They were the restorers of the true line of kings. In the wilder moments of Tudor propogandists' imagination this made Henry VII not just *a* legitimate king. He was the *first* legitimate king for over 800 years.

This, of course, was just imagery. Henry's true claim to the throne came from being the tenuous but just-about-credible heir to the house of Lancaster, which had ruled England for sixty years from the turn of the fifteenth century. He had bolstered his claim immeasurably by quickly marrying Elizabeth, the heir to the house of York, which had usurped the Lancastrians in 1461.

But in medieval England, imagery mattered. And when Elizabeth fulfilled her duty quickly, falling pregnant almost as soon as they were married, Henry and his advisors spotted an opportunity to magnify the ancient heritage of the Tudors in the minds of their subjects. The child must be born in Camelot. And, if he be a boy, he would bear the name of the mighty Pendragon. And so, in the dying days of August, the heavily pregnant Elizabeth of York braved the cobbled streets of England and travelled to Winchester, the city where Camelot had once supposedly stood. And it was there, in the Prior's Great Hall in Winchester, that in the early hours of 20th September, the 20-year-old Plantagenet princess gave birth to the first Tudor prince.[3]

The short life of Arthur Tudor had begun.

According to the heralds of Henry VII's court, news of Arthur's birth led to the 'rejoysing of every true Englisshe man'. Ringing bells could be heard from cathedrals and churches across the country. Many fires were made in the streets.[4] The heralds may have exaggerated the spontaneity of such celebrations. But the joy was genuine enough. A king with a son was a stronger ruler, and a stronger ruler was generally a better one.

In Arthur's case, it was more than that. His birth represented a new hope for an era of peace, because Arthur was not just the heir to England. He was the child of two dynasties and the living embodiment of a fragile peace that the two sides of his family had recently forged. And so, it is not possible to understand the context of Arthur's life, and the huge sense of expectation and responsibilities that must have weighed on his shoulders as soon as he was old enough to understand them, without first exploring the thirty years of dynastic conflict that we today call the Wars of the Roses.

*

Today, we regard the Tudor claim to descend from the ancient kings of the Britons as fanciful. Even at the time, it seemed suspect. Nevertheless, the Tudors were an old family and far more than the grubby upstarts that their enemies dismissed them as.

Throughout the thirteenth and fourteenth century, the family played a prominent role in Welsh politics. They were significant landowners in North Wales and would have enjoyed a similar level of seniority in the Welsh hierarchy, to an earl in the English stratosphere. By keeping one eye on shifting power bases in Wales, and another on events in England, they managed to survive the twists and turns of politics and remain in favour with those that could influence their destiny.[5]

However, at the beginning of the fifteenth century, the Tudors made an uncharacteristic miscalculation. They joined their cousin, Owain Glyndwr, in rebellion against the usurping Lancastrian king, Henry IV. Having been roundly defeated, they would never again recover their power and influence in North Wales.[6]

It was left to the next generation to try and salvage the wreckage. With that in mind, Owain ap Maredudd ap Tudur – better known to English history as Owen Tudor – entered royal service. Owen was born in about 1400 and was no doubt determined to rebuild the family's fortunes. None, however, could have predicted the scale of his future success or the unconventional means he used to achieve it.

By the mid-1420s, Owen had entered the household of Katherine of Valois, the dowager queen of England. Katherine was the beautiful daughter of King Charles VI of France. She was the widow of Henry V, the great war-lord King who had bested the French at Agincourt, and mother to the young Henry VI, who had ascended his father's throne at just nine-months old.

Owen did not remain a mere servant for long. How he caught Katherine's eye remains a mystery. One story claimed that he fell into her lap accidentally at a ball. Another, that the queen saw him swimming naked and that her interest was piqued.[7] Either way, the thrust is clear: the match between Katherine and Owen owed far more to passion than judgement.

The clandestine couple were probably secretly married around 1430 and withdrew from the court.[8] Soon after, in Much Hadham Palace, Katherine again gave birth to a son. The child was named Edmund, probably after Katherine's friend and protector Edmund Beaufort, a powerful nobleman and kinsman of the king. Though he would not live to know it, he would one day become Arthur's grandfather.

Katherine and Owen possibly had as many as four other children together, but by far the most significant in the emerging story of the Tudors was Jasper of Hatfield, born probably in 1431. He would play as big a role as anyone in guiding the Tudors to the throne and securing it thereafter. As we shall see, his role would extend across the generations. He would be more of a grandfather to Arthur than his ill-fated brother was ever able to be.

We cannot be sure to what extent, if at all, the young King Henry VI was aware of his mother's second family during the early 1430s. After Katherine's death in 1437, however, they could be hidden no longer. Thankfully for the children of the match, the king, or those close to him, quickly decided to take charge of the youngsters and provider for their up bringing. Edmund and Jasper were placed in the care of Katherine de le Pole, abbess of Barking Abbey.[9] Here at the abbey, the boys would enjoy a stable and protected upbringing, albeit one that probably lacked much sense of adventure.

Katherine was the sister of John de la Pole, the mighty Duke of Suffolk and chief minister to Henry VI. The choice of guardian strongly suggests the duke's involvement and it is likely that the wily politician had quickly spotted an opportunity. As the King's brothers of the half blood, with no claim to the throne themselves, and totally dependent on royal favour, they could be raised to be stalwart supporters of their sibling's rule. And no king of England had ever needed loyal supporters more than the ailing Henry VI.

Edmund and Jasper's brother, Henry VI, was the most unsuited man to ever wear the crown of England. Ascending the throne at just nine months of age, a council of the nobility had ruled over England – and the English territories in France – fairly stably for the first twenty years of his reign. But kingship was an office of inherently personal authority. At some stage, Henry had to take power for himself. When he did, the problems began.

Historians debate the exact nature of Henry's inadequacy. To some he is a saintly figure, simply uninterested in the mundane mechanics of government. For others, he was the probable sufferer of some kind of impairment that prevented him ever exercising his own will and judgement. Then there are those who simply believe he was a particularly weak king at a time when England needed a mighty one. But all agree that his long reign was an unmitigated disaster.

By 1450 the government led by Suffolk had completely collapsed. Defeats in France and disorder at home, caused rebels to take to the streets and the nobility to turn on the one man whom they probably knew full well had been doing his best to hold together an impossible situation. Suffolk was removed from his post and banished from England. As he set sail, he was unceremoniously murdered by a group of pirates.

Following a brief power vacuum, control of the government was grasped by Edmund Beaufort, Duke of Somerset. Despite being widely blamed for recent military failures in France, where he had acted as commander, he was the king's cousin, confidante and probably best placed to try and steady the ship. Most importantly of all, he had the backing of Henry's wife, the young Queen Margaret of Anjou, who by this time was emerging as a prominent political player.

After the disaster of Suffolk's fall, the Lancastrian royal family needed urgent bolstering. It was almost certainly Somerset and the queen who decided that it was time to bring the Tudor brothers in from the cold. In the Parliament of 1452, both brothers were brought forward and presented as members of the Royal family. Edmund was declared Earl of Richmond, a title with excellent royal pedigree. As befitting the role he was being lined up to play protecting the king's rule in Wales, Jasper was created Earl of Pembroke. Both men were given grants of land and money to help bolster their new status, but as so often in the making of "new men", marriage to a wealthy heiress would be critical.

Before long, Edmund was betrothed to Lady Margaret Beaufort, niece of the Duke of Somerset and a descendant of Edward III. Prior to a birth of a son to the king and queen in 1453, some had even speculated that she was the Lancastrian heir to the throne. Most pertinently, as the sole legitimate child of her deceased father, she was the wealthiest heiress in England.

Edmund knew that to enjoy a life interest in Margaret's estates, he must father a child by her, even if that child were only short lived. In a move that may have shocked contemporaries, he consummated his marriage to the heiress as soon as she was of the minimal canonical age and Margaret fell pregnant when she was just 12 years old. Edmund would never live to see his child born, as he perished of the plague in the November of 1456. Margaret fled to Pembroke Castle and the protection of her brother-in-law. And it was at Pembroke that Henry Tudor, the future Henry VII was born on 28 January 1457. His 13-year-old mother seems to have braved a traumatic birth to bring her son safely into the world. It would be this combination of his mother's bravery and his uncle's protection that would keep Arthur's father safe for the rest of his life. It would ultimately allow him to claim the crown of England.

Henry Tudor was born into an England plagued by political instability. While his uncle could act as a protector and safeguard his inheritance, his proximity to the Lancastrian royal family made him highly vulnerable to the fallout from power struggles over control of the government that dominated the realm throughout the 1450s.

Richard, Duke of York, was one of the richest men in England. Like many in the upper nobility he could trace his descent to Edward III and it could even be argued that he had a better hereditary claim to the throne than the king himself. And this made him a dangerous man.

By the time of Henry Tudor's birth in 1457, York was well established as the leading opponent of Lancastrian government. Following the chaos surrounding the collapse of Suffolk's administration in 1449 and 1450, York returned to London to assume control of affairs. Either by accident or design, he had been outside the realm for much of the 1440s, fulfilling his ancestral role as governor of Ireland. This gave him plausible deniability over the disasters of the proceeding years. York, as both a Plantagenet prince and a man who enjoyed much support among the influential gentry class, naturally saw himself as the man best placed to take the reins. There was just one problem. Somerset had beaten him to the punch.

By the time York arrived in London, Somerset had already taken control of affairs. Like Suffolk before him, Somerset created a puppet-style kingship, around the pliable Henry VI. This allowed the household to direct affairs in the name of the king and, even after the disastrous events of recent years, the name of the king could not easily be challenged.

York moved quickly to establish a rival power base among the commons, the representatives of the gentry class. But with the queen throwing her backing emphatically behind Somerset, there was little his rival could do. Why York, unlike the rest of the nobility, was not prepared to accept this puppet kingship, with the strings being pulled by Somerset and the queen, is not entirely clear. It is possible that the two dukes had a pre-existing rivalry. But it is more likely that he simply sensed an opportunity for power that was too big to resist.

In 1453, opportunity finally came York's way. Following a gruelling regime of travel at the command of Somerset, the king fell into a catatonic state. Somerset's style of government had depended on being able to act in the king's name. With the king unable to communicate, this was clearly impossible. A formal protectorate was proposed and York – as the adult nearest inline to the throne – was selected for the role. Somerset was imprisoned and the balance of power had decisively shifted. As with Somerset's method of government, York's approach did bear some fruit. But it was to be short lived. The king recovered his wits and recognised the son that had been born to Queen Margaret during his illness as his own. Somerset, almost certainly at the queen's instigation, was released and the two regained control of government. York was dismissed. But as all onlookers realised, he was unlikely to go quietly.

Tensions between York and the Lancastrian party, led by Somerset and the queen, were now at fever pitch. It wasn't long before the two sides came to blows. The first armed conflict took place in St Albans in 1455 and an underprepared Lancastrian force were swiftly defeated. Somerset was slain, leaving the queen as the primary Lancastrian leader. For the next few years, reconciliations followed conflicts. Both York and Lancastrian forces enjoyed victories and faced defeats, but at no stage was York ever able to wrestle control of government away from the queen. It was she who retained access to the King.

Eventually, York decided that if he couldn't become the power behind the throne, he had little option but to wear the crown himself. Following a glorious victory over the queen's army at Northampton, York took the king prisoner. Then, at the October Parliament of that year, he made his first open bid for the throne. York, a descendant of Edward III's second surviving son but in the female line, had at least as good a claim to the throne as Henry VI. But to the minds of most of the lords gathered, that was hardly the point. Henry VI was an anointed king and one who had reigned for almost forty years. Anointed kings, they believed, should be replaced sparingly.

A compromise was brokered. Henry VI should be allowed to remain on the throne, but York should succeed him. Given that York was six years older than the king, this can hardly have seemed like the ideal settlement. But his reaction was nothing compared to the queen's. Margaret of Anjou was enraged at this attempt to disown her son. She raised an army and put her rivals to the sword at the Battle of Wakefield. York and one of his sons, Edmund of Rutland were killed. In a final act of revenge, their heads were displayed on the city gates of York.

Margaret's victory was to prove short lived. York's claim to be rightful king of England was quickly taken up by his eldest son, Edward, Earl of March. In February 1461, following a victory in battle at Mortimer's Cross, he rode to London and was proclaimed king as Edward IV. There were now two who were King of England by name. Only a confrontation on the battlefield could determine which was king in deed.

In one of the bloodiest battles on English soil, Edward secured a mighty victory at the Battle of Towton. The nobility had remained loyal to the ailing Henry VI. But the gentry, the class of landowners beneath the aristocracy who were individually subordinate but collectively more powerful, had turned out for York. England, they must have reasoned, needed to be stable again. It must finally have been obvious to them that Henry VI was no longer king in anything but name. Their choice was between a French woman who had become savage and blood thirsty or a full-blooded Plantagenet prince who could bring new hope. The house of York had finally won the crown. But it was a crown covered in blood.

Edward IV had obtained the crown when he was just shy of his nineteenth birthday. Despite his young age, it quickly became clear that he had all the qualities to be first-rate ruler. He was what we would today call 'a people person'. Using his charm, skills, and natural authority, he quickly set about reuniting much of England's governing class and restoring order to the royal finances.

The young king's closest advisor was his cousin, Richard Neville, the Earl of Warwick. Warwick was one of the richest noblemen in England and his family had been stalwart supporters of the house of York ever since the late duke had established himself as a figure of opposition in 1450. He was rightly being rewarded for his service and carving out a crucial role for himself in government.

Warwick knew that the house of Lancaster represented an ever-present threat. The country was nervous about their role in the overthrow of Henry VI who, for all his faults had never been a tyrant. The earl knew that at the first sign of trouble, the landed men of the realm could easily transfer their support back to York's enemies.

Margaret of Anjou remained at large and there was always the distinct possibility that she would be able to draw upon the support of her native France. Warwick knew that, by securing a marriage between Edward and a foreign princess, perhaps even a French princess, England could build an international alliance and help keep Lancaster at bay. There was just one snag. In late 1464, Warwick discovered that Edward had secretly married Elizabeth Woodville, a gentry widow from a Lancastrian family. The earl was enraged that the king had thrown away the chance for a foreign alliance by joining himself to an older woman who was not only socially inferior, but already had two sons of her own from a previous marriage.

Nevertheless, Edward fully intended to make Elizabeth his queen. She was publicly recognised as his wife and the two quickly began to arrange marriages between Elizabeth's many siblings and the high nobility of the realm. This left a bitter taste in the mouth of Warwick and other previously loyal Yorkists.

Edward's choice of wife may not have been to everyone's taste. But marriage, whoever it was to, meant the possibility of a son and heir to secure the house of York's hold on the throne. So, it must have been with a hint of disappointment in 1466 that the queen gave birth to a princess. Known to history as Elizabeth of York, Arthur's mother would become the first of ten children born to the couple. Though it would be some time before Edward IV obtained the son he desperately needed.

Despite the disappointment of her gender, Elizabeth was no doubt a delight to her parents on a personal level. According to Bernard André, a contemporary, even as a girl Elizabeth possessed 'Marvellous piety and fear of God, remarkable respect toward her parents, almost incredible love toward her brothers and sisters, and noble and singular affection toward the poor and ministers of Christ were instilled in her from childhood.'[10]

Perhaps it was these Christian values that fortified Elizabeth throughout her turbulent life. She would know more grief than a princess would typically be expected to face. Yet there is no record of her ever-showing anger, bitterness or even a lack of grace. During her time as queen, foreign ambassadors would be quick to criticise her husband and the court. But none ever found fault with Elizabeth.

Arthur's mother was to gain her first taste of disruption when she was just 4 years old. The Earl of Warwick had grown increasingly dissatisfied with Yorkist rule and the role of himself and his family under it. At some stage, he recruited the king's younger brother George Duke of Clarence to his cause. The two of them orchestrated several low-level rebellions in the north before finally taking the king prisoner and attempting to depose him in 1469. Their bid failed and Edward was soon free. Despite the king's preparedness to forgive the rebels, Warwick and Clarence fled to France. There they formed a most unlikely alliance with the woman who had once been their sworn enemy, Margaret of Anjou.

Despite the unlikeliness of the alliance, a deal was quickly struck. Margaret's son would marry Warwick's daughter, Anne Neville, and the new allies would pool their resources to invade England, free Henry VI – who had been Edward's prisoner for a few years – and restore Lancastrian rule. In a demonstration of how fragile the crown had become; they soon achieved their mission, and the once mighty Edward IV was forced to flee the realm.

Elizabeth Woodville, pregnant and alarmed, gathered her children and fled to sanctuary at Westminster Abbey. Elizabeth of York had gone from being the senior princess of England to a penniless exile. It was not the last time that Arthur's mother would know such a dramatic spin of fortune's wheel.

While the return of Lancastrian rule – known as the Readeption of Henry VI – was a sure low point in the life of Arthur's mother, it was quite the opposite for his father's side of the family. The young Henry Tudor, treated with understandable caution by the Yorkist regime, had long been in the care of William Herbert, an ally of Edward IV's. He seems to have been treated well but would later regard this chapter as one of imprisonment despite retaining affection for his captors.

Henry's beloved uncle, Jasper Tudor could now resume his guardianship. Together they travelled to London. Here, for the first time, Henry came face to face with his namesake the king. According to Vergil, Henry VI, 'seeing the boy, held his silence for a while, studying his character, and then said to the nobles who were present, 'This indeed is the one to whom we and our adversaries must yield our power.' Thus, the pious man predicted that someday Henry would obtain the crown."[11]

But fortune's wheel was soon to spin again. Armed with support from his Burgundian relatives, Edward landed in the north. Before long, he encountered Warwick at the Battle of Barnet. Edward was victorious and the earl was slain. Finally, he faced the queen's forces at Tewkesbury and was again victorious. Henry VI's son, Edward Prince of Wales was killed.

While Edward IV had been enduring his brief exile, Elizabeth Woodville had given birth to his son in sanctuary. The house of York finally had a future to look forward to, and the King was determined that nothing would blight their chances again. After the Battle of Tewkesbury, Henry, Duke of Somerset, the last male line descendant of the Lancastrian house of Beaufort was dragged out of sanctuary and executed. Soon after, the ailing, aged and harmless Henry VI was put to death in the tower, almost certainly on Edward's order. The once proud house of Lancaster was defeated.

Or was it? For it would surely not have escaped the newly reinstated king's notice for long that the blood of Lancaster flowed through the veins of another Henry. And one that, were it not for quick action, would easily be within his grasp.

Henry Tudor, now aged 14, had a claim to the throne which was tenuous at best. He was a descendant of John of Gaunt, the mighty Duke of Lancaster from whom all Henry IV, V and VI had derived their royal claim. However, his great-grandfather, John Beaufort had been born Gaunt's bastard. While he had later been legitimated following the marriage of his parents, a question mark had remained around the ability of the Beauforts to ever claim the throne. To make matters more complicated, Henry's slender claim came through his mother. The whole argument of Lancaster's superiority over York was dependent on the fact that royal claims could not travel through the female line.

Nevertheless, those that still longed for a Lancastrian king could no longer afford to be picky. The house of Lancaster, and their Beaufort schism were both extinguished in the male line. And, while Henry VI had only been the boy's uncle in the half blood – and the non-royal half at that – it helped created an affinity between Tudor and the Lancastrian cause. Should men ever again begin to hope for the cause of Lancaster, it would likely be in Henry Tudor that those hopes were invested.

Fearing for his nephew's safety – and mindful of the threat he was under as a stalwart Lancastrian supporter – Jasper Tudor took Henry into his care and set sail for the continent. The original plan seems to have been to head for France. After all, through Katherine of Valois, both Henry and Jasper could claim to be the blood royal of that kingdom too. But, according to Polydore Vergil:

> 'By chance he was carried to Brittany. And there he humbly approached Duke Francis, explained the reason for his arrival, and entrusted himself and his nephew Henry to the duke's protection. The duke cheerfully received the earls with his hospitality, treated them with honour, kindness, and grace, no differently than if they had been his own brothers, and promised on his oath that they would henceforth be free of harm while they stayed with him, and that they were free to come and go wherever they wished.'

Jasper and Henry's time in Brittany would not be quite as free as the duke's promise suggested. They were political exiles and subject to the twists and turns of Brittany's politics and emerging foreign policy. But for now, they were safe. The continued presence of the Tudors, lying outside Edward IV's grasp was an irritant, but it was little more than that. While a few stalwarts remained loyal to the memory of Lancaster, most now made their peace with the Yorkist rule. Margaret Beaufort, technically the most senior Lancastrian in England, married Thomas Stanley, a close ally of Edward IV and began a slow and steady campaign to see her son rehabilitated and returned to England.

Free from the threat of their external enemies, the house of York was now free to turn on themselves. Edward's troublesome brother George – despite being forgiven his earlier transgressions – continued to cause trouble. Eventually, he was sentenced to death in 1478, supposedly being drowned in a butt of Malmsey wine.

Yet, despite these dramatic interruptions, Edward's second reign had stabilised England as much as anyone could reasonably expect a king to do. The nobility was united and the king's youngest brother, Richard, Duke of Gloucester, enjoyed spectacular success as governor of the once-Lancastrian north on behalf of his sibling. Meanwhile, the king's son and heir, another Edward, was growing up well in Ludlow under the watchful eye of his Woodville relatives.

But this fragile peace was not to last long. In 1483, Edward suddenly fell ill. Within a few short weeks he was dead, just a couple of weeks shy of his forty-first birthday. It was an eventuality that few could have predicted. But what came next shocked contemporaries and would lead to the final destruction of the short-lived house of York.

The queen immediately instructed her brother, Anthony, Earl of Rivers, who was with her son in Ludlow, to bring the prince to London. However, on the way, the young Edward V – as he now was – was intercepted by his uncle the Duke of Gloucester. With superior forces, Gloucester quickly apprehended the young king and had his supporters taken into custody. He then travelled to London with Edward and had him placed in the tower.

On the face of it, Gloucester had done little wrong. He had been named as Protector of the Realm in Edward IV's will. While he might have been a little heavy handed in his treatment of the young king's uncle and half-brother who had been bringing him to London, he was doing nothing more than ensuring that the Woodville family – who had a reputation for being grasping – would not deprive him of the important role he had been instructed to carry out. The Tower of London was a royal residence. Ostensibly, there was nothing sinister about his decision to house the young king there.

But the queen knew better. 'Thinking that there was nothing of honesty in this, she took her remaining children and the marquis [her elder son by her first marriage], to save them from the impending danger, and concealed herself in the asylum at Westminster.'[12]

Not to out done, Richard gathered the great lords of the realm and turned on the charm. The Woodville may never have enjoyed great popularity at court, and, unlike his brother Clarence, Richard had always been loyal to Edward IV. He quickly convinced the nobles that the queen had overacted. All he wanted was to ensure his nephew's succession. It was imperative, he argued, that the young King's brother was present at the coronation. He asked some of the Lords to convince the Queen of his sincerity. After great difficulty and only after 'giving many promises' the Queen surrendered her younger son, Richard, Duke of York. Elizabeth clearly did so with great reluctance. Vergil later wrote that 'the innocent lad was wrenched from his mother's embrace.'[13]

Elizabeth had made a fatal mistake. With both boys in his possession, Richard finally showed his true colours. Acting with his ally, the Duke of Buckingham, Richard 'summoned armed men, in fearful and unheard-of numbers, from the north, Wales, and all other parts then subject to them.' On 20 June, Richard was proclaimed King. In order to justify this naked power grab, 'It was set forth, by way of prayer, in an address in a certain roll of parchment, that the sons of king Edward were bastards, on the ground that he had contracted marriage with one lady Eleanor Boteler, before his marriage to queen Elizabeth.'[14]

As far as pretexts go, it was a flimsy one. But despite his devotion to Elizabeth Woodville, Edward IV had been a notorious womaniser. The notion that he may have contracted a secret marriage was just-about credible. After all, wasn't that precisely how his marriage to Elizabeth had begun? Quite what evidence Richard had stumbled across to trigger this revelation has never been clear and, in truth, it hardly mattered. The newly proclaimed Richard III had the military advantage. Supporters of the sons of Edward IV had recently been executed. There were few left alive who were prepared to oppose him.

But those that were had not quite given up hope. Men still loyal to the memory of Edward IV began to meet secretly to plot how to free his sons, the boys best known to us as "the princes in the tower". Before long, these plots became known and, after a short time, Richard would have realised that his attempts to bastardise the boys had not been enough to quell their support. The young Edward V and his brother Richard were drawn deeper into the tower. They would never be seen again. Debate rages to this day as to how the princes met their death, or whether they met their death at all. But given that the princes were high-security prisoners, guarded by men loyal to the king, it is highly likely that the traditional view, that they were killed on the reluctant orders of Richard III, is as close to the truth as we are ever going to get.

Elizabeth Woodville, still languishing in sanctuary, would soon have become aware of the probable fate of her sons. Richard's usurpation had caused her to lose her status as queen dowager and her daughters to be declared bastards. Any hope of restoration must have died with the news that her sons had likely succumbed. But her hopes were about to be revived by the plan of another mother.

Margaret Beaufort, mother of the exiled Henry Tudor, reached out to Elizabeth through their mutual physician, Dr Lewis. Margaret suggested that her son, from the house of Lancaster should marry the queen's daughter Elizabeth of York. The two rival houses would be united, and together they could attract enough support to overthrow Richard and take the crown.

The dowager queen readily agreed. Margaret and her agent, Reginald Bray quickly began attracting others to their cause. In a real coup for the campaign, the powerful Duke of Buckingham who had been one of Richard's early supporters defected to the Tudor cause. He led the rebellion against Richard as Henry Tudor readied a fleet and set sail from Brittany.

But the campaign was a failure. Richard soon put down the rebellion and Buckingham was executed. Henry returned to Brittany without having set foot in England. Nevertheless, the initiative had established him as a rival claimant for the throne. Men now fled to join his exile court. It would surely be just a matter of time before he would strike again. Richard knew this full well and began dishing out punishments on those he suspected of involvement.

One person who could no longer afford to wait for Henry's next attempt was Elizabeth Woodville. Following public promises from the King that he would not harm her or her daughters, she departed sanctuary and seemingly reconciled with Richard. From our vantage point, it is easy to see how Elizabeth had little choice. As we shall see, there is reason to believe that some of Henry's closest supporters never forgave what they considered to be a betrayal of their cause.

Following a change in the political mood music in Brittany, Henry and his exile court fled to France. Here, they obtained the support of the French King for a second attempt at an invasion. In the summer of 1485, they again set sail and this time, Henry landed successfully in his native Wales. They progressed through the principality with little disruption. Eventually, Henry and his moderate force encountered the superior Royal army at Bosworth Field.

The events of the Battle of Bosworth are difficult to recreate. It is far from clear why Richard, with a superior force, was unable to defeat the Tudor army with relative ease. We do know that the Stanley brothers – Thomas, Henry's stepfather, and his brother William – did not enter the fray and remained on the sidelines. Eventually, William Stanley entered the field and declared for Tudor. Richard's forces were routed and the King himself was slain. William Stanley, the saviour of the hour, picked up the fallen, bloody crown and placed it on Henry's head. Henry Tudor had begun life as a fatherless noble and spent much of his youth as a penniless exile. Now he was King of England and founder of the most prolific dynasty in the nation's history.

Chapter 2

The Once and Future King

Henry Tudor was a lucky man. Against all the odds, he had defied Richard III's superior force at Bosworth and in the space of a few hours, transformed himself from obscure exile to King of England. His fiercest support had come from men who had once been loyal to the famed Yorkist King, Edward IV. They had risked life and limb to give Henry his shot at the crown. All they asked in return was that he agree to marry the beautiful and charming 19-year-old princess, Elizabeth of York. It was hardly the bitterest pill to swallow.

Elizabeth of York would have been an attractive choice to any King, regardless of the circumstances. Years later, a Spanish ambassador, who was sent to England to find fault with the Royal family, could find nothing to criticise in Elizabeth, whom he described as "a very noble woman and much beloved."[1] Across all the accounts of her life, her beauty, bounty, and graciousness form an undisputed legacy.

Yet, despite this catalogue of qualities, there may have been fears in the earliest months of the new reign that Henry himself was having his doubts. As he prepared for his coronation on 30th October, the role of Queen consort had to be written out of the ceremony. Henry was to be crowned alone. Then, the newly enthroned King quickly summoned a Parliament where it was confirmed in law that the throne belonged to him and his descendants. The law makers may have believed that Henry's rule was dependent on a future marriage, but the law itself now said otherwise.

Whatever fears did abound however, were shortly to be eased. On 10 December, the Commons dispatched their speaker, to beseech the king to: 'take to himself that illustrious lady Elizabeth, daughter of King Edward IV, as his wife and consort; whereby, by God's grace, many hope to see the propagation of offspring from the stock of kings to comfort the whole realm'.[2] Henry quickly obliged and, 'at last, upon the eighteenth of January was solemnised the so long expected and so much desired marriage between the King and the Lady Elizabeth.'[3]

Much has been made of this six-month delay between Henry's victory at Bosworth and his marriage to the Yorkist heiress. Had he really been considering trying to go it alone? But whatever else the Tudor King was, his history had made him a pragmatist. He knew full well that holding his crown would be a tall order, whatever the circumstances. Without his marriage to Elizabeth, it would be flatly impossible.

It's possible that, having accepted the necessity of his marriage, Henry felt it important to establish a degree of independence before embracing the union. Everyone knew that his only real claim to the throne was matrimonial. But people would tolerate a degree of indulgence in his own dynastic and military significance.

There was also a practical need for Henry and Elizabeth not to rush their nuptials. Under the reign of Richard III, Parliament had recognised the supposed illegitimacy of Elizabeth and her siblings. Under law, they were deprived of all rights on inheritance. While no one really believed that Elizabeth was a bastard, it remained a legal reality. And what Parliament had decreed, only Parliament could overturn.

There was no merit in a marriage between Elizabeth and Henry while the princess's status was dubious. Only Parliament could reverse Elizabeth's fortunes. And only a King could summon a Parliament. Henry had little choice but to be crowned alone. The wedding itself passed almost without note. Today, royal weddings are a great spectacle. Arthur himself would enjoy a wedding accompanied by much pomp and pageantry in the years to come. But this was unusual. Most weddings in the fifteenth century, even royal ones, were low key affairs rather than great state occasions.

The real festival for the new queen would be her coronation. As 1486 dawned, orders were made for 'tawnings of ermyns', 'canapye stavez' and 'cherez of estate' all 'agenst the coronaction of our soverayne lady ye queen'[4] Plans for Elizabeth's big day were in motion, and it looked set to be a grand affair. Yet, the coronation was quickly shelved. The most likely reason is that it was already obvious by the beginning of Lent that the queen was with child.

Pregnancy was no bar to participation in public life. Fifty years later, Anne Boleyn was crowned when visibly with child as a sign of fruitfulness. Elizabeth, however, seems to have endured terrible illness during and after pregnancy. Despite being thrown together in what can only be described as a political marriage, Henry and Elizabeth soon fell deeply in love. The King was probably already falling for his young bride and keen not to push her into a public ceremony when she was unwell. And all concerned, of course, were desperate to protect the safety of the child.

The fact that Elizabeth fell pregnant so quickly, and that Arthur was born just eight months after the wedding has raised more than the occasional eyebrow over the centuries. Had the new king and queen really waited quite as long as it first appeared to enjoy all the benefits that marriage had to offer?

If Henry and Elizabeth had slept together after the 10 December 1485, but before 18 January, there would have been nothing improper about it. Even by the standards of the day. Under church law, a verbal agreement to marry, followed by consummation was enough to constitute a valid marriage. In the upper classes, where inheritance mattered and the legitimacy of heirs had to be beyond doubt, this was usually accompanied by a marriage ceremony. But it was not strictly necessary.

After Henry had pledged to marry Elizabeth in December, she was styled and treated as queen. They were man and wife from that moment. The ceremony that followed was simply a public acknowledgement of that canonical truth.

Nevertheless, it is unlikely that either Henry or Elizabeth would have wanted to take any risks with the legitimacy of their future children. For the new Queen, memories of her public disgrace under Richard III were still fresh in her mind. It was the secretive marriage of her own parents that enabled people to question its validity. This is a mistake that she would never have wanted to repeat. Henry himself, knowing full well the challenges any son of his would face in securing the throne, would have done nothing to create further complications.

It is far more likely that Elizabeth conceived straight after the wedding and that Arthur was born a little premature. As we shall see in the next chapter, arrangements for his christening were a little rushed with a central figure failing to show up on time. The queen's confinement – the time when women withdrew from the world to prepare to give birth – was shorter during her first pregnancy than it was with the birth of Princess Margaret three years later. Preparations for Arthur's nursery at Farnham perhaps suggest that there was a nervousness about moving the child too far.

Whatever the circumstances of Arthur's conception, both mother and father must have been ecstatic and relieved that Elizabeth had proved so effortlessly fertile. According to the court poet, Bernard André, they were far from alone. He wrote that the news brought 'sublime joy for the church, good cheer for the court, and incredible delight for the entire kingdom.'[5]

For Elizabeth at least, the news must also have stirred feelings of trepidation. She knew full well how a family could fall from the fountain of royalty to the charity of churchmen in a matter of days. The hopes for her new family were largely vested in her ability to bring this child to term and to somehow ensure that he be a boy. The sense of pressure must have been overwhelming.

At some stage in the pregnancy, Henry VII decided that his son was to be born in the city of Winchester. A strange but illuminating choice. Even by English standards, Winchester was ancient. The city was of Roman design and probably of Celtic origin.[6] It had served as the administrative capital for Anglo-Saxon England. While no one could doubt that it was prestigious enough to host the birth of a prince, it was far from the practical choice. The city had seen better days. A venue to act as the queen's great chamber was eventually found. But getting it up to scratch for the birth clearly required significant investment.

William Damys, page of the King's bed was paid 40 shillings, 'for the carriage of divers goods of the king from Westminster to the city of Winchester'. Benjamin

Digby, page of the queen's bed, received a range of sums for 'expenses of himself and servant, attending in the city of London for making, ordering, and preparing certains stuffs for the lady queen against the nativity of the lord prince.'[7]

Yet for Henry, and perhaps Elizabeth too, every penny lavished on Winchester was money well spent. For whatever its practical drawbacks, the ancient settlement had one dazzling attraction: it was the city that had once, so people believed, been known as Camelot. By the time that plans were afoot for the birth at Winchester, Henry must have alighted on a name for the child. His prince would not bear the name Henry for himself and the Lancastrian kings of whom he was so proud. Nor would he be christened Edmund for his father, or John for the Beaufort descendants whose blood had brought the Tudors to the throne. His name would act as a tribute for Arthur Pendragon, the legendary King of the ancient Britons.

It's often said that Henry Tudor claimed direct descent from King Arthur. This book even opens with an allusion to it. But this is an oversimplification. Henry certainly made much of his Welsh heritage and his status as the restorer of the true line of British kings. However, the genealogies published in his time did not explicitly link the family to Arthur. Instead, they stressed Henry's descent from King Cadwaladr, a historically sound figure with a somewhat mythical reputation.

In the literature of the time, which most took as history, Cadwaladr was the last true King of the Britons. Before his death he prophesied that one day, the Britons – or Welsh, as they were now known – would again take control of the isle and return a true Briton champion to the throne. There are few prizes for guessing who Henry VII thought that champion to be.

By virtue of the fact the Tudor lineage 'extends all the way back to Brutus', their descent from Arthur was implied.[8] But it was always the connection to Cadwaladr that was stressed. The great Welsh red dragon had flown over the Tudor army at Bosworth in the form of Henry's standard. At his coronation, his champion rode on a horse trapped with Cadwaladr's arms.[9] Henry, at least at the beginning of his reign, was not happy to be regarded as king simply by marriage or even by conquest. He had to establish an aura of authority. His Welsh heritage gave him the chance to do so.

The birth of a son to the queen was a rare opportunity to magnify this association. And if a nod to their ancient linage could be embodied in his heir, Henry had a chance of making this imagery immortal. The choice of name was paramount. Yet no future English King could possibly be named Cadwaladr. As proud as Henry was of this affinity, he had no intention of truly reminding his people that he was effectively a foreigner. But Arthur was an altogether more appealing choice. It was a common name in England. It had associations with the most glorious days of ancient Britain. And just as importantly as all that, the King who had first held it, was enjoying a popular revival in the English imagination.

The tales of King Arthur had been popular in England since at least the twelfth century. Geoffrey of Monmouth's famed account of Arthur's reign in his work *Historia Regum Britanniae*, brought together different strands of Arthurian legend and wove them together into a rich narrative tapestry. It is from Geoffrey's work, completed around 1138, that many of the fundamental components of Arthur's story derive. His father Uther, his magical advisor Merlin, and his ultimate exile to Avalon.

However, much of what we today see as central to Arthurian legend developed after Geoffrey's time and away from the shores of England. Continental writers evolved the story significantly, creating the knights of the round table, the city of Camelot, the sword Excalibur, and the quest for the Holy Grail. The wealthy in England, of course, were able to get their hands on much of it over the centuries. But many of these elements may not have been widely known.

All this changed in the years before the Tudors took the throne. By 1471, an elusive English knight named Thomas Malory had gathered many of the great continental Arthurian stories and translated them into English. In 1485, William Caxton, one of the pioneers of the printing press, published Malory's work as *Le Morte d'Arthur*. Tantalising tales of Arthur, Guinevere, Lancelot, and Mordred had a wider English audience than ever before.

By choosing Arthur as a name for his heir, Henry knew full well that he was riding what we would call 'a popular wave'. Yes, it was a useful piece of propaganda. It linked his house to the island's ancient inhabitants. But good propaganda had to capture the public imagination. And thanks to Malory and Caxton, the Tudor king could do so spectacularly.

The choice of Arthur as a name may also have appealed to the queen. She had been raised on the tales of Camelot. As a member of the high nobility, she had greater access to the stories than the general population. Her family, the house of York, also alluded to descent from the ancient Kings of Briton as heirs to the Mortimer Earls of March, a family with Welsh roots.

The decision also meant that her son would share the name of her half-brother. Arthur Plantagenet was an illegitimate son of Edward IV, and Elizabeth seems to have been close to him. Yet, while she might have appreciated this association, it was entirely coincidental. The heir to the Tudor dynasty was never going to be named for a bastard. Toward the end of their pregnancies, queens withdrew into an all-female environment. During this 'confinement', Elizabeth required a great chamber that could accommodate her in luxurious comfort. For such a venue, Winchester proved short on options. The first choice must surely have been the Great Hall of the Norman castle. It was here that King Arthur's round table was proudly displayed. In reality, the table probably dated from the reign of Edward I, but few had trouble in believing the more colourful tale of its origins.

Despite its iconic status, there was no feasible way that the Great Hall could serve as the Queen's great chamber. It was in desperate need of repair and totally unsuitable for the birth of a prince. Happily, however, the nearby Priory of St Swithun had received more recent attention.[10]

In her page-turning biography of Elizabeth of York, Alison Weir recounts a story that suggests the queen originally wanted to give birth in the castle. However, upon finding it in such a sad state, she quickly vacated to the Priory. Weir rightly calls this story into question. The castle had been in disrepair for many years. Could it really have come as such a shock to the king and queen?[11] However, it is possible to believe that such an error could occur if the move to Winchester was a last-minute decision and if plans were made in haste. While we have no direct evidence that this was the case, it is certainly plausible.

During the spring of 1486, Henry VII had been on progress across the north, the midlands, and parts of the West of England. At each location he was greeted by great pageants which consisted of spectacular performances masterminded by the leaders of the host cities. The themes and imagery deployed in these performances would give the fledgling King his first inkling into how the people of his realm understood his stature and heritage.

Each performance was naturally incessantly flattering to the King. They generally consisted of actors dressed as heroes from that city's heritage, or a great saint, pouring praise on Henry. The people of York wisely referenced the King's connection to Henry VI, his saintly Lancastrian uncle of whom he was immensely proud. And throughout the country, churchmen read a bull from the Pope asserting that together, Henry and Elizabeth were the heirs to the two previously feuding houses of Lancaster and York.[12] From a constitutional perspective, the core narrative of the Tudor dynasty was clearly cutting through.

But throughout the pageantry, very little reference was made to Henry's connection to the ancient Kings of Britain. And pageantry was a medium that should have lent itself to exactly that kind of imagery. The people of Worcester had been planning a reference to Cadwaladr, but for some reason their performance was shelved. Despite references to his heritage at Bosworth and the coronation, England simply wasn't getting the message.

As he reflected on his progress, Henry may have decided that it was time to up the ante. He knew that his connection to ancient Briton was only ever going to be imagery. Yet imagery mattered to medieval monarchy. The decision to treat the birth of his first child as a relaunch of that campaign may have been one that he came to just a matter of weeks before it was due to take place. Whether rushed or otherwise, there could be no economising in the scale of luxury or comfort that given to the queen. Her chamber was 'hanged with rich arras'. All windows but one were to be covered so that there may be 'light whenever it pleaseth her'. The floors were carpeted and the pillows on her royal bed were 'furred with ermines and bordered with velvett.'[13]

These comforts were the best that a fifteenth-century woman could hope for. They did little however, to mitigate the great danger that Elizabeth was about to face. Childbirth may have been a woman's greatest duty, but it was also her gravest threat. Death in the line of duty was common and Elizabeth herself would succumb to it some seventeen years later. In 1486 however, her hope would surely have been that God had brought her this far. He would carry her through the ordeal and bring her baby into the world. She at least had the comfort of her mother, and probably her eldest sister Cecily with her. Both would act as 'gossips' – people who would tell the world of the birth when the child arrived and then play a leading role in the christening.

Also present throughout was the king's mother, Lady Margaret Beaufort. How comforting Elizabeth found the presence of her mother-in-law is anyone's guess. She was at least someone that the queen already knew well. The historian, however, should be very grateful for Lady Margaret's involvement. It is thanks to a note in her own book of hours that we know that Arthur came before 1:00 am in the morning of 20 September.[14]

Elizabeth's life had already been unusually turbulent. She had twice fled to sanctuary, seen her father deposed and watched as her uncle publicly bastardised her before probably murdering her brothers. Since the moment she fell pregnant, she knew that the eyes of the world were upon her. Her husband was desperately hoping she delivered a son, and she would have suspected that some in her own family were praying that she failed in that mission.

Over the spring and summer of 1486, Elizabeth had faced her greatest test. She had passed with flying colours.

Chapter 3

A Christian Prince

Thanks to the labours of his wife and the hand of fate, Henry VII had secured a son and heir within thirteen months of taking the crown. It was another stroke of luck for the ever-fortunate King.

Perhaps by now, Henry was growing used to things going his way. If so, he was about to learn that whatever his successes at battle, at bed or in council, there was one foe that no English king, save perhaps for Canute, could ever hope to tame. The inclement English weather.

On the day of Arthur's christening, the heavens opened. England's ruling class, dressed in their finery, and jostling to be noticed, were soaked to their skin as they approached Winchester Cathedral. It was supposed to be the greatest day of triumph since the coronation. It looked set to be a wash out. The christening took place on 24 September, four days after the prince's birth.[1] This was an unusual delay. Baptism usually had an urgency about it. Under the teachings of the church, a child was born a heathen. Should they succumb to death before purification, they risked eternal judgement.[2]

As we have already seen, Arthur had arrived on the scene earlier than expected. His christening was destined to be a moment for national celebration and time had to be given for the remainder of England's upper class to decamp to Winchester. A short interval was necessary.

However, the delay also serves to suggest that Arthur was broadly fit and well. As we shall see, there may have been some concerns about the implications of his early arrival to his health. But they could not have been grave. Had there been any fear that the boy was likely to perish, they would have baptised him straight away.

The courtiers and churchmen responsible for the great event could do nothing about the weather. Nor could they do much to mitigate late arrivals. What they could control, however, they managed with aplomb. Winchester Cathedral was decked out in the splendour appropriate to the occasion. The body of the church was hanged with 'clothes of arras', or tapestries.[3] We don't know what images filled these fixtures, or whether images featured on them at all. But it's tempting to imagine that at least some depicted scenes from the popular Arthurian tales. After all, memories of Camelot were what the entire occasion had been designed to evoke. In the middle of the Cathedral was 'ordeigned and preparede a solempne fonte', with seven square steps leading up to it and a rich canopy hanging over it.[4] Arthur's arrival was a moment of Tudor triumph. It was essential that everyone should see it.

For Elizabeth, this ceremony marked a moment of great relief. For Henry, it was a symbol of vindication. Yet neither of them was present to witness it. Kings and Queens kept away from the baptism of their children. After the child himself, it was the godparents that were the stars of the show. Anyone that risked outshining them was expected to keep their distance.

The choice of Arthur's Godmother may have taken some by surprise. By the autumn of 1486, it was already clear that Lady Margaret Beaufort, mother of the King and survivor of the Wars of the Roses, was being lined up to play the leading matriarchal role in the new Royal family. Surely, the role of Godmother was hers by right?

Henry VII, however, had not risen to prominence by being predictable. Rather than hand this glittering prize to his own mother, he gave the task to the dowager Yorkist queen, Elizabeth Woodville. Margaret did not even attend. This has led many to believe that by the time of Arthur's birth, his grandmothers had become bitter rivals.

Elizabeth Woodville was one of the most controversial women to ever be crowned Queen consort of England. Not only was she a woman famed for a scandalous marriage that shocked the political establishment. She herself was the product of one.

Elizabeth's mother had been Jacquetta of Luxembourg, daughter of the Count of St Pol, an influential landowner in Northern France. At age 17, she had married the 44-year-old John of Lancaster, Duke of Bedford and uncle to the English King Henry VI.[5] Bedford died just two years after the marriage leaving Jacquetta both a young widow and the first lady of the English court.

Jacquetta was young, rich and beautiful. She did not remain single for long. By 1437 she had contracted a secret marriage to Richard Woodville, who had been a knight in Bedford's service. Jacquetta fell instantly pregnant, and the marriage would soon be exposed. The couple were fined £1000 for marrying without the King's consent, but soon pardoned by the typically gracious Henry VI. At around this time, Elizabeth – the first of fourteen children – was born at Grafton Manor in Northamptonshire.[6]

Despite her mother's continental connections to Royalty, Elizabeth was regarded as a member of little more than the well-off gentry. When she was about 15, she made a respectable marriage to Sir John Grey of Groby. The couple produced two sons, Thomas, and Richard. But what may have been a contented family life did not last long. Sir John was killed fighting for Lancaster at the Battle of St Albans in 1461. This left Elizabeth the widow of a man who had fought against the newly triumphant house of York. She was squarely on the wrong side of the political divide.

Elizabeth would soon turn her fortunes around in spectacular style. In 1464 she shocked the political class when the young Yorkist king, Edward IV unveiled her as his new wife. The high nobility could do no more than watch with disbelief as this commoner-Queen was crowned in Westminster Abbey and react in horror as her low-born family were promoted to positions of power.

If Elizabeth Woodville was born on the fringes of England's nobility, Arthur's other grandmother hailed from its upper reaches. Lady Margaret Beaufort was the daughter of John Beaufort, Duke of Somerset. The Beauforts were a branch of the Lancastrian Royal family though their origins were slightly dubious. They descended from John of Gaunt, the fourteenth century Duke of Lancaster, but through his liaison with his mistress, Katherine Swynford. The couple were later married, and their children legitimised by both Pope and Parliament. While a question mark remained over their eligibility to succeed to the throne, by the early fifteenth century, they were clearly established as leading members of the high nobility.

Despite this almost-impeccable pedigree, Margaret's early years were highly tumultuous. She was born in 1443, and less than a year later, her father died in disgrace. This left her both a wealthy heiress and a little girl with no real protection.

By the time she was 7 years old, she was married to John de le Pole, son of the Duke of Suffolk, the king's chief minister. Suffolk's enemies deliberately misconstrued this marriage as an attempt by the duke to secure the throne for his son. Henry VI was then childless and by primogeniture descent from John of Gaunt, Margaret was the next in line to succeed, though it is doubtful many truly saw it that way. This, among other charges, led to Suffolk's downfall and death and implicated Margaret, entirely against her will, as the pawn in a plot to unseat her cousin the king.

Given the age of Margaret and John de la Pole, the marriage could be quickly dissolved. As we have seen, this left those close to the king free to marry Margaret to Edmund Tudor Earl of Richmond and Henry VI's half-brother. Tudor wasted no time in getting Margaret pregnant and himself killed. Aged just 13, she found herself both a mother and a widow. For the rest of Margaret's life, her energies and priorities were focused on her son, Henry Tudor. As soon as it was decent to do so, she married into the powerful Stafford family. By this stage the Wars of the Roses were in full swing. As members of the flailing Lancastrian dynasty, the young countess knew that she and her son were vulnerable to the rise of the house of York. She must have hoped that the Staffords, who were among the greatest landowners in England, could do something to protect them.

When Edward IV eventually took the throne in 1461, Margaret swallowed her Lancastrian pride. She and her husband made their peace with the new regime and were quickly restored to favour. We can only guess at what she made to the King's scandalous marriage to Elizabeth Woodville. She was likely as shocked as everyone else, but the affairs of the house of York were not Margaret's primary concern. She was fast becoming a shrewd pragmatist. And she may well have admired Elizabeth for exhibiting similar behaviour.

After the death of her husband Henry Stafford in in 1471, Margaret married Thomas Stanley, a wealthy midland landowner and mainstay of the Yorkist court. This would have brought Margaret more into Elizabeth's orbit. She seems to have made a good impression. In 1480, at the baptism of Princess Bridget, the youngest of the Royal York children, she carried the babe to the font. A mark of honour and an indication of trust.

In the months before Edward IV's sudden death, it seemed like Margaret had made significant progress in her only real aim: the rehabilitation of her son who had been in exile for over a decade. Margaret was on the verge of securing his safe passage back to England and the restoration of his earldom of Richmond, which had been taken from him some years before. But as the king unexpectedly perished, his agreement with Margaret evaporated.

Richard III's usurpation of the throne was a disaster for both Margaret and Elizabeth. The dowager queen lost her status and her sons. And with only a shaky grip on power, the new King could not afford to be merciful to a rival such as Henry Tudor. Without realising it, Richard had sown the seeds of a powerful alliance against him.

According to Vergil, it was Margaret who made the first move. She and Queen Elizabeth both employed the services of Dr Lewis of Caerleon. To Margaret, he had also become something of a confidante. Once rumours of the death of the Princes in the Tower were circulating, Margaret shared a scheme with the physician. A marriage between her son and Princess Elizabeth could intermingle the blood of York and Lancaster and that, in these circumstances, 'King Richard, regarded by all men as an enemy of his nation, could easily be cast down from all honour and deprived of his crown.' Lewis consented to 'secretly deal with the Queen about this great enterprise.'[7]

Elizabeth readily agreed. Both women set about recruiting supporters to their children's cause. Before long, their plot joined forces with the rebellion of the Duke of Buckingham, a former supporter of Richard's who had turned against the King. The mothers' hopes would soon be crushed. Richard saw off the rebellion and the rebels were punished. Margaret was stripped of her lands and effectively placed under house arrest. It was difficult to see how Margaret and Elizabeth's plan could ever be resurrected.

Richard quickly moved to neutralise his sister-in-law. He promised publicly to keep her and her daughters safe if she left sanctuary. Richard now seemed secure on the throne, and it looked like he had seen off the Tudor challenge. Sanctuary was no place to raise her children and whatever her feelings toward Richard, his offer must have seemed like the best one on the table. She had little choice but to accept. Yet, to many that were supporting the Tudor cause, and had given up everything to do so, Elizabeth's reconciliation with Richard was a betrayal they could never forget.

It's possible that from this point on, Margaret harboured some ill feeling toward her one-time collaborator. Henry's mother had risked everything for their shared enterprise. Elizabeth, on the other hand, had taken the easy way out at the first sign of trouble. Of Arthur's two grandmothers, Margaret had always been faithful to the path that had led to his creation. Elizabeth had almost destroyed it. Yet, it was traitorous Elizabeth rather than faithful Margaret who had been chosen to be his Godmother and spiritual guide. Should we see Margaret's lack of attendance at the christening as a snub?

Such a response would be understandable but it seems to fly in the face of Margaret's character. As a great survivor herself, she knew full well the power of pragmatism. Whatever her personal feelings, it was crucial that the Tudors were seen as a legitimate Royal dynasty. The presence of their predecessor Royal family bolstered credibility. As a mother herself, she would have understood Elizabeth's predicament. So why then, did Margaret fail to attend the christening of her first grandchild? The answer perhaps lies in understanding the importance of precedence and the role that Margaret was destined to play in enhancing her own son's credibility.

Throughout Henry VII's reign, Margaret was treated like a Princess. She was given precedence before duchesses and would speak, act, and write with sovereignty. But there was no scenario in which she could be given precedence over Elizabeth Woodville, who had once been crowned Queen of England.

Precedence and pre-eminence clearly mattered to Margaret. As her son's reign progressed, she would appear at public ceremonies wearing 'like mantel and surcott as the queen, with a rich corrownall on her hede'[8] She walked just a pace behind the queen, and by the end of the reign, was signing herself "Margaret R", an allusion to the regnal style.

But there was more significance to Margaret's status than high-born vanity. Henry VII claimed to be the Lancastrian heir to his half-uncle, Henry VI. As we have seen, at times he was even at pains to associate himself with the ancient Kings of Britain. He, Henry, had to be seen as every bit as royal as his wife. And for that to be credible, his mother's status must be bolstered in tandem. It was through Margaret that he claimed descent from Edward III. If she were merely a "countess in the corner" at great state occasions, what would that say about his own heritage?

While Henry clearly recognised the wisdom in having Arthur's Yorkist grandmother act as godmother, he could hardly let his own mother be so publicly acknowledged as inferior, and this is probably the clearest answer we're going to get as why Margaret declined to attend.

Had Elizabeth of York given birth to a girl, there would have been two godmothers present at the font. Margaret and Elizabeth could probably have stood shoulder to shoulder, with a slight nod toward Elizabeth's superior status being just about tolerable. But baby boys, even princely ones, were permitted just one godmother. The King perhaps judged that it was best for Margaret to wait behind. After all, the King and Queen themselves were not attending in order not to overshadow the godparents. Ironically, Margaret's absence enhanced her status.

While Margaret Beaufort's lack of appearance has been much discussed over the years, few seemed to have noticed another Lancastrian no-show at the big day. Arthur's great-uncle Jasper Tudor was nowhere to be seen. Jasper Tudor was the second son of Owen Tudor and Katherine of Valois. He was born around 1431 and from a young age was raised by nuns and priests under the orders of his half-brother, Henry VI. Always grateful to his half-brother for rescuing him from obscurity, he quickly became a stalwart defender of the Lancastrian cause in the wars of the roses. Though his military contributions in the early years were sporadic at best.

After the Yorkist victory in 1461, he fled to exile. Due to his status as a cousin of Louis XI he soon found refuge in France, while he waited for an opportunity to strike. The unexpected defection of the Earl of Warwick in 1469, set the scene for the readeption of Henry VI and Jasper returned to England to help secure his brother's regime. At this stage he assumed custody of his teenage nephew, Henry, taking him into exile in Brittany when Edward IV returned to power in 1471.

After his ground-breaking victory in 1485, one of Henry's first acts was to reward his faithful uncle. Jasper was restored to his earldom of Pembroke and given the title "Duke of Bedford" as well as extensive grants of land. His fortunes were further bolstered by his marriage to Katherine Woodville, widow of the duke of Buckingham and sister to the queen dowager. As well as having the advantage of giving Jasper access to Katherine's extensive jointure, it served as another York-Lancaster wedding, underlying a theme of unity and family ties which would underpin the narrative of the new Tudor court.[9]

Jasper had guided the Tudor dynasty from peril to power. How could he fail to be present at a moment of their triumph? Arthur was entitled to have three godfathers. Is it not staggering that the duke wasn't one of them? Whatever his personal feelings toward her, it's unlikely that Jasper was reluctant to share the stage with Elizabeth Woodville. He had been happy to marry her sister when the price was right. Elizabeth might have felt some reluctance about playing opposite such a fierce Lancastrian, who had caused her husband so much grief over the years. But this too, seems like an unlikely reaction from a woman who had been pragmatic enough to make peace with Richard III.

The writer is tempted to imagine, but the historian must avoid filling a vacuum left by an absence of evidence. There may have been a political or family reason that Jasper failed to attend. Perhaps he was just ill or too far away to reach Winchester in time.

While Jasper was a strong candidate for lead godfather, he was hardly the only one. There was another man who had been every bit as loyal to the house of Lancaster, despite having far less to gain from it. John de Vere, the thirteenth Earl of Oxford.

John de Vere was the son of a Lancastrian loyalist who had been executed by Edward IV in 1462. Despite almost certainly despising the Yorkist usurpation of the throne, the young Earl decided to bide his time. He feigned loyalty and was soon rewarded by a King who was keen to win over the nobility.

In 1464 he was awarded all his father's estates, giving him access to a wide patrimony in East Anglia. Once his inheritance was safely in his hands, he started using it to plot against the King that had restored him to it. He was accused of conspiring with Lancastrians as early as 1468 and was instrumental in negotiations between the Earl of Warwick and Queen Margaret of Anjou.

Rewarded for his loyalty, Oxford served as a senior statesman in the brief return of Henry VI. He bore the sword of state at the ceremony that restored the crown to Henry VI. The Lancastrian regime started to crumble, but Oxford's loyalty didn't. He commanded the right wing at the Battle of Barnet, fleeing to France after defeat.

Even then, he never gave up the fight. It simply wasn't in his nature. He sailed to Essex to raise mischief. He seized ports in Cornwall. He committed to an ongoing campaign of piracy. Eventually in 1474, after desertion by his men and a wound to his eye, Oxford was finally captured.[10]

Edward IV had been content to leave Oxford imprisoned in Calais but when Richard III tried to move him to England in 1484, the earl escaped. He soon joined a jubilant Henry Tudor in France. The Tudor cause now boasted a man of impeccable Lancastrian pedigree and exceptional military experience. It was Oxford who led the famously successful Tudor vanguard at the Battle of Bosworth. While his story is often confined to a footnote, he was as crucial to Henry VII's remarkable victory as a Jasper Tudor or a Margaret Beaufort.

Oxford was the perfect candidate to stand godfather. He was from the old blood of the realm, a Lancastrian loyalist and had already proved his devotion to the Tudor cause. There was just one problem. He was running dangerously late.

The Earl had been in Langham in Suffolk when news reached him that the prince had arrived earlier than expected. Though he surely set off straight away, the severe rain had made his journey treacherous. The ceremony had yet to begin but there was still no sign of one of its leading participants. News reached the cathedral that the earl was within a mile. While this would soon prove to be an optimistic estimate, it was judged that it was safe to begin.

Arthur's own entry was preceded by a great procession. In a carefully choreographed performance, the ceremony's key actors marched into the Cathedral in reverse order of precedence. Their procession would have been steady and solemn, with still no sight of the Earl of Oxford, it's tempting to imagine each participant ambling along even more slowly than they otherwise might. The first to enter were men of little note who must have been pleased as punch to land a role in what was essentially a performance. The henchmen, squires and gentlemen and yeoman of the crown each carried with them an unlit candle in each hand.[11]

Next came the members of the Royal Chapel. At its most basic, the chapel was a travelling choir who moved with the king. But it was also an establishment within the Royal household which was responsible for wider spiritual wellbeing. Few details of the Royal Chapel from the early Tudor period survive. If as seems likely, it was based on the model established by Edward IV, then it consisted of twenty-six chaplains and clerks, two yeoman of the chapel and eight children – young boys whose voices had yet to break.[12] Following the chapel were 'certen knyghtes and esquiers'. Then came the king's herald followed by the sergeant at arms. All those that had entered so far must have felt deeply honoured to be taking part. But they would also have known that they were little more than the warmup acts. Their presence had set the stage. Now it was time for the stars to take it.

The Lord Maltravers was the first of the nobility to enter. He was the queen's uncle and heir to the Earldom of Arundel. With him was Thomas Stanley, Arthur's step-grandfather. Stanley was enigmatic, mysterious, and difficult to trust. Without his support, Arthur's father would never have come to the throne.

Thomas Stanley was one of the most skilled survivors of the fifteenth century. Born to a family with a substantial landed base and connections at court, Stanley came into his inheritance in 1459 just as the Wars of the Roses were reaching fever pitch. On the face of it, he was loyal to Lancaster. At Queen Margaret's command he raised 2000 men ahead of the Battle of Blore Heath. But his forces never actually entered the battle, aiding the Yorkist cause substantially. Just a year later, he enraged the queen by supporting the disinheritance of her son and serving on a Yorkist dominated council.

Neither side could depend on Stanley's loyalty for long. In 1470, he lent troops to support the Lancastrian restoration of Henry VI. When the wind began to blow in the other direction, he was again quick to turn his coat. Thankfully for the Stanleys, Thomas's brother, Sir William, had been among the first to rally to Edward IV. It was probably William that pleaded his brother's cause. No doubt anxious to keep the powerful Stanleys onside, Thomas was forgiven and appointed steward of the King's household in late 1471.

At first glance it seems as if Stanley simply turned his coat to whoever looked likely to be the victor. However, it's possible to detect a more sophisticated strategy than that. In the late 1450s, he had married Eleanor Neville, daughter of the Earl of Salisbury and sister of the Kingmaking Earl of Warwick. The Nevilles had been the earliest supporters of the Yorkist cause and it had been Warwick that had abandoned them ten years later. Throughout the early segment of the wars, Stanley seemed to have pursued a strategy of shadowing the Nevilles – albeit cautiously and at something of a distance.

It could well have been this willingness to follow the political path of his in-laws that first attracted Margaret Beaufort to Stanley. After being widowed in 1471, she was in the market for a husband and protector, as well as someone who could fight the corner for her newly exiled son. At this stage, Margaret would have held no hopes that her son would ever challenge the house of York for the throne. But she was embarking on a campaign for his return and restoration. She needed a husband with connections, credibility and perhaps a little flexibility to help her in her cause. Stanley was the perfect choice.

The couple married soon after 1471 and Margaret's investment soon paid dividends. In the reign of Richard III, as we have seen, Margaret was a leading member of the rebellion against Richard. Had it not been for Stanley's assurance that he could control his wife, Margaret would have almost certainly faced full attainder. Like Edward IV before him, Richard was probably worried about alienating the regionally powerful Stanleys. It seems unlikely that the King actually trusted Thomas.

This lack of trust clearly manifested itself in Richard's decisions, ahead of the battle of Bosworth, to hold Stanley's son, Lord Strange, hostage. It was probably for this reason that Thomas did not enter the battle, hanging between the two armies, just as he had at the battle of Blore Heath over a quarter of a century before. Eventually, Thomas's brother, Sir William Stanley entered the field and helped to bring about a decisive victory for Henry Tudor. It was probably William Stanley that picked up the bloody crown from the battlefield and placed it on his step-nephew's head.

We'll never know how Henry truly felt about his stepfather's lukewarm support. But Stanley was well rewarded with, the 'creation of Thomas, Lord Stanley, as earl of Derby, to him and the heirs male of his body issuing', a title that his descendants still hold to this day.[13] He was also confirmed as constable of England and high steward of the duchy of Lancaster. His status as Arthur's godfather was simply the latest in a long list of honours.

After Stanley's procession came his son, Lord Strange, carrying a pair of 'gilt basons' with a towel folded over them. The Earl of Essex followed, carrying the 'salte of gold covered'. Lord Neville, heir to the Earl of Westmorland entered with a taper 'garnished with iiii wrethen bowtest and bowles'. Up next was the young Earl of Essex who carried the "say of salt".[14]

As we shall see as we continue to explore Arthur's story, Royal children were expected to participate in very public ceremonies from a young age. The 11-year-old Anne of York, the Queen's sister, was to be no exception. She entered the cathedral with a rich crimson cloth pinned to her chest and hanging over her arm. While this cloth may have looked decorative it also had a practical purpose. It would be used to dry the baby's head after his baptism.

The young Princess was accompanied by Sir Richard Guildford and Sir John Turburvill, who on the left hand was bearing the staff of office. Guildford had been an early supporter of the Tudors, through his and his family's connections to the Beauforts. He had joined Henry Tudor in exile after 1483. Now, as his prominent position accompanying a young Yorkist princess demonstrates, he was embarking on a career of reward.[15]

At the procession progressed, the assembled guests must have been growing impatient. No doubt still cold and damp from the rain, they would have been eager to catch their first glimpse of the prince. Finally, Arthur, 'wrapped in a mantel of cremesyn cloth of golde furred with ermyn' was carried in by his aunt, Cecily of York.[16]

To bear the heir to the throne to his baptism was an awesome privilege. Cecily, as a princess of the blood was an entirely appropriate candidate. But Arthur was also a newborn baby. It must have been some comfort to his mother to know that, if she had to give her son over to the world so quickly, that it would be to the loving hands of his aunt that Elizabeth entrusted him.

Cecily knew full well that Arthur was the most precious jewel she had ever clutched in her arms. Absolutely nothing must go wrong. Thankfully for 17-year-old Princess, support was close at hand. The Marchioness of Dorset bore the prince's train. Cecily's brother, the Marquess and her cousin, the Earl of Lincoln gave 'assistance to my lady Cecill'. A great canopy of estate was carried over Arthur by his great uncle Edward Woodville, the Lord la Warre and Sir John Arundel.

Originally, the party had been scheduled to process from the cloister of the abbey and enter through a little door to the west end of the cathedral. On the day itself, they found they had to travel a little further. The weather was too 'cowled and fowell' to be at the west end near the door and Cecily had to bring Arthur quickly but carefully to the south end.[17] The Queen dowager was at her place at the font but there was still no sign of Oxford. Word reached the cathedral that the earl was less than a mile away. It was worth hanging on a little longer. So, they waited. And they waited. For three long hours the nobility of England sat shivering in the cold as Princess Cecily no doubt anxiously tried to calm a chilly and disgruntled baby. Eventually enough was enough. The king sent word that the ceremony should proceed. The Earl of Derby and Lord Maltravers were to act as godfathers at the font.

It's often said that Derby and Maltravers had to act as emergency stand-ins due to Oxford's tardiness. But this isn't quite right. Both men had brought gifts for the prince, which was the special obligation of the godparents. While a boy only enjoyed one godmother, he was blessed with three godfathers. Two would serve "at the font" and another would act at the child's confirmation which would follow straight after. It is likely that Oxford and Derby had been scheduled to appear as Godfathers at the font, with Maltravers acting as godfather at the confirmation. If so, Maltravers had secured a slight promotion.

Arthur was christened by John Alcock, Bishop of Worcester, Peter Courtenay, Bishop of Exeter and Thomas Langton, Bishop of Salisbury. Alcock had been a tutor and advisor of the young Edward V during his time as Prince of Wales and his involvement stressed the continuity between Arthur and his late uncle. Courtenay had been a supporter of the rebellions against Richard III in favour of Henry Tudor. He was already being lined up to be Bishop of Winchester and an important figure in Arthur's early years. Langton, on the other hand, had supported Richard III right up until Bosworth. His inclusion showed that Arthur's birth heralded a new era of reconciliation. Previous crimes could be forgiven. Provided, of course, that everyone behaved themselves.

Medieval christenings were quite the ordeal for a youngster. Arthur had already had salt put in his mouth. Now the bishops immersed him in the font and the little Prince would surely have cried out in confusion. But that wasn't the only thing that made this a moment of great drama. As Arthur was dipped in the water, the officers of arms threw on their coats and the henchmen set their torches a light. After four days living in the squalor of sin, Arthur was now a sanctified Christian.

The main occasion was complete. And, in yet another serving of comic irony, it was at precisely this moment that the Earl of Oxford entered the Cathedral. The herald does not record whether or not he looked windswept and dishevelled. But the reader will be forgiven for imagining him drenched in rain, soiled in mud and thoroughly out of breadth.

Elizabeth Woodville swept up her grandson in her arms and walked him to the high altar. As she laid him upon it, the sounds of "veni creator spiritus", a haunting Gregorian chant, filled the cathedral as the king's Chapel sung and the organs played. The Earl of Oxford, quickly briefed on his new role as godfather for the confirmation, took the prince in his right arm and the Bishop of Exeter confirmed the child. If anyone worried that the muddy earl would ruin the baby's garments, perhaps they were reassured to remember that Princess Anne was still on hand with a towel.

Beside the altar lay a cloth, where the presents of the Godparents were proudly displayed. At a christening, only the godparents gave gifts, but they nominated another to present them to the recipient. In this presentation of gifts, we witness yet another opportunity for symbolism. The Yorkist Queen gave a cup of gold, presented by Sir David Owen, uncle to Henry VII. The Earl of Oxford, Lancastrian stalwart, gave a pair of gilt basins. These were born by Sir William Stoner, a man who had prospered under Edward IV. The Earl of Derby, that cautious but early supporter of the house of York gave "a riche salte of golde covered", presented by the Beaufort loyalist Sir Reginald Bray. Finally, Lord Maltravers, brother-in-law to Elizabeth Woodville, gave a "cofer of gold" which was born by Sir Charles Somerset, a cousin to Margaret Beaufort. This York-Lancastrian symmetry was hardly a coincidence.

Finally, after the singing of the anthem of St Swithun, Cecily returned the prince to the nursery and the precession followed her out. Back in the loving and safe arms of his mother, the King and Queen bestowed the blessing of Almighty God, Mother Mary, and St George on their little, longed-for prince. For Arthur, the ordeal was finally over but for everyone else the party had just begun. Back in the church yard, there were set 'ii pipes of wyne, that every man mygtht drynke ynow.' The King of England had been blessed with a healthy son and a future for his dynasty. Whatever his later reputation as a miser, for today at least, the drinks were on him.

Chapter 4

Diseased Minds

Arthur's birth was a happy occasion for the people of England. For the vast majority of people, it mattered little which king sat on the throne. It mattered greatly, however, that he did so stably. The birth of a male heir could only serve to make things better.

In the weeks following the prince's birth, Bernard André, the court poet extolled the people to:

> "Come celebrate the child's birth, O Muses, and the noble offspring born of illustrious royalty. To celebrate the festal day, wreath your hair with a comely flower, O English, and crown your brows with garlands.
>
> Let the pipe blow, let boys and young girls dance and stir and air with applause. And let happy London celebrate festive games. Behold, they royal child Arthur arises, the second hope of our kingdom, sent from heavenly Olympus.
>
> Sprinkle the ground with branches green and twined with flowers, and let bright fires prolong the dying day. The celebrated and happy feast approaches for the English. Let the multitude and the court shout hurrah.
>
> Let them prepare tables for feasting and fill their glass, let them drink wine from a full bowl, and let each one drink with his cup to the prince's name. And you parents, your brows bound with triumphal laurel, offer worthy prayers to God at the altars so that whatever you ask on your son's behalfs, Henry, he may grant it.
>
> Nor let the solemn feasts cease in the temples, but let the high priest of Christ, gowned in his shepherd's band and cloak attend to the sacrifices as of old. Then let the priests chant fitting hymns with great praise and entreat blessed spirits to favour the boy, that he may magnify the splendid deeds of his parents and exceed his ancestors in piety and arms.
>
> And the boy will prosper, for he shows promise of these things. While the Morning Star draws forth the heavenly bodies of the

dawn, while the Evening Star bends Phoebus to the western waves, and while the star-bearing heaven follows its fixed cycles, let us then revere the annual festival of such a storied day, let holy incense and spices, and fruit of wealthy Arabia burn in our hearts.

Let the guardian spirit himself come witness his own honours and let his brow drip with pure nard."[1]

It's curious to note that, despite all that effort that the king had made to ensure his son was born in Winchester, the official court poet made no allusion to the ancient British connection. Throughout his reign, Henry seemed to struggle to instil this imagery into the minds of the humanist intellects he had imported into his Kingdom. Before long, he probably realised that he was on to a losing battle. After all the fuss of his birth and baptism, Arthurian mythology seems to have played no major role in the rearing of the prince.

If the king was frustrated that André and other court poets seemed to "miss the memo" on Camelot, this would have paled by comparison to the joy and relief he felt at his son's birth. After the christening, the court remained as Winchester for a few weeks. The Queen was suffering an 'agu' and needed chance to recover. Once Elizabeth was back on her feet, however, they moved to Farnham Castle, which was to act as Arthur's new home for at least six months. Farnham Castle was the residence of the Bishop of Winchester. It was about halfway between Winchester and Westminster and seems to have been chosen as a nursery for Arthur in something of a hurry. It is likely that there were some concerns about Arthur's health as a result of his prematurity. The King and Queen may have been reluctant to move him too far, too quickly.

After settling in their boy at the safe and secluded castle the Royal couple removed to 'Grenewiche, and ther they kepte the solempne fest of Al Halowes'.[2] For Elizabeth in particular, the parting must have been heart breaking. She was more than aware of the realities of Royal parenting. Motherhood happened at a distance, and this was especially true in relation to the eldest son. But being prepared for such remoteness does not mean that it was any easier to face.

Despite the distance, Arthur would never be far from his mother's thoughts. She would visit him in January and oversee the appointment of his household. And, as we shall see, when the house of Tudor faced its first major crisis, it would be the protection of Arthur that was his mother's overwhelming priority.

Over the last eighteen months, fortune's wheel had spun decisively in Henry VII's direction. But he was not a man to rest on his laurels. Having been 'vexed by evils ever since coming to manhood' he knew full well that celebration could quickly crumble to crisis.[3] The first Tudor King is often remembered as a man of intense paranoia. That word, however, is slightly misleading. It suggests someone whose fear or suspicions are unfounded. This was hardly the case for Henry. Though he enjoyed extraordinary luck in overcoming the schemes and plots of his enemies, such devices were rarely far away.

As 1487 opened, Henry became aware of plot against him that risked engendering everything he had worked for. News reached the King that the Irish nobility had abandoned their loyalty to the Tudors and were playing court to a small boy in their keeping. This boy, so they claimed was none other than Edward, Earl of Warwick, the son of George, Duke of Clarence. As the royal nephew to the late York Kings Edward IV and Richard III, the child was probably the last remaining York Prince with breath in his body. This dark news, or something quite close to it, was the nightmare that Henry had been dreading since his first day on the throne. Edward of Warwick was the only man left alive in the male-line descent of Edward III. Or, to put it another way, he was the only person in existence who both was, and could beget, a Plantagenet heir to the throne.

From a strictly legal standpoint, the young earl had no claim to the throne to speak of. Following years of disloyalty, his father, George Duke of Clarence, had been sentenced to death by the duke's brother, Edward IV. Clarence's sentence was accompanied by an act of attainder, a legal device which prevented the descendants of the offending party from claiming any inheritance through their disgraced parent. Besides, Parliament had already bestowed the throne on Henry and his descendants.

Henry knew full well that such constitutional niceties rarely mattered. Particularly if the spirit of revolution was in the air. He himself had been under attainder when he defeated Richard III at the Battle of Bosworth. Through no fault of his own, Warwick's very existence represented an alternative path to the succession. If the English political class ever decided that Henry's days were numbered, Warwick was most likely the man they would turn to.

It was for this reason, that Henry's very first act after emerging victorious from battle had been to bring the young lad into his custody. He dispatched one of his loyal men to apprehend the young earl and take him to London where 'the poor lad, born for misfortune, was immediately imprisoned.'[4] He had remained in the Tower of London ever since.

The good news was that Henry knew straight away that whoever the Irish were paying court to, he was an impostor. The real Warwick was safely in the Tower. The bad news was that many might well believe he had escaped. Rumours to that effect had recently circulated and it seemed logical that if the boy was to escape Henry's clutches, Ireland would be his destination. The house of York was popular in the country. Warwick's father, Clarence had even been born there. Many would be only too keen to provide the boy with shelter and support.

The King must have been enraged, anxious and despondent. Arthur's birth was supposed to have ended the bloodshed. He and the queen had given the country a

York-Lancastrian Prince that all could unite behind. Now, just months after Arthur's birth, conflict once again, seemed inevitable. It was time to prepare for battle. On 2 February, the king gathered a great council together at Sheen.[5] His first step was to ensure that no men fled to Warwick's banner simply because they had no other option. That meant it was time to bring a number of rebels back in from the cold.

In the early days of Henry's reign, Francis, Viscount Lovell, a close friend and loyalist of Richard III, had led a minor uprising against the newly crowned king. The Duke of Bedford had calmed this rebellion easily enough and Lovell had fled to safety. Inevitably, those men involved in the rebellion had been living under a cloud ever since. Some were suspected of aiding and harbouring Lovell. Without a way back to favour, Henry knew that these men would be forced into the arms of the latest Yorkist pretender. He issued an amnesty for prior offences.[6] He that repented, could be forgiven. Now it was time to prove that 'the false opinion that the boy was in Ireland might be erased from men's minds.'[7] According to Hall, the young Earl of Warwick was shown 'in the cytie and other publique places'. Later, the boy was brought from the tower through 'the moost publyke and vsuall stretes of London' to St Paul's cathedral and showed "him selfe openly to everybody in the procession".[8] If any were tempted to support the mysterious boy in Ireland, they must do so in the full and certain knowledge that they were backing a pretender.

But as Henry was about to discover, it is impossible to convince a man of something that he has already decided not to believe. Or as Vergil put it, 'this medicine did nothing to cure their diseased minds.'[9] And from Henry's point of view, there was no mind more diseased than that of John de le Pole, the Earl of Lincoln.

John de la Pole was a senior member of the Yorkist Royal family. His mother, another Elizabeth of York, was sister of Edward IV and Richard III. As a young man, he had played a prominent role at court during both reigns, being created Earl of Lincoln in 1467. After the death of Richard III's son, Prince Edward in 1484, Lincoln was appointed to the prestigious roles of Lieutenant of Ireland and President of the Council of the North. These may have been signs that the now childless King envisaged Lincoln as his successor, although no heir was ever formally designated.[10]

Richard's defeat at Bosworth was inevitably a blow to Lincoln but initially he stayed loyal to the new Tudor regime. He failed to join Lovell's rebellion, even helping to punish wrong doers in its aftermath. He was often in the King's presence and, as we have seen, played a high-profile role at Arthur's christening.[11]

Yet, despite this outward display of loyalty, huge questions remained over the Earl's true intentions. When his cousin Warwick was brought into council to speak with the lords present, it was largely for Lincoln's benefit. It was a strategy that failed.

Almost immediately after the council meeting, Lincoln fled to Flanders. Here, he was reunited with Thomas Lovell, both of whom quickly pledged their support to the supposed earl in Ireland. By this stage, Lincoln would have known full well that his true cousin was safely in the tower. The boy in Ireland was nothing more than an impostor. The fact this failed to perturb Lincoln may suggest that it came as no surprise. The Earl of Lincoln might well have been part of the conspiracy from the beginning. Flanders, or more specifically, the Duchy of Burgundy, was no random destination for either Lincoln or Lovell. In Burgundy they knew they would find protection from Lincoln's aunt, Margaret of York.

To the extent that Arthur ever knew anything about his great-aunt Margaret, hers was a name that he would have been brought up to despise. She was the third daughter of Richard, Duke of York and became a valuable asset on the European marriage market when her brother, Edward IV, took the throne in 1461. Six years later, aged 22, she left England for Burgundy and married its Duke, Charles. Despite her geographical distance from her homeland, she was rarely out of English affairs, mediating between her warring brothers and using her influence to shape an English foreign policy favourable to the Burgundian cause.[12]

We will never know how Margaret felt about the decisions of her youngest brother, Richard III, to overthrow her nephew, Edward V, to take the crown for himself. But she bitterly resented Henry Tudor's seizure of the throne and refused to recognise his legitimacy as King of England.

Lincoln and Lovell immediately set about convincing Margaret to support the cause of 'Warwick' in Ireland. In reality, she needed little convincing. She too, may have been involved with the conspiracy from a much earlier stage. Readily, she agreed to fund an army. What may have started out as a fanciful rebellion was quickly becoming a credible campaign.

Upon hearing that Lincoln had fled, Henry had to finally face that battle was inevitable. He 'sent captains of war in all directions with orders to prepare and assemble an army, so that with the entire multitude they might make an impression on that place where he decided his enemies would come.'[13] Fearing also that more men may cross to Flanders, he began to 'defend the entire eastern coast with garrisons, guardians and watchmen.'[14] News of Lincoln's defection seems to have shaken Henry. While he had probably always had his suspicions about the Earl, he might genuinely have thought that Arthur's birth would be enough to solidify Yorkist support. Now, it was time for the King to turn his ever-active suspicions to other members of his wife's family. After all, if Lincoln had paraded his loyalty at Arthur's christening, and turned his back on him so quickly after, could any of the prince's kinsman truly be trusted?

As old wounds readily reopened, the king dispatched his stalwart ally, the Earl of Oxford to arrest the Marquess of Dorset, Henry's own brother-in-law.[15] Dorset was Arthur's uncle. He was no blood relative to either the Earls of Warwick or Lincoln. Nevertheless, as we shall see later, he had probably never enjoyed the king's full trust. Henry had been let down once too often. From now on, he was taking no chances.

Events would soon prove that Henry's mistrust of Dorset was misplaced. And regardless, he soon had more pressing matters to distract him. By early May, Lincoln and Lovell had reached Ireland, armed with 2000 German soldiers supplied by the Duchess of Burgundy. They quickly located the young pretender and caused him 'to be proclaimed and named king of England, after the most solemnpne fassyon as thoughe he were there of the verye heyre of bloud royall lynially borne and descended.'[16]

We can hardly blame anyone in Ireland for now sincerely believing that the boy in their custody was genuinely the Earl of Warwick. The Earl of Lincoln himself had recognised the boy as his cousin. What reason was there to doubt that he was truly a Yorkist Prince? The news that Lincoln had reached Ireland was yet another blow to the King but by the time his own military preparations were in full swing. He had set up base in the midlands and a number of lords were with the king at Coventry. He commanded them to go and raise men from across the country. It was time to prepare for a fight.

The great magnates of the realm were well placed to guide Henry on military matters. But there were other issues to discuss which were just as pressing. On these matters, there were only a handful of people he could trust. Henry headed to nearby Kenilworth Castle. From there, he wrote an urgent dispatch to the queen's chamberlain, the Earl of Ormonde:

> 'Right trusty and right welbeloved Cousin we greete you wele, and have tidings that our Rebelles landed the fifth daye of this moneth in our land of Irland. Whefore, and forasmoche as we have sent for our derrest wif and for our derrest moder to come unto us, and that we wold have your advis and council also in oche matiers as we have to doo for the subuyng of our Rebelles, we praie you that, yveing your due attendaunce upon our said derrest wif and lady moder, ye come with thayme unto us; not failing herof as ye purpose to doo us Plaisir. Geven undre our Signette at our Castell of Kenelworth the 8th dye of Maye.'[17]

Henry was enduring his first moment of crisis. Now more than ever, he needed his wife and his mother by his side.

Elizabeth and Margaret Beaufort, quickly responded to the King's summons, reaching the secure fortress of Kenilworth by mid-May. The Queen was not to remain there for long. Whatever else the Royal trio discussed, it is highly likely that they hatched a plan to deal with the worst-case scenario: the King's death on the battlefield.

At the end of May, the queen departed Kenilworth and headed to Farnham. Whether it was her idea to join her son, we shall never know. But it is hardly likely that she needed much convincing. With her husband's throne facing its gravest threat, her separation from her child must have been overwhelming. But there was more to her mission than maternal concern.

Ahead of the Queen's departure, a detachment of the Royal household was sent ahead to Romsey Abbey, eight miles north of the Solent. Historian David Starkey notes that they were probably under instruction to, 'prepare an escape route abroad for the queen and the prince if things went badly.'[18]

At just six months old, Arthur had little chance of holding the throne if his father succumbed on the battlefield. Henry, however, understood well that a Prince in exile was never truly out of the picture. The evidence suggests that in the event of the King's death, Elizabeth was to take Arthur to the continent and establish a court in exile.

As an infant, Arthur could do nothing to help his father directly. Yet, for as long as there was breath in his body, the hope of the Tudors could live beyond Henry. The fact that the perilous task of preserving the Tudor dynasty was bestowed on the Queen shows just how much trust already existed between the Royal couple. As the years went by, it would become clear just how effective a partnership they had forged. Elizabeth's role in the crisis of 1487 shows that the foundations of the King and Queen's relationship were already established.

On her journey from Kenilworth to Farnham, Elizabeth was joined by Peter Courtenay, Bishop of Winchester. This was clearly a sensible choice. Farnham was Courtney's castle. He possessed the local knowledge and influence to help the Queen navigate any tricky situations she encountered.

But by assigning Courtenay as her principal councillor, the King was once again conveying his trust. Though an early defector to the Tudor cause, Courtenay had been an Edward IV man through and through. Had there been even a hint of suspicion about the queen's loyalty, she would have been assigned a Lancastrian minder. There was also one other distinct advantage in ensuring the Queen was in the company of a Bishop. In the event of Henry VII's demise, Courtenay could ensure that Arthur was quickly crowned King. Though the boy would never grow up to become King of England, it is staggering to think how close he came to that accolade before he was even old enough to know what it was.

As Elizabeth travelled to Farnham with haste, we can only imagine what she might have been feeling. Her cousin was leading a campaign against her son, financed by her aunt and in the name of another cousin. Whatever loyalty to the house of York lingered in Elizabeth's heart surely died on the road to Farnham.

The Queen reached Farnham on the 11 June.[19] While her proximity to her son must have been a comfort to Elizbeth the presence of the queen can have only added to a sense of crisis and drama. During the days after Elizabeth's arrival, plans for an emergency departure must have been frantic. Fortunately, it seems that they were soon abandoned. Within days, happier news had reached the queen.

After the Queen's departure, the King headed to Coventry where he waited for his men to join him. The sense of apprehension must have been overwhelming. Less than two years previous, he had been nothing but a rank outsider. Yet, due largely to the failure of England's landowning class to turn up and fight for their anointed King, Henry had snatched victory from the jaws of defeat. Now *he* was the anointed King. He faced a foe who claimed to be far less of an outsider than Henry had ever been. His very survival depended on the loyalty of men he barely knew. It must have been an agonising experience.

Mercifully for Henry, his fears could soon be calmed. First, came the Earl of Shrewsbury with a large company of men. Next, arrived the King's stepbrother Lord Strange and John Cheney, both 'commanders of great military glory, together with a number of other skilled men at arms.'[20] Then, responding to Henry's summons came the 'noblest and stoutest men' from the nearby counties before the leading men from more distant regions finally arrived: the Nevilles, Latimers and Norrises. Thus, as Vergil surmised, 'hour by hour the royal army was wonderfully increased'.[21]

By this time, 'Warwick's' army had landed in the north. Under the command of the Earl of Lincoln, it progressed through Yorkshire, consisting primarily of Irish soldiers and the 2000 German mercenaries supplied by the Duchess of Burgundy. In a worrying sign for the rebels, their ranks do not seem to have swelled significantly by the time they encountered the Royal army, just outside a small Nottinghamshire village called Stoke.

Henry had once again placed his army under the command of the trusted Earl of Oxford. They formed the Royal troops into a triple battle line. The vanguard, with Oxford at its head, charged forward to engage Lincoln's forces. The battle lasted for more than three hours. Margaret of York had evidently secured quite the captain for the German troops. Even those loyal to the Tudor cause described the commander, Martin Schwartz as "a high-born German outstanding for his skill in war."[22] 'Not many men' said Vergil, excelled 'Martin Schwartz in power of mind and body.'[23] But for all Schwartz's valour, the Royal army had three distinct advantages. The first was superior numbers. The second, was a superior strategy. Oxford organised the men in such a way that only the vanguard ever engaged the enemy, with the remaining troops topping up the fighting force as was necessary. And the third was that the Irish too in 'accordance with their national custom' fought 'with bodies unprotected by any armour.'[24] Despite their bravery, they were soon overcome.

To the King's great frustration, Lincoln perished on the battlefield. With the rebellious earl dead, it would be challenging to establish the facts of the matter and ascertain who else had been party to the conspiracy. After victory however, the young boy, posing as the Earl of Warwick was quickly apprehended. It was time to establish the true identity of the boy, who had come so close to bringing the house of Tudor to its knees.

According to later Tudor-era chroniclers, the boy was named Lambert Simnel, the son of an Oxford joiner. He had been the pupil of a man called Richard Simons, "a base-born priest to whose heart cheats and windles were dear from the outset, but otherwise not unlearned."[25] It was the priest, apparently, who had concocted the plan. Rumours of the survival of Edward IV's sons persisted into the reign of Henry VII. Simons believed that if he could present the child in his charge as one of the Yorkist princes, he could secure the throne for the boy and a great church office would be the priest's reward.

But when he heard tell that Edward, Earl of Warwick had escaped from the tower, he decided to change tack. He coached the young Lambert in the art of royalty and trained him to effectively pose as the young nobleman. When he felt confident that his charge was up to the task, he took the lad to Ireland to secure support for his cause.[26] This retelling, directly or otherwise, is based on government sources. We would be wise to treat it with caution. Nevertheless, in his book, 'Henry VII and the Tudor pretenders', Nathen Amine demonstrates that the somewhat unusual names of 'Lambert' and 'Simnel' were both in use in England in the fifteenth century.[27] There is little reason to doubt that this boy – who was promptly forgiven and given a job in the Royal kitchen – was who Royal sources claimed him to be. What seems far more suspect, is that this great campaign originated from nothing more than the scheme of a pesky priest. There is no conclusive evidence that Yorkist loyalists, such as Lincoln, Lovell and the Duchess of Burgundy, were its true authors. But it is hard to dismiss the possibility. What we can be sure of is that, had the campaign been successful, the Earl of Lincoln would never have put Simnel on the throne. According to Vergil, Lincoln's plan had been to lead Lambert to England and, if victorious, quietly replace him with the real Earl of Warwick once they reached London. The young prince would then be declared Edward VI and England would once again be under the rule of a Yorkist King.[28]

It's difficult to see how Vergil could have known this conclusively, though it certainly makes sense. But we must also entertain an even darker possibility. Could it be that, in the event of success, both Warwick and his impersonator would have disappeared quickly? In that eventuality, the next logical York heir to the throne would surely have been Lincoln himself.

In some sense, the Battle of Stoke was a more significant occasion in the establishment of the Tudor dynasty than Bosworth. What happened at Bosworth field remains a mystery. Historians still don't really understand how Henry won. Stoke demonstrated that the Wars of the Roses really were over, even though it would be years before that was apparent. When a King was acknowledged as a legitimate and competent ruler, the landed class came together to repel any threat to his sovereignty. That is precisely what had happened.

After years of turmoil, the Tudor strategy of uniting the houses of York and Lancaster had proved successful in its primary mission. England had accepted the settlement. And this was in no small part because Henry and Elizabeth had managed to embody their dynastic alliance in the form of an heir. Arthur, though he was too young to know it, had been a fundamental part of the Tudor victory at the Battle of Stoke. He represented the future of stability and the union of York and Lancaster. And the men of England had risked life and limb to secure it. As he grew from infant to child and become cognisant of his great destiny, the pressure to honour the sacrifices made in his name must never have been far from his thoughts.

*

The tumultuous events of 1487 had threatened to uproot the foundations of Arthur's life and dramatically disrupt his destiny. The infant prince, sleeping and growing peacefully in the sanctuary of Farnham Castle, was blissfully unaware of the chaos engulfing his family.

However, the Simnel crisis may be linked to an event that would affect Arthur profoundly and personally. His relationship with his grandmother and godmother, Elizabeth Woodville.

As we have seen, upon becoming aware that the Irish were agitating against him, the king called an emergency council. According to both Vergil and Hall, at the February council meeting, it was 'determined that the lady Elizabeth wife to King Edwarde the IV shoulde loase and forfeyte al her lands and possessyons, because she had voluntarily submitted her selfe and her daughters wholy tyo the hands of kynge Richarde, contrarye to the promes made to the lords and nobles of thys realme.'[29] In what Hall is very clear was an act of punishment, Elizabeth was to live a 'wretched and a miserable lyfe' in Bermondsey Abbey.[30]

On the face of it, Vergil and Hall's reasoning simply doesn't add up. Why would the King take this moment to punish his mother-in-law for a "crime" she had committed some three years earlier? Since that time, he had married her daughter, restored Elizabeth to her status as queen dowager and given her pride of place at the Royal court. He had even chosen her over his own mother to stand as godmother at Arthur's christening.

Vergil, writing about twenty years after the event, seems to express surprise at the reasoning. Had not Elizabeth's actions ended up helping Henry? They had led to Richard supposedly attempting to marry his niece, Elizabeth of York, revolting the nation and turning more men to Henry's cause. Besides, both Vergil and Hall find time to note the excellent work the elder Elizabeth had undertaken as queen consort.[31] Even those sympathetic to Henry were not convinced by his judgement.

Francis Bacon, writing some 130 years after the event, was the first to offer an alternative explanation for Elizabeth's banishment. He believed that, just as Elizabeth had once plotted against Richard III, she was now doing the same to his successor. He argued that 'out of the precedent and subsequent acts, is, that it was the Queen Dowager from whom this action [the Simnel plot] had the principal source and motion.'[32]

Bacon had access to sources lost to us. On most occasions, his accusations are worth taking seriously. This is not one of those times. He offers no real rationale for his suspicion. He notes, as even Vergil alludes, that the explanation given – of Elizabeth's previous reconciliation with Richard – lacks plausibility. But that does not, in and of itself, vindicate an alternative.

Is it really likely that Elizabeth Woodville would back a conspiracy to put the son of the Duke of Clarence on the throne at the expense of her own grandson and godson? Elizabeth had been a sworn enemy of Clarence, supposedly once declaring that her children would never come to the throne if the Duke of Clarence lived.[33] Why would she suddenly back his son at the expense of her own descendant?

Whatever her feelings about Henry VII, there is no claim that Elizabeth would have preferred to Prince Arthur's. Save, of course, that of her own sons. But Elizabeth knew full well that her sons were dead.

Or did she?

Historian Matthew Lewis has put forward an intriguing theory. What if the boy crowned as King Edward in Ireland was not an impostor claiming to be Edward, Earl of Warwick? What if he was another Royal, Yorkist, Edward? What if he was Edward V, one of the princes in the tower, himself? If that were so, it would certainly explain Henry's suspicions toward Elizabeth Woodville and her son, the Marquess of Dorset.[34]

Lewis explores this theory in his excellent book, *The Survival of the Princes in the Tower*. As he does so, he skilfully exposes how little we truly know about many of the events surrounding the Battle of Stoke and the authenticity of the so-called Simnel boy that Henry would later put to work in the Royal kitchens. Nevertheless, Lewis's suggestion that Edward V could have been at the centre of the campaign, relies too heavily on puzzling comments by Bernard André. Writing about the events leading up to the Battle of Stoke, André wrote.

> 'While the cruel murder of King Edward the Fourth's sons was yet vexing the people, behold another new scheme that seditious men contrived. To cloak their fiction in a lie, they publicly proclaimed with wicked intent that a certain boy born the son of a miller or a cobbler

was the son of Edward the Fourth. This audacious claim so overcame them that they dreaded neighed God not man as they plotted their evil design against the King. Then, after they had hatched the fraud among themselves, word came back that the second son of Edward had been crowned king in Ireland.

When a rumor of this king had been reported to the king, he shrewdly questioned those messengers about every detail. Specifically, he carefully investigated how the boy was brought there and by whom, where he was educated, where he lived for such a long time, who his friends were, and many other things of this sort. Various messengers were sent for a variety of reasons.

At last [blank] was sent across, who claimed that he would easily recognise him if he were who he claimed to be. But the boy had already been tutored with evil cunning by persons who were familiar with the days of Edward, and he readily answered all the herald's questions. To make a long story short, through the deceptive tutelage of his advisors, he was finally accepted as Edward's son by many prudent men, and so strong was this belief that many did not even hesitate to die for him.'[35]

To Lewis, this represents a slip of the tongue for André. If it were indeed a 'son of Edward IV' in Ireland, the government would have perceived that as a bigger threat than the presence of Warwick, or someone pretending to be him. As such, so the theory goes, the official accounts were crafted to claim that the rebellion was in the name of Warwick, not in that of his more threatening cousin. After all, the vast majority of what we know about the beginnings and development of the plot comes from government sources. Writing years later had André, who must have been privy to the real story, forgotten that it was a secret?

Lewis himself accepts that André was partially confused. Though he stated the boy was posing as Richard, the younger of the princes in the tower, this makes little sense. The Irish had crowned a 'King Edward'. If he were a son of the late Yorkist ruler, it must have been the elder.

This theory simply asks too much of André. All at once he is required to have been trusted enough to be told the real story but unreliable enough to betray it. His memory has to have been sufficiently sharp to remember the essence of a secret truth, but scatty enough to forget a fundamental fact.

If André had been privy to the real story, one that was presumably not widely circulated, surely, he would have understood the significance of maintaining the pretence? Would he really have mentioned it so carelessly? Especially in a text he was writing to give to the King. It is much more credible to assume that André, who was writing years after the event, was muddling some of the facts of the Simnel campaign in 1487 with the Perkin Warbeck plots of the 1490s. In that far more serious conspiracy there certainly was a pretender claiming to be Edward IV's second son. And he too would begin his campaign in Ireland.

André is rarely a reliable source when it comes to specifics. As a blind man, he was dictating chunks of text to a scribe. He left many blank spaces that he intended to fill in when he had checked his facts. The copy of André's work that survives is what we would call a "work in progress". To construct a theory out of one of his fairly regular, first-draft blunders, is to build a house on very shaky sand.

There is no reason to believe that Elizabeth thought either of her sons were involved in the plot. Or that she suspected the boy in Ireland was pretending to be anyone other than Warwick. As such, it seems unlikely that she ever leant the campaign her support. So why then, was she seemingly punished at the moment the campaign was gaining momentum?

Some historians have argued that, despite the timings, Elizabeth's banishment had nothing to do with the Simnel affair. The queen dowager's change in status, they suppose, came down to money. Elizabeth's lands were given to her daughter, whose coronation was finally on the horizon. She needed to be given her jointure as Queen and Henry clearly felt the Royal finances were insufficient to support both a wife and her mother.[36]

Money clearly played a part. With Henry VII, it usually did. Since coming to the throne, he had bestowed land on both his mother and mother-in-law. By 1487, he had already intervened more than once to protect the landed settlement of his wife's grandmother, the Duchess of York. The reign of the King's beloved uncle, Henry VI had been undermined by the saintly ruler's inability to control patronage and prevent wealth flowing into the hands of the Royal household members. While he himself was too young to remember, Henry VII would have known full well how such perceptions of corruption had damaged the monarchy. Something had to give. His mother-in-law was the most obvious target.

But can we really dismiss the timings of the decision as a mere coincidence? Henry's council made the decision just as the Simnel plot was heating up. He completed the paperwork at the same time as he was gathering his armies for confrontation. Surely, it is reasonable to believe there is some connection between the impostor Prince in Ireland and the demotion of the queen dowager.

Historians have paid too little heed to the reasons for Elizabeth's banishment that were actually offered by near contemporaries. Yes, there is a certain lack of logic to the King punishing his mother-in-law for something that happened three years earlier. But we are too quick to forget that when a new crisis strikes, it quickly revives memories of its predecessors.

The official orders which authorised the treasurer and chamberlain to remove lands from the queen dowager make it clear that Henry is acting on 'the advise of the lords and other nobles of our counsall'.[37] This chimes with Vergil's claims that Elizabeth's actions had betrayed, "those lords who, turning their backs on all the fortune they had in England, had, chiefly at her behest and for her sake, crossed the sea to Henry in Brittany."[38] Both sources, and the later writing of Hall, suggest it was certain lords of the council, rather than the King himself who were baying for Elizabeth's metaphorical blood.

Let's pause and consider how recent history had played out from the perspective of Henry's loyalist supporters. Primarily, these were men, like Oxford, who had either been loyal to the Lancastrian cause throughout the Wars of the Roses. Or, they had been loyal servants of Edward IV who had been unable to make their peace with Richard III's usurpation. The one thing they had in common was that they had risked everything to join Tudor in exile. Their primary hope had been that Henry would marry Elizabeth of York and claim the throne as her husband. Or at least, draw enough support on the basis of the betrothal to make good his claim in battle.

This entire plan depended on the queen dowager standing firm and keeping her daughters away from Richard's prying hands. At the first sign of trouble, she buckled under the pressure. Unlike them, she was not prepared to risk everything. She reconciled to Richard. She put her own comfort and survival above the cause they had sacrificed so much for. And by allowing Richard to negotiate a marriage for the young Elizabeth of York, she had come close to hammering the final nail in the Tudor coffin.

Finally, in 1485 at the Battle of Bosworth, victory came for these patient men. When it did, Elizabeth was not punished. She was restored, enriched, and given pride of place. It was she who acted as godmother at Prince Arthur's christening. A christening which staunch Lancastrians such as Margaret Beaufort and Jasper Tudor did not even attend. Was there to be no retribution for Elizabeth's act of betrayal?

Of course, our vantage point helps us to see this differently. In reality, as 1484 dawned it must have seemed to Elizabeth Woodville that the Tudor cause was lost. A life in sanctuary was not sustainable for her many daughters. Richard could be on the throne for the next twenty or thirty years. Making peace with him, on the proviso that she and her daughters would be safe, was her only real option.

But in the heat of revolution, it is equally understandable why Henry's supporters reacted with anger. The king was right to ensure a high-profile role for his Yorkist in laws at crucial court occasions. The whole Tudor dream could only work if Elizabeth and her children were restored to wealth and status. But nor could those who had been loyal through thick and thin be casually alienated.

Henry's victory at Bosworth had papered over the cracks of his broken alliance with Elizabeth Woodville. Most were probably happy to focus on the glory of the victory and to celebrate its spoils. But could it be that the Simnel plot had reopened old wounds? The King realised that there were Yorkist elements that would never accept him as ruler. Perhaps he needed to send out a signal that disloyalty was not easily forgotten.

Even in this context, the king had to be careful not to alienate those who might be tempted to rebel. As we have seen, his first act in the February council was one of amnesty. Though they would have understood the logic of it, this must have jarred with the faithful. Once again, they had to welcome back into the fold those that had betrayed them. Was their price, spoken or otherwise, that at least one head had to figuratively role?

Elizabeth was the obvious choice. Her reconciliation with Richard had been high profile. Her punishment for it could be equally so. Yet, few were so loyal to her personally that it was likely to provoke much of a reaction. The chances that Henry ever seriously suspected his mother-in-law's involvement in the Simnel conspiracy are slim. But there is every chance that the whole episode had reminded him exactly who his friends were.

When he reached his decision about the queen dowager's future, thoughts of Arthur cannot have been far from his mind. After all, it had been less than five months since his maternal grandmother had been lined up to play a significant role in the prince's life. She had acted as godmother. Her daughter had carried him into the cathedral and her son had supported them both. Almost everyone involved in the proceedings had a connection to the dowager queen by either blood or marriage. There is every reason to think that this was done, at least in part, to remind all assembled that this little babe was Edward IV's grandson and the true heir to the house of York.

Like the king's household, Arthur's establishment would always maintain a high degree of York-Lancaster symmetry. When the king later formed Arthur's council, many of those who had served Edward V were reappointed. Many of his crucial officers had served Edward IV and even Richard III.

But after 1487, is it just possible to detect the hint of a shift? Months before, the house of York had been out in force to mark Arthur's arrival. But few of them would play a meaningful role in his upbringing. It would be Henry VI's brother, Jasper Tudor who kept a watchful eye over Arthur's government of Wales in its earliest days. The man later appointed to act as his chamberlain was Margaret Beaufort's nephew. The prince was to be taught and educated by a man with a thoroughly Lancastrian understanding of recent history.

From now on, Arthur's inner circle would be tinted more by the red rose than the white. What place in it could there really be for his Yorkist grandmother?

Chapter 5

The King's Most Dear Son

Privacy was not a concept that Arthur would ever know. Even from his youngest months, there would be times when he must be on public display.

This remarkable requirement is clear from the fact that from birth, he was gifted two cradles. One was for everyday use and housed in his inner chamber. The second was the "cradle of estate", which was used when the infant prince resided in his outer chamber and had to dress to impress.

The cradle of estate was nothing short of a masterpiece. It was covered in crimson cloth of gold, with pommels of sliver and gilt. Graven with the coat of arms of the King and Queen, the cradle stood proudly on a floor carpeted with cloth of gold and furred with ermine. The arms of the King flew fiercely above it.

Though young, Arthur slept on a mattress and two pillows. He was given a pair of fustian, a kind of hard-wearing thick cloth and a pane (or blanket) of scarlet furred with ermine and bordered with blue velvet upon velvet of cloth of tissue. His head sheet was covered in cloth of gold and furred with ermine.[1] There could be no mistaking the fact that the boy sleeping soundly among this finery was the son of a king.

Mercifully for the little prince, use of the cradle of estate was probably kept to a minimum. While children were expected to grow up fast, even in medieval England they were still allowed to be children. When a baby was baptised, their godparents pledged to keep them from fire and water until they were seven years old.[2] This reflects an acceptance that, for these first crucial years of their life, a child needed a special degree of nurturing and shelter from the wider world.

As a Prince, Arthur was never going to be shielded from the public glare for a full seven years. But for the first two or three, the business of courtiers, ambassadors and petitioners could be kept from his door. There was to be some peace in Arthur's early life. Even if he probably never remembered it.

Arthur's relative remoteness in his early years must have been a blessing for the boy. But it is a source of frustration for the biographer. Due to his absence from the life of the court, and a lack of surviving records, we have no way of knowing where he spent his childhood.

As we have already seen, after his baptism in Winchester, Arthur's parents settled him at Farnham Castle. Arthur was still at Farnham six months later, when the people of the town wasted no time in petitioning the King for a licence for a 'perpetual chantry of one chaplain to celebrate divine service at the altar of the Blessed Mary in the north side of the said church'.[3]

The inhabitants claimed concern that, despite the town being host to 2000 men and women, their spiritual needs were under resourced. They surely reasoned that Henry VII would look favourably on a request from the town where 'the king's firstborn son Arthur is now being nursed'.[4]

Farnham may have served as Arthur's home for the first six years of his life. With the exception of its distance from London, it boasted all the required qualities. It provided a degree of seclusion but was large enough to accommodate the prince's expanding household. While originally constructed in the 13th century, the previous Bishop of Winchester, William Waynflete had invested in significant improvements.[5] Arthur's needs would naturally develop as he grew. But for now, Farnham was fit for a prince.

In July 1488, two Spanish ambassadors were invited to meet the infant prince who was staying '12 miles from London'.[6] Farnham is a far greater distance from Westminster than that, so it's possible that by this time Arthur and his household had relocated. However, it's just as likely that Arthur had been temporarily moved nearer, in anticipation of the ambassadors' visit.

Ahead of his creation as Prince of Wales, a herald's account of the proceedings records that Arthur came by water from 'Ashehurst to Shene' ahead of the ceremony. It's not clear which 'Ashehurst' this refers to or whether this was Arthur's home or simply a stop on his journey. But there's no Ashurst that fits the twelve-mile journey from Westminster, which suggests it was not the place that the Spanish ambassadors inspected him.

So, while it's possible that Arthur and his household relocated from Farnham before he was 2 or 3 years of age, it's equally plausible that Farnham remained his main base. He just might have been more nomadic than is generally assumed.

While we can't be sure exactly where Arthur's household was located, we happily know much more about its shape and size. On 1 February 1487, the King set aside 1000 marks (£666) for 'expenses of his moost dere son the prince'.[7] This was a staggering sum. Not dissimilar to the annual income of some barons and probably on par with what an adult earl might spend on his establishment. It shows just how seriously the fiscally conservative king took the upbringing of his son.

The most senior member of Arthur's initial household – and the most significant person in his young life – was the lady mistress. By September 1488, payment records show that this role was occupied by Lady Elizabeth Darcy. While this is the first recorded mention of her appointment, she was probably already in place by the time of Arthur's birth.

Elizabeth Darcy was the most qualified person in England for the job. She had performed the same service for the children of Edward IV. Her appointment was Elizabeth of York's decision, but the king would have needed little convincing.

Lady Darcy was a widow from the knightly class. At first glance, it might seem like such a prominent position should go to a woman of more advanced rank. However, it was common for someone of Darcy's station to occupy such a role. While wellborn enough to be entirely respectable, women at her level were more likely to have played an active role in the upbringing of their own children. She still wouldn't have been involved in the nitty-gritty of running her offspring's nursery, but she would probably have kept a close eye on it. A great lady of the realm would have been able to outsource even that. As such, a woman of grander rank would not have had the skills needed to ensure the smooth running of Arthur's fledgling establishment.

According to Chaucer, lady mistresses were usually of mature years. They were selected for their virtuous character. This might be because they had always been virtuous, or more colourfully, because they had previously succumbed to temptation but, upon realising the error of their ways, chose to forsake 'the olde daunce' forever.[8]

In the case of Lady Darcy, we can safely assume that she was among the former. There would have been no questions about the character, or the past of a woman selected to rear two future kings. Her duties would have been broad. She would have overseen every aspect of life in the nursery, supervised the nurses that tended Arthur and even given some direction to the male members of the household.

It was a huge job, and she was well rewarded for it. She was paid £20 a year, a significant sum supplemented with regular bonuses. In late 1488 she was granted a yearly gift of 'one tun or two pipes of red wine, to be had yearly at the port of London.'[9] Nurturing the heir to the throne, it would seem, was thirsty work.

In the earliest months of Arthur's life, Darcy was supported by a nursery nurse. Initially this was a wet nurse, responsible for feeding the thriving prince. Later, she would have continued responsibility for his feeding but was scrutinised by a physician, instructed to stand over the nurse at every meal to see 'what moate or drinke shee gave the child.'[10] When the Prince was three and a half years old, the king granted an annuity of £20 to Katherine Gibbs, "late nurse of the king's first-born son". It is likely that Katherine served as Arthur's nurse from the time of his birth until he was old enough to need her no longer.

Also under Darcy's supervision, were four chamberers or 'rockers'.[11] Initially they would have rocked Arthur's cradle and, as he grew older, assisted in other duties. Earlier in the century, the 2-year-old Henry VI could boast a principal nurse, a day nurse, a laundress and two others of unspecified duties.[12] While the roles of Arthur's nurses may have been less formalised, between them they would have fulfilled a similar range of functions.

The nurses that tended to Arthur were likely women of reasonable birth, but below the gentry class. This was reflected in part by their lower, but still significant wages. An Agnes Butler and Evilyn Hobbes secured salaries of 33s 4p for their services. Alice Bywymble was paid just 28s 6p. However, all might have looked forward to greater rewards to come. Richard II, Henry VI, Edward IV and Henry VII had all made generous gifts to their nurses.[13] It was a role that could lead to a lifetime of recognition.

Women were at the centre of Arthur's world for the first three years of his life. His nephew, Edward VI would later complain about how long he had been subject to the rule of petticoat. Future King or not, the requirements of tending to an infant, to the medieval mindset, required a feminine touch. Nevertheless, it did not cost 1000 marks a year to employ a lady mistress and a handful of women. And, to the mindset of the fifteenth century, there were tasks that only men could fulfil.

Details of which men served Arthur in his earliest years or what their duties were are scant. Records show that Robert Bluet, William Wangham and John Hoo were all servants to the prince by 1489, along with a further nine men who are unnamed.[14] Although lumped together on a solitary payment record, these men were from different social backgrounds and presumably fulfilled vastly different functions.

John Hoo seems to have been a member of a landowning family. He was perhaps on hand to start guiding Arthur to the path of knightly pursuits. Something which, as we shall see, would have begun as quickly as it was physically possible to do.

On the other hand, William Wangham was from the lower orders. Ahead of preparing Arthur's nursery before his birth, Wangham was paid 16 pence for 'the making of two parrs of coverlets'.[15]

While retaining a man like Wangham in Arthur's household might strike some as odd, there was certainly enough work to do. Throughout his infancy, Arthur was splendidly attired. His father made a grant from the Royal wardrobe of 'divers robes, tunics and ornaments, things and stuffs for the said lord prince.' His 'mistress-nurse' was also sent 'damaske, satyn, sarsynette, fustainne, furrure or ermyns, black bogi; with sheets of holand cloth, brusshis, corchettes, tapettes, iron hammers.' The household was clearly expected to craft this all into glorious attire for the young Prince. While Lady Darcy probably had some skill in doing so, she might well have required the assistance of a master craftsman.

According to the ordinances later laid down by Henry VII for the raising of Royal children, 'Yeomen and groomes must bee charged to awaite upon the chamber.'[16] This was almost certainly the case in Arthur's household. No payment records survive as to who carried out these tasks, but the gentry-level men already mentioned are strong contenders. Given their role in helping prepare and serve food to the heir to the throne, they would have been men who enjoyed the highest degree of the king's trust. In March 1488, Thomas Poyntz, one of the King's esquires for the body was granted forty marks a year for services to the King and 'to Arthur the King's first-born son.' It is likely that it was the king's own close servants who were dispatched to attend on Arthur, perhaps on a rotation basis.

Other payment grants suggest that the link between Arthur's household and his father's were well established. Later in February 1489, a similar grant for both services to the king and Arthur was awarded to John Whytyng. Later in that year, after Arthur's creation as Prince of Wales, Whytyng was appointed as Arthur's sewer, a role that consisted of helping prepare and bring the prince's food.[17] It is likely that this was always part of his duties.

Bernard André, the man who would one day assist in Arthur's education would later write how Arthur's intellectual gifts were apparent from a young age.

'So great was his natural vigour that without any tutelage or help he displayed to his guardians the promise of his virtues out of his native goodness'.[18]

Those rearing the boy may have taken umbrage at the claim that Arthur progressed 'without any tutelage or help'. But perhaps they would have agreed that the prince was a natural student.

The formal education of boys did not usually begin until the age of about 5 or 6 but by that age, Arthur had already achieved a 'swift and thorough knowledge of the first principles of literature.'[19] He probably began studying in some kind of structured form at about the age of 3. John Nele would later serve as the dean of Arthur's chapel, but even at the early stage, the prince's household would have contained chaplains. It could have been these men that gave Arthur his first instruction in letters and introduced him to literature. Or it may have been gentlemen in the household, Lady Darcy herself or some combination of all of them. It's also possible that an unnamed tutor was present in Arthur's household at a young age.

But education for the nobility was not just about the academic. Being raised in the knightly tradition had a strong physical component. To start with, this probably consisted of basic exercise. Edward IV had instructed, when his son was 2, that the prince should enjoy exercise and recreation twice a day.[20] Given Arthur was being raised by the same mistress, we can safely assume that he enjoyed a similar routine.

In his earliest years, Arthur's outdoor play would have consisted of the usual childhood games of the time. He might have fashioned a horse from a peeled wand and rode it like children today would a hobby horse. He could have made a sailing ship out of a piece of broken bread.[21] As he weaved his own imagination into the games and activities of his infancy, those supervising him at play may have gained their first sense of Arthur's interests and personality. Did he make a sword from a twig or blade of grass as it's tempting to imagine his brother Henry VIII doing? Or did he build a church out of stones and discarded sticks, like a gentle Henry VI may have done?

Over time, this outdoor recreation would have given way to more formal physical education. And that time probably arrived quickly. By the time of his creation as Prince of Wales, just after his third birthday, he was skilled enough to ride a horse during the ceremony. Arthur must master the knightly pursuits quickly and those rearing him knew that there was little time to waste.

The more physical Arthur was encouraged to be, the greater the risk of bumps and bruises. Perhaps in recognition of the boy's burgeoning career as an athlete, the King appointed a new doctor, Stephen Bereworth to serve as the prince's physician. The doctor was granted an annuity of £40 out of duchy of Cornwall lands "in consideration of the grantee's cordial affection and good service to the king, and in reward for his medical attendance upon Prince Arthur, the King's first-born son."[22]

The wording of this grant is unusually warm. And, on the face of it, the salary seems large. Afterall, it was double what Lady Darcy was receiving. Both of these points have given rise to speculation that Arthur's health had recently been at risk and that Dr Bereworth had intervened to save his life.

We should not indulge in such speculation too liberally. Forty pounds was certainly a large sum. Some members of the landed class would have drawn less annual revenue from their estates. But it was not unprecedented for a Royal doctor. Arthur's household seems to have included a physician from day one. Bereworth's appointment probably just marks a changing of the guard. It is of course possible that Arthur suffered more worrying bouts of ill health in his earliest year. Childhood illness is far from uncommon and it's difficult to know what toll his prematurity took on his early development.

However, if Arthur had experienced any kind of urgent medical assistance in the early part of 1488, we can be confident that there were no physical signs of illness by the July of that year. That month, two Spanish ambassadors were invited to visit the prince. So confident were the English in his appearance that they invited the visitors to inspect him naked before watching him sleep. The ambassadors cheerfully reported back that 'he appeared to us so admirable that, whatever praise, commendation, or flattery, anyone might be capable of speaking or writing would only be truth in this case.' So confident was the King in the strength of Arthur's physicality that he wished the ambassadors to take Arthur's 'figure, image and appearance to Spain.' [23] Had Arthur been fragile, sickly, or even small for his age, the King would hardly have been so confident.

Impressing foreign ambassadors was part of the theatre of international relations. To show the strength of a dynasty, embodied in a thriving, healthy heir was too good an opportunity to miss. However, the Spanish ambassador's inspection of a young, naked Arthur was a moment of even greater significance. While he was not yet two years old, his father had already opened negotiations for the prince's marriage. The marriage of a king, or a future king, was one of the primary diplomatic levers that empowered a nation to exert influence in the game of European affairs. It was a game that England had been out of for several decades.

By taking a domestic bride, Edward IV had shut down the possibility of a strategic marriage. Edward V had been too young for negotiations to be finalised and Richard III had come to the throne as a married man. Political realities meant that Henry VII's marriage was a done deal before he even took the crown. Now, with the wars of the roses finally settled, Arthur could search for a bride among the palaces of the continent. Recent English policy had focused on relations – or tensions – with France, Brittany, and the low countries. However, by the mid-1480s it was becoming clear that European power was heading south. A marriage between Ferdinand of Aragon and Isabella of Castille had effectively united two of the major territories of Iberia. The Kingdom of Spain was emerging on the European stage as a force to be reckoned with.

An alliance with Spain would give England the chance to emerge from her own internal conflicts and take her place on the world stage. Crucially, if Arthur could be married to one of the daughters of the Spanish or Catholic monarchs, as Ferdinand and Isabella were known – who could dare question that the house of Tudor was anything less than first-rate European Royalty?

Fortunately, for Henry, the shape of Spain's emerging foreign policy did include a role for England. Even more fortunately for Arthur, the Spanish monarchs had four daughters. One, the Infanta Catalina was just nine months older than the English heir. She would become known in English history as Katherine of Aragon. Being close in age, was not of primary importance when it came to marriage negotiations. Indeed, Katherine would end up married to Arthur's younger brother Henry who was some six years younger than the princess. Nevertheless, where such niceties could be accommodated, they could help create the sense that the stars were aligning.

Henry made the first move. In March 1488, the King issued a commission to 'John Weston, prior of St John of Jerusalem in England, John Gunthorpe, Dean of Wells, Christopher Urswik, Great Almoner, Thomas Savage, Doctor of Law, and Henry Ainsworth, Doctor of Law, to conclude a treaty of alliance with Ferdinand and Isabella of Spain, to settle all pending subjects of dispute, and to confer on the articles regarding the assistance to be given to one another by the contending powers.'[24]

A marriage between Arthur and Katherine wasn't mentioned. Yet, the embassy would have known that their mission was to test the waters for such a match. And they seemed to get a warm response. About a month later, Ferdinand and Isabella commissioned Gonzalvo de Puebla, the half-crippled lawyer and diplomat to 'conclude a treaty of marriage between Princess Katherine and Arthur, Prince of

Wales'[25] De Puebla would later be posted to England on a more permanent basis and become an important figure in Arthur's world. Larger than life, and perhaps a little workshy, the ambassador was loathed by many of his fellow Spaniards. Henry VII however, seemed to develop great affection for him. It is likely that Arthur did the same.

However indelicate it seems to us today, in the fifteenth century it was impossible to discuss marriage without debating money. De Puebla was under strict instructions to agree 'the marriage portion, and the conditions of its payment and repayment in case of the dissolution of the marriage' and to 'concert the amount and conditions of the jointure to be given by Henry to the Princess Katherine.'[26] Dr de Puebla, accompanied by another ambassador called Juan De Sepulveda quickly set sail for England. By early July, negotiations had begun in earnest.[27] The early stages of the negotiation, between the Royal parties themselves, largely centred around grand statements of respect and affection. But when the ambassadors met behind closed doors, it was time to get down to business. The gloves came off quickly. In bat for the Spanish were de Puebla and de Sepulveda. Representing the English were Richard Foxe, Bishop of Exeter and Giles Daubeney, an experienced diplomat.

The parents of rich women were expected to pay a marriage portion to the family of their daughter's future husband. The price that Ferdinand and Isabella must part with was always likely to be a sticking point. The English began by asking the Spanish to propose a sum. This wasn't going to wash with De Puebla. It had been the English, after all, that had first solicited the marriage. Would it not be more becoming for them to name the price?

Foxe and Daubeney went in high. They asked three times the sum that the English ambassadors had hinted at when they visited Spain. De Puebla reacted with mock amazement and quickly went for the jugular. Why were the English being so unreasonable? Given what happens every day to the Kings of England – a subtle dig to the turmoil of the Wars of the Roses – it was a wonder that Ferdinand and Isabella should consider giving their daughter to England at all. The Spaniard later reported back that "this was said with great courtesy, in order that they might not feel displeasure or be enraged."[28] Yet it is tempting to wonder whether the Spanish men's "great courtesy" had been quite so well received.

Foxe and Daubeney dropped their demands by a third. The Spanish stalled. Perhaps two or four persons should be selected as umpires. The English could not brook such a delay. They lowered their original demand by half. De Puebla would only concede a quarter. The match would be so advantageous to the King of England, he maintained, that he ought to content himself with that. The English disagreed. Besides, what were the Spanish panicking about? The King and Queen of Spain would not need to fund it out of their own pocket. The money would come from their subjects. There was surely room to be generous. Henry's negotiators had clearly done their homework. They referred to old treaties with France, Burgundy, and Scotland. Compared to these incidences, the marriage portion they were seeking was modest indeed.

History seemed to be failing the English but perhaps economics could help. They turned their talk to the exchange rate. England was an expensive place. The smallest English coin was worth eight Spanish marvedis. And they refuted the Spanish's claims about a lack of safety. There was not "a drop of blood in existence" from which any danger might arise.

Eventually the marriage portion of 200,000 gold scudos was agreed. Every scudo was to be of the value of four shillings and two pennies. How this compared to the original demands is unclear, but both parties seemed able to live with it.

Money was still firmly on the table. Next up for discussion was the jointure, the lands and revenue that would be bestowed on Katherine if Arthur predeceased her. The English offered a third of the revenue of Wales, Cornwall, and Chester, with the best towns, villages, and castles to be selected for her. This would be equivalent to eighty gold crowns.[29]

The Spanish pushed for a greater dowry in the event that Katherine became queen. The English flatly refused to raise the stakes. They insisted that 'there is no country in the world where Queens live with greater pomp than in England, where they have as many court officers as the King.'[30] The Spanish relented quickly. Dowries or jointures were usually between a fifth to a third of the landed estate in question. What the English were offering was already on the generous side. Nevertheless, before the ink was dry on the treaty, the English would offer more still. The negotiating teams also poured over a variety of other issues. Shared foreign policy objectives. Trade implications. Customs for merchants. Though on these they seemed to reach no firm conclusions. Toward the end of the year, Henry decided to up the ante. On 11 December, he commissioned:

> 'Thomas Savage, doctor of civil laws and chancellor of the marches, and Richard Nanfan, a knight of the king's body, to treat with the counsellors and commissioners of the king of Castile, Ligeoun, Aragoun, and Sisillia, and his queen-consort, for a perpetual league of peace and friendship between them and the King of England; and also for the espousal and marriage between the King's son, Arthur Prince of Wales, duke of Cornwall, and earl of Chester and Katerine, one of the daughters of the said king and queen of Castile, &c; with powers to make terms respecting the provision and dowry of the princess, the time and mode of her passage to England, and her establishment and treatment in the said country.'[31]

Negotiations continued throughout the early months of 1489 until eventually at Medina del Campo, both sides ratified a detailed treaty on 26 March.

The wording of the treaty serves as a sharp reminder that this marriage was not about love or affection. Flowery language may have been sprinkled into the preamble, but the future union of Arthur and Katherine was fundamentally about politics, commerce, and foreign affairs.

It is not clear at this stage, how committed the Spanish truly were to fulfilment of the marriage. When the children were as young as Arthur and Katherine, such agreements could easily be broken off before the couple reached marital age. As we shall see, this treaty was not the first that would have to be negotiated before Arthur could truly be sure of his marriage prospects. It's possible that, at least on the Spanish side, no one truly expected this engagement to come to fruition.

Nevertheless, a roadmap for the young Royals' eventual nuptials was set out in the document. Arthur and Katherine were to marry *per verba future de proesenti*. This meant that the couple would commit themselves when they reached the appropriate age. A minimum of 12 for a girl and 14 for a boy.

However, the treaty had to be careful in its language. While arranged marriages were the norm for the upper classes, forced marriage was forbidden by the church. The parents could commit that they would "employ all their influence with their children that the marriage be contracted as stipulated."[32] But they couldn't make a commitment on their child's behalf. Of course, in reality this made no practical difference. Neither infant would ever be able to escape the commitments their parents had made on their behalf unless their parents decided they should. And to the fifteenth century mindset, it would be puzzling if either of them would want to.

The marriage portion – which had been such a bone of contention at the early stages of negotiation – was set at 200,000 scudos, each scudo to the value of four shillings and 2 pennies. A fourth however, could be payable in ornaments and jewels belonging to the princess.[33] This compromise seemingly solved a sticking point early in the negotiations as to whose responsibility it was to ensure that Katherine was appropriately kitted out.[34] Katherine's dowry was settled at a third part of the revenues of Wales, Cornwall, and Chester. It was specified that should she become Queen her dowry would be greater.[35]

Arthur was still too young to understand what a marriage was. Nevertheless, his parents had all but committed him to one. From this point on, those caring for him must have filled his young head and heart with stories of a beautiful princess beneath the Pyrenees. One day, she would traverse the ocean and join Arthur where they would rule together over a prosperous Kingdom. It must have seemed like a fairy tale. As he grew however, Arthur would soon learn that to truly win the hand of your princess, you had to slay a number of dragons.

The ratification of the treaty of Medina del Campo was a major diplomatic coup for Henry VII. The Spanish had responded to his advances quickly. The treaty was concluded in less than a year. It was clearly an agreement that both parties valued, even if they had different expectations for its long-term prospects. But negotiating the treaty would prove to be the easy bit. Henry VII had secured his immediate foreign policy objectives in forging a continental alliance and, by extension, being recognised as a legitimate prince of Europe. But the Spanish had their objectives to, and during the negotiation of the treaty successfully locked England in to supporting their military objectives.

The driving force behind Spanish foreign policy at this point was the French-Breton wars that had been brewing for most of the decade. Francis II, Duke of Brittany, had died in 1488, leaving just a teenage daughter, Anne to succeed him. The French King, Charles VIII, claimed with some legitimacy that the young duchess was his ward, giving him feudal rights to determine her marriage. Should he marry her himself, Brittany would be fully annexed to France. The power of Ferdinand's arch-rival would be substantially increased.

The Spanish were determined to clip France's wings. And this meant forming an alliance against Charles to prevent him taking what he wanted by force. Ostensibly their objective was the protection of Brittany rather than the containment of France, but few were confused as to their driving motivation.[36] Henry VII had no desire for war with France. He owed them much for their assistance in his conquest of England. And unlike his eventual successor, Henry VIII, he had no aspirations to establish himself as a great war lord. During the treaty negotiations he had attempted to avoid binding commitments. But he knew full well what was expected of him.

Henry signed a separate treaty pledging protection to Brittany. Parliament agreed to raise a tax of £75000 to fund 10,000 Archers to 'provide for the defence of this realm against its ancient enemies.'[37] The tax was far from popular. Risings in the north were so violent that the Earl of Northumberland was murdered, and it took public hangings to restore order.[38] To many, it might not have seemed like these sacrifices were worth it. Lord Willoughby de Broke led a force of 7000 troops into Brittany in March to bolster the Duchy's defences. But they did little more than scuffle and most were home by the end of the year. Henry, however, had proven that when his allies needed him, he was prepared to commit men to their cause.

To say that Henry went to war purely to secure Arthur's marriage would be a drastic oversimplification. He had his own clear interest in the outcome of Brittany's future. But in one way or another, it is true to say that all his military actions were about protecting Arthur's future. Once again, though he was barely old enough to hold a toy sword in his hand, Arthur's destiny was being shaped and preserved by battle. Even the innocence of his childhood was protected by drops of blood.

*

The long months of 1489 had paved the way for Arthur's dynastic and political future. But it also marked the year which would signal the beginning of great personal change for the prince. In about February of that year, the Queen fell pregnant. It is not clear why there was a relatively long gap between Arthur's birth and the second conception. It could be that there was trouble conceiving but it is more likely that following a difficult pregnancy with Arthur she needed considerable time to recover.

Arthur's status in the family was about to change. He would go from only child to elder brother and no longer would be the only Royal babe of the realm. It could have been the prospect of a second son that caused Henry to think about confirming the seniority of the first. But for whatever the reason, during the parliamentary session in October, 'the king remenbring on his furst beogten sone was not yet created prince.' He determined that on Saint Andrew's Day – 30th November – Arthur would be brought before the lords of the realm and created Prince of Wales.[39]

The chapter of relative peace and seclusion that had marked the first three years of Arthur's life was over. Princes could not stay children for long.

Chapter 6

The Prince of Wales

Arthur's earliest memory is something we can only guess at. Had he lived to become an old man, he may have confided recollections of his infancy in a friend or confessor. His early death deprives us of such reflections. But surely, we can be confident that whatever else filled his early memory, recollections of the last days of November 1489 were vividly among them. For these were days when he traversed the river Thames, riding the beautifully adorned Royal barge. Spanish merchants fired guns in tribute to his approach and the craftsmen of London lined the banks of the river in anticipation of his arrival. Boats, guns, and festival. What little boy would fail to be fascinated?

Just a month before Arthur's intrepid journey, Henry VII had ordered letters to be sent to the great landowners of England and the 'sonnes and heires of divers of the great estates of this royaulme' commanding them to come to Westminster on St Andrew's Day, 30th November. Arthur was to be dubbed a knight of the bath and created Prince of Wales.[1] By Arthur's time, the title of Prince of Wales had long been associated with the eldest son of the King of England and it was always created alongside the Earldom of Chester. Today it remains a title that the sovereign can only bestow on the heir apparent, which they invariably do.

Ironically however, when the title was first given to an English prince it may have had an altogether different purpose. The first English Prince of Wales was Edward of Caernarfon, son of Edward I, who would grow up to become the ill-fated Edward II. The elder Edward ensured that his son was born in Caernarfon, the ancient castle of historic significance in Wales. It is highly likely that the King was planning for this boy to be a prince devoted to Wales from the beginning, as a signal of English domination over the principality.

At the time of his birth however, the younger Edward was not his father's eldest son or his heir. His elder brother Alfonso still lived. It could be that the ever-cunning war lord was preparing to leave the rule of England to one son and Wales to another. If so, it was a short-lived plan. Alfonso died later that year and Edward became the heir.

By Arthur's time, the title of Prince of Wales did not have a happy recent history. Edward of Westminster, son to the hapless Henry VI was disinherited as a child. He died on the battlefield trying to reclaim his position. The future

Edward V enjoyed a successful tenure as prince but lasted just a matter of weeks on the throne before being overthrown by his uncle, Richard III. Richard's own son, Edward of Middleham perished as a child, just seven months after receiving the title.

As time would tragically show, Arthur was to fare no better than his unfortunate predecessors. But as 1489 drew to a close, such fears were far away, and all eyes were focused on a glorious future. The boy was now betrothed to a Spanish princess and was about to become an older brother. It was time for him to take his place as a great man of the realm. At least for the purpose of ceremony.

Arthur arrived at Sheen on 21 November. The festivities around his creation did not commence for another four days. It is likely that this time was spent preparing the boy for what was to come. He probably spent time among many of the great men who would be participants in the ceremony. The next few days would be gruelling for any 3-year-old. The more familiar he became with the key players, the smoother everything would run.

On Wednesday, the 25th, he boarded the King's barge which had been 'ryally prepared' for the occasion. From Sheen, he journeyed down the Thames, setting sail for Mortlake, to the sound of trumpets as minstrels played. It must have all been rather exciting. Between Mortlake and Chelsea, the Royal barge was joined by other vessels, no doubt splendidly attired, and carrying the great men of the realm. These 'lords espirituell and temporell' entered Arthur's barge 'in their own parsonne'. Arthur would finally encounter some familiar faces. The Bishop of Winchester, whom he would have known well from Farnham, along with his step-grandfather the Earl of Derby and his godfathers the Earl of Oxford and the Earl of Arundel (who had been styled as "Lord Maltravers" at Arthur's christening).[2]

There is no suggestion that Arthur was accompanied by a nurse or Lady Darcy. It's possible that one was present but not mentioned. Yet, appearances were everything in proceedings such as this. A woman, particularly one of little rank, would have looked quite out of place. It's more likely that one or a collection of Arthur's male servants were present, perhaps dressed as a yeoman or a sergeant-at-Arms. After all, the boy could hardly have been totally unsupervised for the first leg of the journey.

At Chelsea, Arthur and the great lords in his company rendezvoused with the Mayor of London. Rather than climb aboard the Royal vessel, he escorted the prince in his own barge, spectacularly decorated in Royal banners. We don't know which flags flew a top either vessel but it's likely that the red Welsh dragon and Cadwaladr's arms were among them. Arthur's own arms depicting the feather of the Prince of Wales were almost certainly flying. Strictly speaking, he was not yet entitled to use these badges, but they would already have been created in anticipation of his elevated status. This was likely their first outing in public.

At Lambeth they met the Spanish ambassadors. Spain was understandably keen to show an interest. By this stage Arthur was engaged to the Spanish Infanta, Katherine of Aragon. With the Spanish ambassador were many Spanish merchants 'in shopbottes, shutting gownes in nombre and after casting apples – as it had bene in fighting on the see with targes – all in rejoishyng of the princes coming.'[3] Quite what this looked like is hard to fathom. But it must have seemed an impressive display to the infant prince.

Eventually Arthur landed by 'the King's Brigg'. From there, all the way to the King's bench in Westminster Hall 'the worshipful craftes of London stood in order on both sides'. To the extent that Arthur understood that all this was for him, he must have realised that he was very special indeed. Arthur proceeded to join his father, who was in the 'the great chamber of the bricketoure '[4] We don't know whether they were alone or what was discussed. Nor, do we really know how well Henry and Arthur knew each other at this stage. One thing is for sure: those responsible for Arthur's care would have impressed upon him that this was a moment for best behaviour! Although the week's festivities were to centre around Arthur's creation as Prince, this would be preceded by an occasion that was almost as grand. The admittance of Arthur, and other worthy postulants into the noble Order of the Bath which would take place in Westminster ahead of the main event.

The Order of the Bath and the ceremonies that surround it are of ancient but obscure origin. Elements of the tradition, such as being fully immersed in water, clearly have connotations to baptism. It is likely that the order's foundations were religious as much as noble. The practices associated with the Bath may have begun as a way of ensuring that knights from the top-tier of families received a more prestigious induction. The making of a knight required a simple dubbing with a sword, and it was probably felt early on that a bit more fuss should accompany the knightly of the elite.

By at least the coronation of Henry IV in 1399, Bath had emerged as a distinct order of chivalry. Men were dubbed into it at great occasions such as coronations, weddings or in the wake of great victories.[5] The premise of the order seemed to revolve around ceremony, making it the perfect accompaniment to great occasions. While we know that Arthur would later become a knight of the equally prestigious Garter, no account of his induction into that noble order survives. His creation as Prince of Wales, however, represented a wonderful opportunity to induct those who were next in the pecking order.

Service to the King was among the first duties of a knight. On the eve of their creation, all the postulants would have a chance to demonstrate it. Each of them played a public role in a great feast, providing for their lord's every need. Arthur held his father's towel during dinner. All eyes would have been firmly fixed on him and there could be time for wriggling, fussing or sulking. His discipline, at such a young age, must have been remarkable.

Arthur was destined to join the order with nineteen other worthy candidates. Among the gentry postulants there seems to be no rhyme or reason as to who was chosen. They were simply those that were deemed to deserve the honour. This was the next great occasion where the King could bestow it. But with the noblemen that accompanied Arthur through the process, a little more thought seems to have been given. The prince represented the future. Those that would be knighted with him, were those that would share it. After the prince himself, the most senior knight was the young Earl of Northumberland. The boy was aged just 11, having come into his inheritance after the murder of his father earlier in the year. Joining him was William Fitzalan, Lord Maltravers. This is not the same Lord Maltravers who had acted as Arthur's godfather at his christening. By this time, he had succeeded to the Earldom of Arundel, vacating the junior Maltravers title for his son to enjoy. Maltravers was also aged about 11. While Arthur was significantly younger still, it is clear that the intention was to knight him among those that could be just-about considered his own generation.

The herald that recorded the proceedings notes that 'Lord Gray Ruthyn' was due to be knighted. But this is a slight mistake. Lord Grey Ruthin was George Grey, the son of the Earl of Kent. He was much older than the others and had been knighted at the coronation of Richard III. It was surely Grey's son, Richard, also aged 11, who joined Arthur at the ceremony. To be fair on the herald, it was a minor mistake. Just six months later, George succeeded to the Earldom. By the time the herald was writing up and editing his notes, the young Richard would have been known by the 'Grey Ruthin' courtesy title.

A 'Lord Stourton' was also named as a nobleman due to be knighted. He was much older than Arthur and the others, breaking the pattern of youth. It could be that he was long overdue for the honour and simply had to be accommodated. Or perhaps the ever-cautious King felt that, given the complexities of what was to come, at least one older man should be among them. These noblemen were being prepped to one day serve Arthur and bolster the success of his reign. But for now, they assisted the boy in serving his father. Stourton carried the water, Northumberland took the say and Maltravers and Grey held the basins. The more junior knights carried the dishes. At this stage in his life, Arthur still spent much of his time under the maternal care of women. Male officers within his household had probably taken on more significant roles with every passing year, but Lady Darcy and Arthur's nurses would still have acted as his primary carers. Now the young Prince found himself saturated in masculinity without a mother, a mistress or a nurse in sight. It must have felt very grown up.

Once the King had finished eating, Arthur and his fellow knights could finally satiate their appetites. Arthur was waited on by Thomas Brandon and Thomas

Brereton. Both men hailed from families that were prospering under the Tudors. This association of service to the heir showed they were destined to rise higher still.

As we have seen, a cleansing ritual, similar to baptism was the heart of making a new knight of the Bath. The night before their dubbing, the men would each immerse themselves in a bath of warm water. As night fell, these baths were assembled and drawn. Most were placed in the Parliament chamber. However, the baths of the three young noblemen – Northumberland, Maltravers and Grey – were placed in the entry between the Parliament chapel and the chamber. This was probably a reflection of their seniority. Each of these boys was an earl or the heir to an earldom. Arthur's bath was kept separate even from the nobility. Almost certainly as a mark of precedence. It was prepared in the King's closet. His distance from the others also served a practical purpose. Away from judging eyes it is likely that he could again be tended by the nurses that knew and treasured him.

The men – heralds – who wrote about the Arthur's knighting ceremony did so with a certain objective in mind. They were masters of ceremony. They wanted to keep a clear record of how things were done so that the proper order could be replicated in the future. They gave detailed descriptions of who performed what role, what precedence they were accorded and the setup of the ceremony. But they didn't feel the need to trouble themselves with detail of the ceremony itself. As such, what was almost certainly an elaborate and theatrical ceremony was simply summed up by one line: 'the king in his parson gave them the advertisement of theordre of knygthode.'[6]

Thankfully, the later knighting of Arthur's younger brother, Prince Henry, was better recorded. We can safely assume that the two ceremonies followed a similar trajectory. All postulant knights had the advertisement of knighthood read to them – a form of words which made their commitments clear. Usually, these words would have been read by the Earl of Oxford, as the great chamberlain of England. But on this occasion the King recited them himself.

Standing before Arthur, who was stripped and placed in his bath of warm water, the King issued his instructions. Arthur was to be strong in the faith of the Holy Church, protect all widows and oppressed maidens and to love and defend the King with his power.[7] Arthur must already have viewed his father as a figure of awe. An almost mystical lord whom he would see on occasion and revere by routine. The words must have made as powerful an impression on Arthur as if they had been delivered by God himself.

The king then dipped his finger in the water and made a sign of the cross on his son's shoulder, which he then proceeded to kiss. Arthur was lifted out of his bath and dried. Once the King had read the advertisement to the remaining postulants, they would all have proceeded to St Stephen's Chapel to keep vigil until the early hours of the morning.[8]

The long vigil was part of the usual traditions for the knighting ceremony. But on this occasion, all the men present had reason to be extra vigilant at prayer. And none more so than Arthur. News reached them that the queen was in labour. Arthur was probably too young to know just how risky a business this was for his mother. But he was old enough to understand that a brother or sister was on the way and was surely excited about the prospect. The fervency of the postulant's prayers was answered. 'Upon six of the cloke that same night, she was delivered of a princess.' [9] Arthur had become a big brother. But for now, he had another, more pressing transition to focus on. In the early hours of the morning, after a night at prayer, Arthur would have made his confession. Quite what sins such a young man would have to confess is a mystery, but it was a ritual he was used to. And then, after receiving his absolution, the exhausted boy would finally be permitted a few hours' sleep until daybreak.[10] Arthur would certainly need his rest. Once awake, the prince was 'convead thoughout saint stephen's chappel to the other end of the stairs toward the vicars logings, where he took his hourse.' The Earl of Essex, Arthur's cousin, was assigned to look after the young prince as he and the other postulants 'roode aboute the standard in the pales in to Westmynster hall'.[11] Mercifully, it was not a long ride. Essex bore the prince's sword and spurs.

As we have already seen, the King was due to knight some twenty men. Arthur, of course, was the star of the show and none would have resented this. Afterall, it was dazzling honour to be inducted into the order on the same day as the future King. They must have each hoped that it would create a lifetime affinity with the man who would one day become the fount of all honour and the forger of their fortunes.

When they arrived in Westminster Hall, Arthur was led to the King's presence by the Marquess of Berkely and his godfather, the Earl of Arundel. The Earl of Oxford, the chamberlain of England, took the sword and spurs from Essex and presented the right spur to the King. Henry commanded the Marquess of Berkley to set it on Arthur's right heal. As he did, Arundel set the remaining spur on his left.

The King then reached for his sword. With what we must assume was great and tender care, he dubbed his son's shoulders. Since birth, Arthur had born the title 'Duke of Cornwall' but had generally been referred to as 'My Lord Prince'. Now he was a knight of the Order of the Bath.[12]

After the King had 'dubbed al thos knyghtys' – the herald mentions as something of an afterthought – Arthur was taken to the King's closet. Here, he relinquished his sword and his spurs and was dressed in the robes of estate. From the closet he was 'led into the Parlement chambre to the kyngis presence by the marques of Barkeley'. By this stage, Arthur must have been exhausted and it is entirely possible the Marquess carried him in his arms. Behind him, also in great robes were his godfathers, the Earls of Arundel and of Derby, who carried his cape, coronet, and golden ring upon a golden robe. Behind them, came the Earl of Shrewsbury bearing a great sword with the pommel facing the ceiling.[13]

Frustratingly, the herald simply records that Arthur was 'create as acustumed.' To gain a sense of what the creation ceremony really looked like; we will have to use our imagination. Thankfully, the apparatus that was brought in with Arthur gives us a clue. The great Lords with him, at some stage, would have affixed the cape to his shoulders. His father must have placed a gold ring on his finger and the coronet on his head. His father would have fixed the sword to his belt. After the ceremony, the King departed. No doubt he was eager to set eyes upon his new-born daughter. However, the main reason was one of precedence. It was finally time for Arthur to be the main man. A status he could only achieve with his father's absence. The Prince of Wales proceeded to host the great men of the realm for a feast of celebration. Here, Arthur sat under the cloth of estate in the Parliament chamber. Among him were the newly created knights, the older of whom were presumably keeping a watchful eye over the infant prince. Not far away, were the nobility, including Arthur's godfathers, the Earls of Arundel and Derby. Arthur, no doubt with help, 'licensed them to ett ther mett'.

Finally, it was time to cry the prince's largess: an announcement of a gift that Arthur, like all good princes, made to the poor. The precise form of wording used on this occasion is unrecorded. But based on previous ceremonies, it is likely that a herald – probably Garter King of Arms – rose to his feet and cried: 'the high and mighty Prince, the King's son, Prince of Wales and Earl of Chester, largess' before stating the amount the prince had surrendered.

How much did Arthur understand about any of the events in which he had so ably starred? As with so much about the young boy's inner thoughts, we cannot be sure. But the vivid colours, the sensational sounds, the rich clothes and the journey by barge and horseback must have left a lasting impression. He must have recalled at least fragments of his creation ceremony for the rest of his life. It must have convinced him of the uniqueness of his destiny and may, once again, have caused the incredible burden on his shoulders to feel heavier still.

From the vantage point of the twenty-first century, where comparatively little is expected of youngsters, it seems unfathomable that Arthur could have performed the series of events with the ease and independence that the heralds record. Over a three-day period, he emerged into the court, served at a feast, kept an all-night vigil, and rode to his creation ceremony. And seemingly all among relative strangers, none of whom had any real childcare experience.

It is possible that the relatively vague account of the ceremonies omitted to mention times when special allowances were made for Arthur's youth. Or even moments that he was absent altogether. It is certainly possible that he was excused much of the vigil. Talk of Arthur being 'led' to various stages of the proceedings by various great men, could imply he was carried. While we can't rule out the presence of Lady Darcy or Arthur's nurses at any of the proceedings, it remains highly unlikely. The ceremony surrounding the Order of the Bath was inherently masculine. Men were stripped naked. The presence of a nurse waiting in the wings would be quite out of place. Though, as we have seen, this may have been why Arthur's bath and bed were kept separate from the others.

Even if there was more support for Arthur than the herald's account suggests, these days of constant performance must have been intensely gruelling. And this, more than anything else, shows how rigorous and disciplined Arthur's upbringing must have been. The dating of grants and payments to Arthur's servants, in the months leading up to his creations, show that his household was gradually acquiring a more masculine dynamic. To perform the duties required of him, such as riding on his own horse, standing still as spurs were affixed to his feet and a sword was dubbed on his shoulders, must have necessitated an intense period of preparation.

The sense of pressure on those raising and preparing Arthur for the occasion must have been enormous. It is inconceivable that these pressures weren't in turn, passed on to Arthur. By this stage, the prince must have known that his life was to be one of intense rigour and discipline. Even if, as is likely, he was still too young to really understand why. For all these reasons, no one could describe the early years of Arthur's life as laid back. But they would be the most relaxed and peaceful that Arthur would ever enjoy. Now, at just 3 years of age, he was the Prince of Wales. A title that was far more than honorific. He would have duties to perform and obligations to fulfil. In time his household would have to grow and change to reflect that.

To say that Arthur's childhood ended on 29 November 1489 would be an oversimplification. But it is right to record that his young life would never be the same again.

Chapter 7

The Maintenance of His State

Arthur was now Prince of Wales, Earl of Chester, and brother to the little baby Margaret. We don't know how long he stayed at court after his creation ceremony, but it's likely that he lingered for a few days to be reacquainted with his mother and to meet his new sister.

Of all his siblings, Arthur probably knew Margaret the best. It may be that the two were able to spend some time together before Margaret was joined in the nursery by their rambunctious younger brother Henry. Or it could just be that Arthur felt a special protective bond over the infant sister he had probably met in the first few days of her life. It is unlikely that he was introduced to his following siblings with the same punctuality.

Arthur would soon have returned to Farnham, or wherever he was living at the time. But he could not simply return to nursery. He was now a dubbed knight and an acknowledged Prince. Over the weeks and months that followed, a series of appointments began to transform his establishment into a household fit for the heir to the throne.

Just weeks after Arthur's return from Westminster the King appointed Richard Howell as marshal of the prince's household.[1] The ap Howells were an old Welsh family who had risen at court under the Welsh-born Henry VII. They seem also to have served the powerful Courtney family. This may suggest that the Bishop of Winchester – himself a part of the Courtney clan – had influenced the appointment.

Richard may have been the 'Richard ap Howell' who had been rewarded by the King earlier in the reign. If so, he may have been connected to Joan ap Howell who had a more intimate heritage with the King. Joan had acted as the King's nurse when he was a child and she was well rewarded by her former charge. It is natural to think that Joan's family, who perhaps impressed the King's mother, Margaret Beaufort back in the 1450s, were soon drawn into the King's circle of trust.

It's equally possible that the similarity in names is just a coincidence. Howells and ap Howells had served other members of the nobility as well as previous Kings. There may have been no connection between Arthur's new marshal and the King's former nurse. But it's tempting to think there could have been. In a noble household, the marshal was responsible for outdoor activities. This included the stables, hunting and falconry.² Arthur's physical, knightly training had already begun in earnest. Howell's appointment shows it was time to step it up.

There are hints that Arthur may have responded well to an increase in outdoor pursuits. When he was just 5 years old, the King gifted the prince a bow that cost 6 shillings and 8 pennies.³ Archery was a popular past time, but it was not essential for knightly pursuits. If Arthur was beginning to learn it, it might suggest that he was already excelling elsewhere.

By the end of 1490, John Almor was appointed as Arthur's sergeant-at-arms, with a salary of 12 pennies a day.⁴ At this stage in his career, we might hope that Arthur's law enforcement needs would be relatively low. However, Almor had previously served the King as a marshal of the hall, a role that probably involved keeping order among the more menial staff that worked the kitchens and the halls. It is likely that he performed a similar role in the Arthur's establishment. He might also have taken charge of the prince's own security, which was certainly a crucial consideration. Two other appointments also give an indication as to how daily life was changing for Arthur. John Whytyng has been appointed Arthur's sewer – effectively a waiter – just before his creation as prince. In March Thomas Fisher was appointed yeoman of the prince's cellar.⁵

There was probably still a fluidity between Arthur's household and his father's. John Whytyng would later return to the King's direct service as a gentleman usher to the King's chamber. Others probably also rotated between the two. Arthur's household was now more than a nursery. But it was not yet fully independent. These appointments strongly suggest that Arthur was now eating his meals, in some degree of estate, at the head of his household. This may not have been entirely new. He had behaved impeccably at the feast ahead of his creation. He almost certainly had experience of such occasions and a slimmed-down version was probably a regular occurrence in his household from a young age. Nevertheless, with a sewer of his own, Arthur must have fully weaned by this stage. He had no further use for a nurse.

Katherine Gibbs was retired in April on an annuity of twenty pounds. She had been with Arthur from the beginning. Initially she would have fed him at the breast. Thereafter she perhaps fed him his meats, under the supervision of the doctor, as he started to wean.

How did Arthur react to the loss? Kings tended to reward their former nurses when they had the power to do so. The early bond seems to have created everlasting affection and gratitude. We would be naïve to think that Arthur was not greatly affected by his parting from Nurse Gibbs. But he may already have been old enough to understand that he was a big and important prince. When things were tough or made him sad, he had to face them with the resilience and nobility of the knight he was. Despite the evolutions in his household and the grand show that had been made of his creation, there would still have been a realism that Arthur was little more than infant and required the care that children needed. Though his household had become significantly more male, there is no evidence that it yet included the really senior male officer positions such as steward or Chamberlain. Lady Darcy was probably still in overall charge. In other words, Arthur's household was in transition. It had probably been gradually evolving since the earliest months of his life. But the series of appointments around the time of his creation as Prince of Wales seems to mark a step change.

Household expansions did not come cheap. The records that survive probably only reflect a handful of appointments. And all of this had to be paid for. Just over a year after Arthur had been given the title of Prince of Wales, his father bestowed on him the lands and revenue to match. For "the maintenance of his state in accordance with the nobility of his race and excellence of his name" Arthur was given 'the principality of Wales, to hold for himself and his heirs, kings of England, for ever; together with all the king's lordships and lands of North Wales, West Wales and South Wales.' With the stroke of a pen, the 4-year-old boy had become a very rich man.

*

Henry VII owed his crown to a collection of exceptional people and extraordinary circumstances. His mother, who had helped establish him as a credible candidate and brokered his marriage. His uncle Jasper, who had kept him safe during the hard years of exile. Stalwart supporters like Oxford who had masterminded his military victories.

But, in reality, there was probably no one that had done more to secure the crown for Henry than the French King, Charles VIII. As much as Henry was probably loathe to admit it, without the French sponsorship of his invasion in 1485, he could never have built the basis of an army with which to mount a credible campaign.

It was perhaps for this reason that Henry had no major desire for war with France. In the early stage of the French-Breton conflict, he had tried to broker a peace between those two rulers that had helped keep him safe during the 1470s and 80s. As we have seen however, events took over and by 1489 he had committed men to military activity on the continent. He followed this up with a second expedition a year later and a series of raids along the French coast.

The French must have been apoplectic at what they saw as Henry's lack of gratitude. Though surely realistic about what their support would mean in terms of influence over English policies they would not have expected England's King to turn on them so soon. Charles now needed to find a way of distracting England from causing him trouble. And, thanks to his own experiences with supporting the pretender Henry Tudor, he knew exactly how to do it.

The leaders of Europe knew that with England's recent history, Henry VII was incredibly vulnerable to credible pretenders to the throne. Any foreign power that had access to one, could cause storm clouds to form on the horizon of the fledgling Tudor dynasty. Finding such a pretender, however, was easier said than done. The young Earl of Warwick was still in the King's possession. The Earl of Lincoln had died on the battlefield and his brother was seemingly behaving himself. Yorkist challengers to the Tudors were in short supply.

Late in 1491, this seemed to change. Word reached Henry VII that a boy had appeared in Ireland who was causing a stir among Irish high society. Leading noblemen, including the Earl of Desmond, believed they had rediscovered Richard, Duke of York, son of Edward IV and the younger of the princes in the tower. In reality, the boy was not a prince at all. He would later confess that he was a man called Perkin Warbeck, who hailed from the French town of Tournai. He had sailed to Cork in December 1491 to sell silk. Modelling the expensive fabrics to potential customers, he had clearly cut a dashing figure. For whatever motivation, some simply refused to accept that he was nothing more than a merchant.

At first, people told him that he must be the young Earl of Warwick, who had escaped the custody of the English King. Warbeck denied it. Then, influential men such as the mayor of Cork, John Atwater insisted that he was an illegitimate son of the late Richard III. Again, the boy rejected it. Eventually, no doubt after much prodding by these men of influence, he relented. He was, he confessed, none other than the escaped Duke of York, the rightful King of England.

The 'discovery' of the young duke was, of course, no coincidence. Nor was the timing of it. The French were due to embark on a major phase of their military occupation of Brittany. Military intervention from England could be detrimental. Or at least highly inconvenient. It was time to give the English King a bigger fish to fry.

Charles VIII had in his keeping an English exile named John Taylor. Taylor had been a faithful servant of Edward IV and Richard III. Unlike so many, he had never been able to make his peace with the Tudors. At some point, probably around 1489, he had sought sanctuary in France. Taylor would make the perfect agent to stir up trouble for France's old enemy. The French equipped Taylor with a small fleet, fully decked out in English garb. He set sail for Cork where he had connections to the mayor, John Atwater. His mission was clear: to find a young man to act as an impostor, stir up a rebellion and distract the military efforts of the English.[6] Initially, the plan seems to have been to find another young man to pose as Edward, Earl of Warwick. At some stage, probably because the local Irish men of influence were reluctant to support another Warwick, when it was known the King had the real one in his custody, Warbeck was presented as Prince Richard. Quickly gaining the support of the powerful Earls of Desmond and Kildare, a Yorkist uprising began.

The King dispatched Sir James Ormond, an Irish esquire of the body, to quell the rebellion. He set sail from Bristol with 30 sailors and 200 soldiers. Yet it was to take five months to fully quiet the uprising.⁷ In March 1492, Taylor's fleet took Warbeck to France. Here, Charles VIII greeted him with the full dignity of a visiting Prince. There can have been no doubt in Henry's mind, as to exactly who was behind the conspiracy. Now it was Henry's turn to seethe with anger. No longer, would England's involvement in the continental conflict be measured. If Charles wanted a real fight, Henry was going to give him one. Plans were quickly put in place for an extensive campaign that would see 15,000 men invading the continent.⁸ By this stage, Henry must have known that liberating Brittany from the French was unlikely, perhaps impossible.⁹ But more than anything else, the English King was motivated by revenge. This battle was personal, and the King was going to lead from the front.

On 5 May, The King commissioned the great landowners of the realm to 'array' the men of the counties because 'Charles calling himself king of France intends to invade this realm.'¹⁰ First among these great men, was Arthur.

While the Prince himself was still far too young to be personally involved with the mustering of an army, those in his service would have acted on his behalf. They probably took the opportunity to explain what they were doing and why their actions were necessary. At five years of age, he would not have understood all the complexities, but he was old enough to grasp the basics. Everything in Arthur's life was, in one way or another, about his preparation for Kingship. This opportunity to enrich his knightly education would have been one they were reluctant to waste.

So it was probably at this point, if not earlier that Arthur became aware of the tensions with France and the political circumstances that contributed to it. Did this include an explanation about the actions of the French in harbouring a rival prince? And if so, did Arthur understand that his own destiny was being threatened by a man claiming to be his uncle? Sadly, we shall never know. Preparations for war continued for the next five months until, in October, Henry's fleet was finally ready to set sail. The king was to lead his men in battle himself. Arthur, of course, was not to join him. He may now be the head of an increasingly grown up and manly household, but the battlefield was no place for a child.

Yet, the Prince had a crucial role to play. While at Dover, ahead of setting sail to France, the King granted:

> 'Power to Arthur prince of Wales, duke of Cornwall and earl of Chester, as keeper of England the king's lieutenant there, to grant licensees to elect to conventual, but not cathedral, chapter; to assent to elections, make restitution of temporalities and receive fealties on elections of minor prelates, but not with respect to the greater prelates, without the king's command : and to present to benefices not exceeding the taxation of 40 marks, churches of the taxation of

20 marks and under to which the chancellor is accustomed to present, being excepted.'[11]

Arthur had recently turned 6 years old. And he had just been appointed acting ruler of England. The Kingdom could not be ruled from Farnham. At some point before the beginning of October, Arthur was brought to the place that was then – as it is today – the governing centre of England. The palace of Westminster. Westminster had been a Royal palace since at least Anglo-Saxon times. It had been built up extensively by a succession of Norman and Plantagenet Kings. Though very different to the Palace we know today, it was already the home of Parliament and the setting for grand occasions. Arthur probably knew Westminster reasonably well. Westminster Hall had served as the scene of his creation as Prince of Wales. He had slept in his father's closet the night before. And he had probably visited on other occasions. However, until Arthur's appointment as regent, he would not have spent much time in the "privy chamber" where the King conducted his business. The privy chamber was an innovation of Henry VII and marked a change in the way that the King conducted government. Prior to Tudor rule, the King's household had centred around one two major public elements. The great hall, where the king would eat and conduct business among the nobility. And the presence chamber, essentially a throne room.

Henry VII added the privy chamber: quite literally a private set of rooms. Here he could consult his advisors in private, away from the political pressures of the nobility. For a king who trusted few, it was the perfect set up. However, the forming of the privy chamber was more than matter of interior design. It marked a shift in the style and power of kingship.

There were a number of people that Henry VII could have left as regent ahead of his departure. Both the queen and the king's mother might have seemed like better qualified candidates than a six-year-old boy. But Arthur was the heir to the throne. It was traditional for the King to leave the next in line in charge. The fact Arthur was selected as regent on these occasions, suggests he was considered just-about old enough.

Between 9 October and 13 December, Arthur signed at least eleven documents of official Royal business. Up until now, his experience of court has centred around the spectacular. His creation as Prince of Wales being the most obvious case in point. Though there is no record of it, he may even have started attending other great occasions, such as Christmas. If so, he may have sat with boyish pride as the cry of his largesse echoed down the halls. Now, it was time for him to learn that much more mundane matters were critical to kingship.

The first order of business was to authorise a series of pardons. The prince issued his grace to offenders from London to York, forgiving men for failing to appear before the magistrates' bench. When he had been made a knight of the bath, he had sworn on oath to protect widows. Now he had chance to put his promise into practice, sorting out the financial settlement for the widowed Viscountess Lisle.

But Arthur's time as regent was not all to be marked by grace and favour. He ordered sheriffs to arrest wrong doers in Essex and placed a bond of recognizance on a group of quarrellers in Bristol. Interestingly for a boy engaged to a Spanish princess, he ordered the arrest of a man who had wronged a Spanish merchant. Though if this act of vigilance was ever used to curry favour with his future in laws, there is no record of it.

Of course, Arthur would not have been the driving force behind any of these decisions. While he signed the documents, his hand would have been guided by others. John Morton, the Archbishop of Canterbury, and Lord Chancellor would not, as a church man, have joined the military campaign. He, in all but name, would have been calling the shots in England.

But that doesn't mean that Arthur's time in charge was entirely nominal. The king would have expected these weeks to form a crucial part of Arthur's education. His preparation for what was to come. Those working with the young prince during these weeks would have wanted to ensure that, in as far as it was possible, he understood the decisions being taken in his name. While Arthur probably didn't know it yet, there was soon to be an awful lot more governing and administration to come.

War with France did not last long. England had not the means to liberate Brittany from her neighbour's control. Having secured Brittany, Charles VIII was keen to turn his attention to his ambitions in Italy. He needed the English off his back as soon as possible. Henry and Charles soon signed a treaty of peace. As part of that agreement, the French committed to providing no further support to Henry's rebels. There could be no doubt at all as to whom this referred. Henry VII made one crucial mistake. He failed to obtain custody of the youth posing as his rival to the throne. And, soon enough, Warbeck and his core supporters fled to Mechelen and to the sanctuary of Margaret of York, the great enemy of the house of Tudor.

In France, Warbeck had been doing little harm. No one particularly believed his claims and Charles VIII had little long-term intention of doing anything to further them. But arguably, Henry's very reaction to the situation had given credence to the boy's pretensions. He was now emerging as a dangerous threat. His 'aunt' soon recognised him as Richard of Shrewsbury. Both Henry and Arthur had a powerful rival on their hands. But for all his rival's supposed Royal blood, Henry VII had something that "Richard" did not. A son and heir. Arthur had performed his role as regent capably. Despite his tender years, he had demonstrated that he was a credible front man for government. Now it was time for the Tudor succession to be made more visible. Arthur had been Prince of Wales in name for three years. Now it was time for him to take up the reins of power in his own principality.

Chapter 8

The Marcher Lord

Henry VII had high hopes for his son before he was even born. The heir to a ruling dynasty was a symbol of the future that helped secure the present. But, as Arthur grew, he could also serve a more imminent, practical purpose. Henry's Kingship built on many of the firm foundations laid by his political, if not his immediate, predecessor, Edward IV. The famed Yorkist king had seized control of England at a time when the rule of law had virtually collapsed in parts of the kingdom and the ancient bonds between king, nobility, gentry, and people had become distorted and dysfunctional.

With remarkable skills, Edward set about strengthening the country's governing foundations and establishing order. By the mid-point of his second reign, which began after 1471, he centred his approach to government through what historians call his 'family policy'. His brother Richard maintained order in the north. His Woodville in-laws wielded much influence in the west. And crucially, his son Edward acted as the figure head for what was effectively a devolved government along the ever-troublesome Welsh border.

Henry would have long planned for Arthur to perform a similar role. There were many advantages to him acting as a head of a distinct regional power base. To start with, it created a second power base for the fledgling dynasty. Should the government in Westminster come under siege, another along the Welsh border would be poised to spring into action. And it meant that Arthur could gain experience in government away from the prying and not altogether loyal eyes of a court that Henry VII never really trusted.

The sooner that Arthur could be in situ, the better. At the end of 1492, his brief regency of England had shown that he had the discipline, behaviour, and presence to serve as the figure head of government. When the King returned to England, he knew that it was time for the next seismic shift in Arthur's upbringing.

On 29 March 1493, the King granted commission to Arthur to:

> 'be justice of oyer and terminer in the countries of Salop, Hereford, Gloucester and Worcester and in the marches of Wales adjoining and in Wales, with authority and with power to appoint deputties or substitutes as justices of oyer and terminer, always provided that a

justice of one of other bench be appointed one of the said justices for the counties of Salop, Hereford, Gloucester and Worcester.'[1]

It was a wide-ranging remit. It placed Arthur at the head of the Council of Wales and the Marches which would be based at the historic and formidable castle of Ludlow. Ludlow Castle, which stands today as a ruin, is strategically located near the English-Welsh border. From the early fourteenth century it had been the seat of power for the Mortimers. This mighty family held the title of Earl of March and were among the mightiest of the "marcher lords" that helped maintain order in and around the principality. When the Earls of March were in harmony with the King, they were a huge asset to regional stability. But as both Edward II and Henry VI discovered, when they were at odds with national policy, they were purveyors of chaos.

Ludlow had fallen into the hands of the house of York when Arthur's great-grandfather, Richard of York, inherited the Earldom of March through his mother. It became a crown possession when Edward IV took the throne. He himself had spent much of his adolescence at the castle and was surely familiar with its advantages as a place to grow up as a knight in training.

Mindful of its strategic significance, and the need to secure the largely Lancastrian principality of Wales to Yorkist rule, Edward had revived the council in the Marches of Wales to provide a degree of regional government. At some stage in the 1470s, he dispatched his young son, the future Edward V, to act as its figure head. Just twenty years later, Arthur was to follow in his uncle's footsteps.

It's not clear at exactly what stage Arthur himself was dispatched to join his council and make a home along the Welsh border. However, in April of 1493 he made a nominal appearance on the bench in Herefordshire to dispense justice. In November of that year, the King granted Arthur the lands associated with the Earldom of March, including Ludlow Castle.[2] Instructions to some of Arthur's senior household officers to keep the peace in Herefordshire were issued at a similar time, which suggests that they were in residence. As such it's most likely that Arthur had relocated during the course of 1493, when he was aged either 6 or 7.

By the time Arthur arrived, Ludlow was no longer just a fortress but a splendid residence fit for a prince. Though the original castle seems to date from the late 11 century, most of what Arthur would have encountered upon his arrival was constructed some hundred years later. By 1493, the inner bailey featured a number of towers which collectively provided the prince with a great hall, a great chamber, a closet and a round chapel for him and his household to be at prayer. As well as the range of comforts on offer, the outer bailey was defended by a mighty fortress.[3] Arthur surely felt safe at Ludlow.

Years later, after Arthur's death, the parents of his wife Katherine of Aragon, wrote to Henry VII demanding that their daughter be removed from the "unhealthy place" in which she was staying.[4] This is clearly a reference to Ludlow, and it has led to much speculation that the castle was damp and cold. But it is hardly likely that a king as cautious as Henry VII, or a mother as caring as Elizabeth of York, would abandon their son to a castle that presented any danger to his health.

Ferdinand and Isabella's reference to an 'unhealthy' place was probably made out of concern for the fact that they feared disease was in the air after Arthur's death. And even if they were referring to the conditions of the castle itself, we must remember that their primary source of information was Katherine's Spanish servants. A Spaniard's expectations of an appropriate temperature may have been quite different to that of an Englishman.

Ludlow was the administrative centre of Arthur's government. But it may not have been the place that he primarily called home. At least not straight away. In 1499, two years before he ever met his future wife Katherine of Aragon, Arthur publicly committed himself to her in a proxy marriage ceremony. This occasion took place at Bewdley Manor, which the Spanish ambassador in attendance described as Arthur's home.

Bewdley Manor, called Tickenhill House in sixteenth-century sources, is about twenty miles from Ludlow. The manor house had been rebuilt by Arthur's great-grandfather, Richard Duke of York.[5] At the time of the duke's investment in Bewdley, it was becoming more common for landowners to develop manor houses more designed around comfort, rather than just residing in the great castles which had primarily been built for defence.

As we shall see, Arthur was buried at Worcester Cathedral. This was a relatively long journey from Ludlow. However, it was the nearest appropriate venue to Bewdley, which lacked a church of its own. The main reason for this was probably that Worcester, the burial place of King John, had sufficient pedigree for hosting the remains of great Royals. But it might also reflect the fact that it was near the place that Arthur had truly called home.

Sadly, we don't know enough about Arthur's itinerary to ascertain how he split his time between Ludlow, Bewdley and the other multitude of houses and castles bestowed upon him. But perhaps we can be tempted to speculate that, in his younger years, he spent more of his time in the calmer environment of Bewdley. Ludlow was perhaps just half a day's journey, and he could have made regular appearances to sit on council meetings and host his fledgling court. As he grew older, he may have spent more of his time at the castle, with Bewdley acting more as a retreat when he needed respite or to devote an extended period of time to his gruelling curriculum of study. Certainly, by the time of Katherine of Aragon's arrival in 1501, Ludlow seems to have been his primary residence.

Throughout much of the medieval era, the most senior administrators in the King's government had tended to be churchmen. The extensive studies that prepared them for life in the church gave them great literary and intellectual skill. It was only natural that king's would wish them to apply their formidable powers to matters of state. Arthur's council would follow this pattern.

By the mid-1490s, William Smith, Bishop of Coventry and Lichfield, was in post as President of the Council. Smith seems to have caught the eye of Arthur's grandmother, Lady Margaret Beaufort at some stage in the 1470s. Upon Henry VII's ascension, Lady Margaret seems to have brought Smith into the Tudor circle of trust. A number of prominent church appointments followed, and he was consecrated as a bishop in 1492. He was clearly someone that the king could depend on.

Whatever skill the bishop must have demonstrated, the real success of Arthur's council would be its ability to involve and engage the mighty landowners of the region. As such, great men that Arthur probably knew well such as his great-uncle Jasper Tudor and his godfather, Thomas Stanley, were firmly in his orbit. It was they, rather more than the administrators of the council, who would truly be able to ensure that Arthur's government was a success. At least in its earlier days.

The work of the council, and relationships with his councillors would become more consuming for Arthur as he grew. But when he first arrived at the Welsh border, his primary interactions would have been with the great men of his household – though of course, there was much overlap between the two. Embracing his new household would have felt manly and grown up. It must have been exciting. But it also meant saying goodbye to his old way of life. And for the 6- or 7-year-old little boy, at least one aspect of that must have been heart breaking. From the moment of his birth, Elizabeth Darcy had been the one, stable constant in Arthur's life. In his earliest years, she would have enjoyed unparalleled authority within the nursery. After his creation as Prince of Wales, his household began to transition to a more manly establishment. Yet, Darcy seems to have been retained as the most senior figure.

Although we know little about Lady Darcy, it is clear that she enjoyed the trust of successive kings. There is no hint to suggest mismanagement in the early years of either Arthur or his uncle, Edward V. She was clearly highly capable and well regarded. There is every reason to think she would have remained an asset to Arthur's establishment and his new role as regional power broker.

But this is not how people in the fifteenth century would have seen it. By the age of 6, Arthur had acted as regent of England and was now being dispatched to rule over the Welsh border. Retaining the services of a woman, according to the worldview of the time, would have been seen as demeaning to Arthur's status. Lady Darcy was redeployed to serve Arthur's siblings. While life had already taught him to be tough in the face of change, it is inconceivable that tears did not accompany her departure. Arthur was now to live among the men. And great thought and strategic consideration would have been invested in deciding exactly which men they should be.

John Arundel was appointed to act as Arthur's chancellor. The young prince was one of the greatest landlords in the kingdom. Huge amounts of money flowed in and out of his coffers. Among Arundel's primary tasks seems to have been to manage this catalogue of transactions.

It was evidently no easy task. To manage cashflow, he would have to negotiate loans with the King to cover costs. The distribution of patronage was essential to maintaining ties of local loyalty and that included, making sure people were paid on time. However, Arundel was more than a treasurer. He was probably the crucial lynch pin between Arthur's council and his household. He likely had overall responsibility for the administration of Arthur's vast landed estate.

Such a role required more than loyalty. The man appointed had to be equal to the extensive administrative burden. So, it is no surprise that a churchman was again selected. Clearly, Arundel performed his duties well and would continue to be rewarded. He would later succeed Smith as Bishop of Coventry and Lichfield.

If the role of chancellor was fundamental to the administration of Arthur's household, the position of steward was just as critical to its daily functioning. Sir Richard Croft secured this crucial appointment. This role would have given him day-to-day oversight of the household, with ultimate supervision of the "menials". This was not as offensive a term then as it is today. Though it did effectively mean the same thing, describing those from the lower order who were responsible for the functional aspects of the household such as cooking and cleaning.[6] He would also likely have supervised the middle-ranking officers.

Croft was a man with strong Yorkist affinity who had served Edward IV, possibly from a young age. Unlike many of Edward's adherents, Croft made his peace with Richard III's usurpation and served the king as treasurer. He quickly transferred his allegiance to Henry VII after Bosworth and retained his post. His position in Arthur's household shows just how committed the King was to include every strand of previous allegiance, provided the men in question were now undilutedly loyal. It perhaps also speaks to Croft's competence and his overwhelming qualifications for the role. He held a variety of landed interests near the Welsh border.[7]

From Arthur's perspective, the most impactful appointment was probably that of his chamberlain, Sir Richard Pole. This role gave Pole supervision over the more private aspects of Arthur's household. Of course, as we have seen, 'privacy' for Arthur would never constitute what we might expect from the concept. But there were times when Arthur and senior members of the household would withdraw to 'the chamber' – which in a medieval lord's household was either a room or a suite of rooms – where more private business and recreation could be held. By overseeing the chamber, Pole would have controlled access to the young prince. It was probably he more than anyone else that had personal charge of Arthur.

Such a position could only be given to one who enjoyed the utmost trust of the King. Richard Pole was the perfect candidate. His mother was the half-sister of Margaret Beaufort, making him a first cousin of the king by the half blood. Though from an established gentry family, the early favour that Henry showed Pole represented huge advancement and he had every reason to continue his loyalty. He had been knighted after the Battle of Stoke and continued to rise in favour ever since.

In a scheme probably designed by his aunt, Margaret Beaufort, Pole had married the young Margaret Plantagenet, daughter of the disgraced Duke of Clarence. This was an astronomical match for Pole, and it shows that his loyalty to Henry VII was beyond question. As we have already seen, the young Margaret and her brother, the Earl of Warwick, represented a huge threat to the Tudor dynasty. Margaret's sons would have a credible claim to the throne. When it came to her marriage, the King faced a stark choice. Either prevent her from marrying, which even the King might struggle to do or join her to someone devoted to Tudor rule. Pole would fit the bill perfectly. He was practically the only man that did.

Much of Arthur's household and his council had been intentionally modelled on the precedent of the future Edward V. But there was one crucial difference. When Edward IV had sent his eldest son to Ludlow, he had named the boy's uncle, Anthony Woodville, as the prince's governor. In Arthur's case, no one man had been given overall power over the administration or sole care of the prince's person.[8]

This was a calculated piece of policy by Henry VII. Fears that Edward had been unduly influenced by his mother's family had contributed to his downfall. Henry must ensure that his boy was a prince for the whole of England. No one faction must be able to influence him, or be perceived to have done so, unduly. Arthur's household would have included a multitude of England's gentry, serving their young master in a variety of ways. While it might have numbered in the hundreds, we only know the names of a few. Other appointments included Sir Henry Vernon, who took up the post of comptroller. Such a role does not seem to have been common in great households in the fifteenth century. It probably involved assisting Croft with his duties. Vernon was from a cautiously loyal Lancastrian family, who wielded significant power in the midlands. He himself had managed to serve Edward IV, Richard III, and Henry VII.[9] His position in Arthur's household probably reflects the King's desire to ensure as wide a franchise as possible. Vernon was later replaced as comptroller by Sir William Uvedale, who was a figure of influence on Arthur's council as the boy grew older.

David Philpp was named as vice-chamberlain.[10] If Vernon was Croft's number two, Philpp seems to have been Pole's deputy. Another churchman, Robert Frost, was named almoner. He would have taken responsibility for distributing Arthur's largesse to charitable causes, making him a moral as well as an administrative advisor to the boy. Frost obviously did a good job. He would later take over from Arundel as chancellor.

These names represent just a fraction of the men that would surround Arthur as he transitioned from boy to adolescent. Some would have been much closer to his own age and would have functioned as friends as well as companions. All would have been aware of the tremendous opportunity afforded to them by daily proximity to the future King of England. As well as the consequences of failing to do their duty in nurturing him. As Arthur settled into his new life in Ludlow, events were happening across the channel that would have caused his father to feel anything but settled.

*

Upon reaching peace with France, Charles VIII had agreed to discontinue his support for Warbeck. The French King had only ever envisaged his harbouring of the pretender to serve as a distraction to Henry and he was probably never serious about becoming a long-term champion of the boy's cause. But whether he intended to or not, his creation of the conspiracy had created a monster. And it was a monster that would stalk and haunt Henry, and probably Arthur himself, for the next five years.

Somehow learning that they were no longer safe in the custody of the French King, Warbeck and a group of adherents escaped to the town of Mechelen, which was under the dominion of the dukes of Burgundy. Before long, the young man had come face to face with Margaret of York, the dowager duchess. Margaret quickly recognised Warbeck as her nephew. For the young man posing as Richard, Duke of York, this was more than a stroke of luck. It was a turning point in a campaign that was fast gaining credibility.

Those sympathetic to the Tudors were reluctant to believe that this meeting between 'aunt and nephew' in Mechelen was truly their first encounter. According to Vergil, it was Margaret that had masterminded the whole plot. Warbeck was a boy that the duchess had 'chanced to discover'.[11] She had thought him 'suitable to be passed off as her brother's son Richard Duke of York.' She, Margaret, had coached the boy herself for the role and 'carefully instructed him in matters concerning England, and about the pedigree of the House of York, so that he could afterwards reel these facts off for memory with ease, imitate their manners, and make everybody believe that he was a scion of the Yorkist family.'[12]

Despite Vergil's certainty, there is no evidence that Margaret was involved in the plot ahead of encountering Warbeck in late 1492 or early 1493. In fact, it is quite possible that Margaret truly believed that the boy was her resurrected nephew. The duchess's life had been marred with tragedy. Since leaving England she had known little companionship and much disappointment. And she had had to watch from afar as her family tore themselves to pieces and made way for a dynasty of upstarts to take their throne.[13] Regardless of the credibility of Warbeck's case, Margaret may have believed in him simply because she needed to believe in something.

Margaret's support brought three fundamental advantages to Warbeck's campaign. The first was credibility. Even though the duchess had only met her nephew once before, she was surely well placed to vouch for his veracity.

The second was connections. Margaret would pen passionate dispatches to other European rulers to gain support for her 'nephew'. And before long she would introduce him to her powerful stepson Maximilian, King of the Romans. But more than anything else, Margaret was able to provide Warbeck and his supporters with a base. And from that base, he could launch a rival court.

No one knew more about the power and problems of a rival court than Henry VII. Between 1483 and 1495 his own rival court – first in Brittany and later in France – had swelled to over 500 people representing a significant chunk of the English gentry.

This was the moment of the Tudors' acute vulnerability. Henry VII was not a man that anyone had supported for himself. With the exception of a few die-hard Lancastrians, like the Earl of Oxford, his core support had come from the loyal men of Edward IV. Henry was nothing more than a vessel to return Edward's line to the throne through his union with Elizabeth of York. Arthur was the fulfilment of that deal.

Arthur, the female-line grandson of the old York king was a weak replacement for one of Edward's own sons. And now, miraculously it seemed that one of those boys had not perished in the tower after all. He was alive and flourishing in Flanders. King of a court of his own. A court just waiting for courtiers. Before long, Henry became aware that men were leaving England and joining Warbeck in Mechelen. England's many ports and harbours could never be effectively policed, and the government had no real idea of who was leaving the country and what messages they were bringing back. Given that many of his most senior household men had been Edward's dearest supporters, there were few whose loyalty he could trust.

Spurred on by fear, Henry deployed every weapon in his arsenal. He dispatched agents to the continent to try and discover information on his rival's origins. He brought back to England those who had known Warbeck as a child in the hope of widely discrediting him. He sent spies to the York court in Mechelen to sway men back to his side. He even suspended trade with the Netherlands in a bid to get Maximillian to desist from supporting the boy.

But despite his attempts, it was Warbeck who was winning what we would call 'the war of ideas'. At least on the continent. Maximillian, sensing a world of opportunity continued to give Warbeck's cause credence by taking him on a tour of the low countries. The rival court would never reach the levels of Henry Tudor's exiled following. But it was growing far too big for comfort.

Finally, in 1495, Henry was delivered a stroke of luck. One of Warbeck's early adherents, deserted Mechelen and made his peace with the King. We don't know why Sir Robert Clifford had become disillusioned with the pretender's cause. It might be that the incredibility of Warbeck's pretences had finally dawned on him. Or he may have simply felt that the campaign had lost momentum. But whatever his reason, he returned to England. And he returned with valuable information.

No doubt in exchange for his own life, Clifford handed over the names of his fellow plotters. In the process he incriminated some of the men at the heart of Henry's household. These included John, Lord Fitzwalter, a senior courtier and William Worsley, dean of St Paul's Cathedral. But far more worryingly than any other, Clifford's list of conspirators included William Stanley. The king's chamberlain, and step-uncle.

William was the younger brother of Thomas Stanley, the husband of Henry's mother Margaret. While the elder Stanley had survived the Wars of the Roses by cautiously switching sides as need demanded, William had long been of a more decided Yorkist sympathy. He had been a close ally of Edward IV. Despite feigning loyalty to Richard III, he had probably never forgiven the overthrow of Edward's son. He seems to have worked behind the scenes for the Tudor cause once it became apparent that Henry would marry Elizabeth of York and, through her, restore Edward IV's line to the throne. Unlike Thomas, who remained on the side-lines, William entered the Battle of Bosworth at a crucial moment and helped secure a Tudor victory. According to some accounts, he even placed the recovered bloody crown on Henry's head.

The extent to which Stanley had plotted against the king is unclear. According to Vergil, Stanley had done little more than remark that if the boy in Flanders was truly the son of Edward IV, he would never take up arms against him.[14] But even this was an act of great political naivety.

William Stanley had flourished under the reign of Henry VII. But he was a man "more mindful of the favour he had conferred than that he received."[15] By being appointed the King's chamberlain he had reached the pinnacle of influence at court and his fortune had been bolstered by numerous grants of land. His brother, however, had been created Earl of Derby, while William remained untitled. Given that Thomas was the King's stepfather, this was understandable to most. Yet William may have felt that given his role in securing the Tudor crown, more honour still should have come his way. Unnerved by a potential act of treachery at the heart of his household, the King gave no mercy. Stanley was beheaded on 16 February 1495. It was at this point that Arthur first became involved in dealing with the fallout of the Warbeck affair. Having been attainted by Act of Parliament, Stanley and his heirs lost all right to their land. The King needed to seize it quickly and bring it into crown possession. On 8 February, the King issued a commission to the mighty landowners of that region to, 'inquire of the lands and possessions in North Wales and the marches thereof, and the countries of Chester, Flint and Salop of William Stanley, knight, attainted of his treason, and to take charge of the same.'[16]

As a major landowner in Wales and along the Welsh border, Arthur was the first named nobleman in the commission. Of course, the commission was also granted to senior members of Arthur's household. He was only 8 years old and too young to take charge of such a mission. But he was not too young to understand the implications of what his men were tasked with.

As we have already seen, everything about Arthur's life was about preparation for Kingship. As he approached adolescence, he would have been expected to take greater responsibility for the actions of his government. Those bringing him up, and governing on his behalf, would have taken every opportunity to increase his knowledge of affairs. They would have been very conscious that whenever he came face to face with the prince, that the father was pleased with the progress of the son. As such, we can be confident that, from at least this point, Arthur would have had a grasp of the goings on in Mechelen. He would have known that some men were plotting against his father and that even those closest to the court could not be trusted. He would also have observed a crucial lesson: treason could not be tolerated and any flicker of it, must be snuffed out quickly.

What did Arthur make of the fact that a man claiming to be his uncle was threatening his father's throne? Was he aware of the gravity of the circumstances and the implications for his own destiny? It is probably reasonable to assume that those who gave him information on it, did so in a way that played down the severity of the risk. And there's one thing of which we can be absolutely certain: he would have been told in no uncertain terms that the boy in Mechelen was nothing more than an upstart and a pretender.

Whatever anxiety Arthur did feel about the situation would soon be eased. At least temporarily. On 3 January, Warbeck – with a fleet of ships supplied by King Maximillian – attempted to land at Deal on the east coast of England. Local forces managed to quickly overpower the pretender and prevent a landing, forcing Warbeck to flee to Ireland. It was the first major test of English solidarity with their Tudor royals that Arthur was old enough to remember. And for now, they seemed to have passed.

Images of Arthur

Above left: A portrait of Arthur aged about 11, probably commissioned to celebrate his formal betrothal to Katharine of Aragon in 1497. Now displayed at Hever Castle. (Sourced from wiki common)

Above right: Arthur in his teenage years. The portrait shows him wearing dress from the years after he died, but it is likely based on a lost original. (Sourced from wiki common)

Right: A teenage Arthur depicted kneeling at prayer in the church window in Great Malvern. Images in stained glass windows are rarely an attempt at portraiture, but the depiction of the Prince does bear some resemblance to the Arthur in sixteenth century dress. (Sourced from wiki common. Photo © J.Hannan-Briggs (cc-by-sa/2.0))

Locations

Above: Arthur's arms adorn his tomb at Worcester Cathedral. (Sourced from wiki common. Photo © Irid Escent (cc-by-sa/2.0))

Below: Farnham Castle, which was probably Arthur's main home for the first six years of his life. (Senior Mac Photography With thanks to Farnham Castle)

Above: Ludlow Castle was the centre of Arthur's administration and one of his main homes from the time he was six. The prince died at Ludlow in 1502 and probably requested that his heart remain there. (With thanks to Ludlow Castle)

Below: As well as his residence at Ludlow, Arthur dwelled in a more comfortable manor house in Bewdley, Worcestershire. (Sourced from wiki common)

Above left: The priory gate at Winchester Cathedral which used to be attached to St Swithun's Priory, where Arthur was born. (Sourced from wiki common)

Above right: !King Arthur's! roundtable at the Great Hall in Winchester. Its presence helped create the sense that the City had once housed Camelot. The Great Hall itself proved insufficient to act as the Queen's great chamber and Arthur's place of birth. The roundtable in this image was painted and decorated after Arthur's time. (Sourced from wiki common)

Below: Winchester Cathedral played host to Arthur's chaotic and almost comical Christening. (Sourced from wiki common)

Family images

Elizabeth Woodville, Arthur's maternal grandmother acted at godmother at his Christening. But a Yorkist rebellion six months later ensured she played no significant role in the Prince's upbringing. (Sourced from wiki common)

Lady Margaret Beaufort gave the Tudors their slender claim to the throne. She was a major figure of influence during the reign of her son, Henry VII and seems to have played a crucial role in shaping Arthur's household. (Sourced from wiki common)

Above left: Elizabeth of York was internationally praised for her grace and virtue. Though circumstances forced them to be mostly apart, Arthur was probably never far from his mother's thoughts. (Sourced from wiki common)

Above right: Henry VII was an unlikely King who proved to be a lucky one. Arthur represented all his hopes for the future. (Sourced from wiki common)

Left: Arthur's great-uncle, Jasper Tudor, Duke of Bedford, helped secure Arthur's rule in Wales in the early days of his administration. (Sourced from wiki common)

Arthur's sister, Margaret, was born the same day that Arthur was created Prince of Wales. Years later, their respective marriage negotiations would be intwined. (Sourced from wiki common)

We know little of the relationship between Arthur and his brother, the future Henry VIII. The actions of their great-uncle, Richard III, may have meant that, had Arthur lived, the two Princes could have grown up to mistrust each other. (Sourced from wiki common)

Arthur would not have known his younger sister Mary well as she was aged just six when he died. (Sourced from wiki common)

Arthur's marriage to Katharine of Aragon was first negotiated when they were both infants. When he finally met his wife, he wrote of the joy he felt when he 'beheld the sweet face of his bride'. (Sourced from wiki common)

Chapter 9

So Great the Abundance

Arthur's formal education began before he arrived at Ludlow and Bewdley. In the very earliest years of his life, he achieved 'a swift and thorough knowledge of the first principles of literature'. This early chapter of his education may have been delivered by a tutor. If so, his name is lost to us. It's also possible that he was taught the basics of his letters by clerks in his household, male attendants or even Lady Darcy before a tutor was formally appointed.

The first man, that we know of, to formally take charge of Arthur's education was John Rede, who was eminently qualified for the post. For about six years, he had served as headmaster of Winchester College, one of England's earliest public schools. He was a man associated with 'humanism' or 'the new learning', the emerging intellectual strand that appealed to Arthur's father.[1]

Records surrounding Rede's appointment are light. He must have been in place by 1492, when payment receipts show that 'my lorde Prynce Scolemaster' received ten pounds from the king.[2] But this seems too late to mark Rede's appointment. It's unlikely that Arthur waited until he was 6 to begin his formal studies.

It seems more probable that Rede joined Arthur's household in 1490, the year he vacated his headship of Winchester. He returned to the college in 1501 as warden. The years in between were likely spent in Arthur's service. Arthur, by this dating, would have been about 4 when his formal studies began. This was in keeping with the general, though somewhat flexible, timeline associated with the education of noble boys. A later document from 1500, refers to Rede as Arthur's chaplain. It is possible that he served in a dual capacity.[3]

The precise details of what Arthur studied between 1490 and 1496 do not survive. He would have continued learning grammar, the basic structure of language. He would certainly have studied history and become acquainted with works of poetry. We know that he spoke and wrote Latin well. And there is evidence that he was taught French by a Flemish man called Giles Duwes.[4] While there's no direct proof of it, he must have studied arithmetic to a certain extent, especially given his father's philosophy that a king should be close to the accounts.

When Arthur was about 10 years old, he and Rede were joined in the schoolroom by Bernard André, the man whom the crude record keepers of the 1490s describe as the "blynde poet".[5] André was French Augustinian friar whom Henry VII had probably been introduced to by Richard Foxe, Bishop of Winchester. The king seems to have brought him to England soon after his victory, employing him as a court poet.[6] Like Rede, he was a committed humanist. The two seemed to work well together in their joint endeavours as Arthur's pedagogues.

After the completion of Arthur's formal education at the turn of the sixteenth century, André was asked to turn his attention to a history of Henry VII's reign. It is from this account – sporadic and unfinished – that we gain an insight into what Arthur's education may have looked like:

> 'I boldly assert this one thing, that though he [Arthur] was not yet sixteen years old he had either committed partly to memory or at least had turned the pages of or read on his own the following works: in grammar the writings of Guarino, Perotti, Pomponio Leto, Sulpizio, Aulus Gellius, and Valla; in poetry the works of Homer, Virgil, Lucan, Ovid, Silius, Plautus, and Terence; in oratory Cicero's Duties, Letters and Paradoxes, and Quintilian; and in history Thucydides, Livy, Ceaser's Commentaries, Suetonius, Tacitus, Pliny, Valerius Maximus, Sallust, and Eusebius.'[7]

It's quite a curriculum. But we should take André's words with a pinch of salt. To be considered accomplished in learned circles as the sixteenth century dawned, familiarity with the rediscovered works of ancient Greece was a prerequisite. As historian David Carlson points out, 'The list is self-consciously modish, perhaps intended to demonstrate André's currency with recent developments of Italian scholarship as much as the prince's accomplishments.'[8] Many of these writers were recent rediscoveries. Both manuscripts and printed versions of the books in André's list were hard to come by. The grammars André describes were written by the prominent Italian humanists of the mid-late-fifteenth century.

However trendy the teaching of ancient Greece may have been, Arthur was a Christian Prince. He needed a thorough grounding in theology and both André and Rede were well placed to instruct. André seems to have developed a commentary of St Augustine's *Civitas Dei*, specifically for Arthur.[9] *Civitas Dei* serves as one of the most influential texts for Western Christianity. By exploring it with his tutor, Arthur would have gained a foundational understanding of many of the church's fundamental doctrines including original sin and the struggle between good and evil.

André lavished praise upon Arthur's qualities as a student. Even before his formal education had begun, "with each passing day the prince's virtues became more apparent". When Rede took up the reins as tutor, such were Arthur's talents that "there was little effort on either part." At the end of his formal education,

'So great was the abundance, the opulence, the bounty, and the generosity of everything, that I can scarcely tell it in words.' Though he proceeds to have a good go. Servants flatter royalty. People tend to speak well of the dead. By the time André was writing, Arthur was a dead royal. And of course, André wanted to ensure that his time as Arthur's tutor was well regarded. Nevertheless, even allowing for flattery and poetic exaggeration, it is likely that Arthur was a capable student.

André's account of Arthur's education features in his work about Henry VII's life, which he was ultimately planning on presenting to the King. The intention was that it would be widely read, including by those that had known Arthur at Ludlow. Few would have known the specifics of the curriculum. André had a little wriggle room to play that up. But many, including the king, would have known if Arthur was bright and intellectually able.

Had Arthur been a slow student, André would naturally have remained silent about it. He would have found some other aspect of Arthur's virtue or ability to boast about. If he wanted his work to have credibility with contemporaries, he would have stuck close to the truth. His account of Arthur's intellectual prowess may be an exaggeration, but it is unlikely to be an invention.

Life at Ludlow and Bewdley consisted of far more than study. While the energies of all those charged with Arthur's care were focused on his preparation for Kingship, there was considerably more to that task than books could instruct, or tutors could teach. In Arthur's employ were a lute player, minstrels and trumpeters. Entertainment must have been lavish and lively. This entertainment would have been enjoyed by the household. But as he began to emerge into adolescence, Arthur's establishment would have started to function as a satellite court, drawing upon the regular attendance of the landowners in Wales and around the Welsh border. Theatre and spectacle would have been at its centre.

As the Prince matured, he would have learnt that these celebrations were about far more than just fun and frivolity. As Prince of Wales, Arthur must keep order within his principality. As Earl of March in all but name, he must secure the Welsh border. The formal work of his administration in discharging with justice will be explored later. However, keeping the peace in a later medieval or early modern state was about far more than legal institutions or hearings. It depended on a subtle but crucial network of affinity and connection between the great magnates of a region and other, lesser landowners. The better Arthur was able to forge these strands, the better the cogs of his government could keep order. It was a lesson in the subtle but crucial aspects of managing the nobility and gentry that his father had never had chance to learn. The son must be given ample opportunity to improve upon the father.

To this end, it was also crucial that Arthur was afforded opportunities to build a network of relationships with young men of his own age. Those that would be the major landed power brokers of his own generation. He almost certainly employed teenage boys as "henchmen", who would perform a range of non-descript duties and perhaps even share in elements of his upbringing. While these would have provided a degree of companionship, they would largely have been drawn from the lower ranks of the gentry. Arthur's closest friends needed to be from its upper reaches.

In about 1496, the year that Arthur achieved his tenth birthday, he was joined in his household by a range of worthy young men who were about his age. There had probably always been other youngsters at Ludlow and Bewdley. But Arthur's emergence into adolescence seems to have been accompanied by the creation of a more intentional set of young men around him.

Gerald FitzGerald, called Lord Gerard in contemporary sources, was the eldest son of the Irish Earl of Kildare, the man who had given early support to Perkin Warbeck. While forgiven by Henry VII for his disloyalty, his eldest son was effectively being kept by the king in surety for the earl's good behaviour. Lord Gerard was probably raised from that point in Arthur's household. While in some senses he was a prisoner, he seems to have grown close to the prince, of whom he was very close in age. It is also likely that at least one, if not two, sons of the Marquess of Dorset were in the prince's household. They would have been Arthur's first cousins and their presence with the prince might help guarantee the obedience of their father, whom Henry VII never seems to have trusted.

At around this time, two gentlemen servants were also appointed. Anthony Willoughby, the son of the Lord Chamberlain and Maurice St John, a great-nephew of Margaret Beaufort. Both these men were about five years Arthur's senior which may have helped create a more balanced dynamic. Arthur was the prince and, of course, the master. But he is also likely to have been somewhat in awe of these slightly older boys. Perhaps he was even keen to impress them.

If later evidence, given thirty years after Arthur's death, can be believed, these young men may have formed something of a what we would call "a friendship group" around the young Prince. They supposedly shared bawdy jokes and boyish banter. Of course, senior officers, such as Richard Pole, would always have kept a firm eye on things. No real mischief would have been tolerated. But there would have been a sense as Arthur grew older, that even Royal boys must occasionally be boys.

As welcome as such light relief surely was, Arthur seems to have enjoyed at least one friendship where there were real moments of closeness. Gruffydd ap Rhys was the son of crucially important Welsh landowner, Sir Rhys ap Thomas. The family were important supporters of the early Tudors and Gruffydd had been sent to serve Arthur and form a similar bond of loyalty to that forged between their fathers. Like most of Arthur's close servants, Gruffydd – who was also about five years older than the prince – played a key role at boy's funeral. But more astonishingly, when he died in 1521, he managed to be buried near the prince in Worcester.

An anonymous poet, who seemed to have some knowledge of the friendship between the two young men, captured his understanding of Gruffydd's feelings after his death:

> 'To my olde master now wyll I be gone,
> Prince Arture, with hym styll to abyde.
> Ytt slaketh my sorowes to thynke vpon
> My chance ys to lye soon ye to his side.
> What sulde I more wyshe yn thys worlde wyde
> Buy ynreste perpetuell to make merye
> With the noble Prynce in eternall glorye?'[10]

Given his life in Ludlow and his absence from many historical records, Arthur often comes across to us as a lonely and isolated figure. To at least some extent, that must be true. The only people who were his social equals were those he was rarely permitted to see. But fragments of evidence from his time on the Welsh border create hope that some of his life was happier and more supported than we might otherwise fear. Arthur had friends. And with at least some of them, he was really close.

Ever since the reign of Edward III, the eldest son of a King had been automatically entitled 'Duke of Cornwall'. Though he was rarely styled as such, Arthur had possessed the accolade from birth and was a mighty landowner in the county through the possessions of the duchy of Cornwall. The Cornwall of the fifteenth century, like the Cornwall of today, possessed a strong sense of independent identity. It was the only real pocket of England where a strong Celtic presence survived. In Arthur's time, about half the county's population still spoke Cornish as their mother tongue.

This sense of independence was underpinned by a strange legal set up. Tin mining was Cornwall's major economic activity. Under laws dating back to King John, swathes of the country were regarded as 'Stannaries': administrative areas that had their own assembly and enforced laws that protected miners from taxes and other obligations. To all intents and purposes, these 'stannary laws' counted out large parts of Cornwall from the king's control. And it made it considerably easier for many men to avoid paying the king's taxes.

To a centralising King like Henry VII, this was never likely to sit well. In 1496, the King suspended the laws and privileges associated with the Stannary towns. Local discontent soon began to fester. It's possible that the King discussed these measures with Arthur before making the final decision. While landowners had no formal power over the laws where their land was concentrated, a king would typically look to them to enforce them. Ideally, local magnates needed to be singing from the same hymn sheet. However, even if this was a topic that the prince discussed with his father, it is unlikely that he had any real input into the decision. Not yet 10 years of age, he had no local knowledge of his duchy. Nor was Arthur yet of an age where he was likely to question his father's judgement. He surely had no idea of just what trouble his father's measures were about to cause.

After his disastrous attempt to invade Kent in 1495, Perkin Warbeck, still posing as Prince Richard, had set sail for Ireland. Hoping to raise the men in revolt and secure troops for an invasion, he was disappointed to find that since he was last in the country, Henry had managed to sure up his own support against the pretender. This time around, Ireland represented more danger than opportunity. He and his supporters fled to Scotland and put themselves at the mercy of James IV.

The Scottish King was only too happy to secure this opportunity to make trouble for his English neighbour. Whether he truly believed that the young man was Richard Plantagenet, we shall never know, but he was more certainly prepared to act the part. He provided Warbeck and about 1400 supporters with Falkland Palace near the east coast, to use as a base. Even more remarkably, he provided his new charge with a wife in the form of Lady Katherine Gordon, a daughter of the Earl of Huntley. As ever, there was a price. He made Warbeck promise that if he became King of England, he would return Berwick to Scotland, a border town that the English had seized in 1482.

In September 1496, James IV and Warbeck invaded England. Warbeck was riding as Richard IV of England. He had issued a manifesto denouncing Henry Tudor's misgovernment and councillors of low birth. He must have been praying desperately that the men would flock to his banner.

Just as the men of Kent had spontaneously repelled the pretender, those of the north failed to rally to his cause. He had attracted no support from the English near the border and he soon fled from the fight, leaving the Scottish King to complete some minor pillaging before returning to his kingdom.

Perkin Warbeck had now attempted two invasions of England. Both had failed spectacularly with the pretender failing to raise even a whisper of support. But rather than draw comfort from his enemy's embarrassments, Henry overreacted with uncharacteristic flare and to catastrophic effect. The English King issued orders for more than £170,000 of taxes to be collected and for a seismic force to be assembled. James IV was about to learn that Henry VII was not a Tudor to be trifled with.

Men across England must have grumbled at the heavy burden of this tax. For the people of Cornwall, it was the straw that broke the camel's back. Cornwall, in the farthest south-west corner of England was under no threat from the Scots.

Paying to defend the Northern border was of no benefit to them. And they were still smarting from the king's suspension of the Stannary laws the year before.

The Cornish rose in revolt. Led by the local power brokers including Lord Audley, Bodmin's MP Thomas Flamank and a local blacksmith, Michael Joseph an Gof, they headed for London. On their journey through Devon and Somerset, others disgruntled at the tax joined them. The rebels were neither well-resourced nor well organised. They should never have made it past Devon. But with the King's eyes firmly focused on Scotland, there seemed to be no loyal magnets left in the West Country who were willing or able to repel them. Some 10,000 men reached Blackheath, near London before the King and his men were able to intercept them on 17 June.

When the fighting actually came, there was no real contest. The Royal army outnumbered the rebels, probably by two to one. The rebels were quickly defeated and the leaders, rounded and executed. But is should never have come to that. The extent of Cornish discontent must have finally become clear to the King. And so, it must also have played on the mind of the county's young and absent duke – Prince Arthur. Warbeck sensed an opportunity. He set sail for Cornwall, possibly at the invitation of the rebels, landing at Whitsand Bay on 7 September. By the time they left the country, his numbers had swelled to 8000. For the first time in his life, Arthur's inheritance was truly under threat.

This time, the King was ready for them. Despite the strength of Warbeck's numbers, they were boldly rebuffed by the Earl of Devon, the king's brother-in-law. The earl routed the rebels to Taunton, where on the 19 September they engaged the Royal army. At the sight of the Royal standard, many of the rebels quickly retreated. Before long, Warbeck would have known that the odds were hopeless.

Perkin managed an escape to Hampshire and took sanctuary at Beaulieu Abbey. He was soon recognised. Even the safety of sanctuary could never protect him. On the condition that his life be spared, he surrendered. Perkin Warbeck was a man who had plagued Henry VII. He must have been a great and continuing source of anxiety for Arthur for as long as he could remember. And he was finally in the Tudors' custody.

*

With Perkin Warbeck finally a prisoner, Henry VII must have felt safer on his throne than ever before. Not only was his great rival now in his keeping. The young pretender, even at the height of his threat, had proved unable to gain or sustain significant support for his cause across the country. The people of England, it must have seemed, had finally made their peace with Tudor rule. If this was how the King felt about his success, then foreign observers agreed with him. A Spanish ambassador wrote that the crown was "undisputed, and his government strong in all respects." But while Henry had gained the loyalty of his people, he would never gain their love.

Arthur, however, was a different story. According to the Spanish observer, "they love the prince as much as themselves because he is the grandchild of his grandfather. Those who know him love him also for his own virtues." [11] While Henry remained "disliked", Arthur was held in great affection. And the experience of meeting the prince only seemed to increase his standing among the people. Rather than react with jealousy toward his son's popularity, Henry chose to maximise it to the full. From about the age of 12, Arthur would increasingly leave the solitude of Ludlow and Bewdley and show himself to the people of the realm.

In the summer of 1498, Arthur was visiting English-owned Calais, though we know nothing of the details. The Spanish ambassador would also later note that Arthur was on a tour of his principality, though this likely means his dominion as a Marcher lord rather than Wales itself. He also visited Chester on at least one occasion. Two accounts survive that give more details of two of Arthur's high-profile visits. In October 1498, the Prince made an entry into Coventry where he was greeted by the spectacle of pageantry that the town had become famous for. During the performance, Arthur was greeted by his namesake, King Arthur who encouraged him to subdue his enemies and force them to do him homage. The Queen of fortune then appeared to the eleven-year-old prince and advised him to put his faith in her majesty. St George, who was probably Arthur's patron saint, also found time for an appearance. [12]

But beneath the festival of pageantry, Arthur's visit served a more practical purpose. During his stay he was called upon to settle a dispute between the corporation of Coventry and cathedral priority.[13] In theory, Arthur had no jurisdiction in the area. The fact he was asked to intervene shows how far his influence was growing. Just a few months later, Arthur was received in style in the city of London. The prince was 'honourably accompanied with many lords, knights and worshipful men" and "his sword was carried through the city by Sir Gilbert Talbot.' The craftsmen and tradesmen lined the streets from Bishopsgate to St Paul's. Arthur rode past them 'clad in crimson velvet bordered with cloth of gold, and after him rode six followers all clad in crimson velvet without borders'

The next day, the mayor gifted Arthur with a pair of gilt basins and a pair of large gilt pots. In what reads like a heavily prepared speech, Arthur offered the following words of thanks:

> 'Father mayor, I thank you and your brothers present here for this great and kind token, which I trust in time to come I will deserve. And because I cannot thank you enough, I shall ask the king's grace to thank you; and for my part I shall not forget your kindness.'

On paper, Arthur's words don't read like a great moment of oratory. But according to the chronicler they were 'spoken with such good deliberateness and such a confident expression that the hearers were amazed, considering his tenderness of his age, which at that time was no more than twelve years of age.' [14]

Arthur was adjusting to a life of public affairs. Not only is this a sign that he had won the affections of the people. He must also have gained the trust of his father. By the time he approached his teenage years he was fast becoming an ambassador for the Tudor cause and the competent figure head of a sophisticated regional government. Perhaps most importantly for Arthur, his maturing years granted him the opportunity to spend more time at court. This, in turn, enabled him to be closer to his family: a family that he may have been more tightly woven into than is commonly imagined.

Chapter 10

A Rose Between Thorns

'Family life' was a concept with which Arthur would never be familiar. Even by the standards of the day, he was raised at a distance from his parents. While his siblings were able to share a childhood together, Arthur was always destined to be absent and remote. Nevertheless, it's possible that the young Prince was more tightly woven into the fabric of his family than his geography, status and circumstances might initially appear to suggest.

The question of how much Arthur's parents saw of their progeny in his youngest years is almost impossible to answer. Admirable attempts to reconstruct an itinerary for Henry VII are based on examinations of the dates and locations that official documents are issued from. While it's an assumption that the king was always residing in the same place, it's not an unreasonable one.

Such a paper trail gives little reason to think that Henry and Elizabeth saw their son with any regularity. But this is probably misleading. After all, Arthur's parents could hardly just "drop in" to wherever he was staying. Hosting the king and queen was an ambitious undertaking, even for the grandest of households. Ahead of a visit by the Royal couple in 1487, the Bishop of Winchester had invested significant sums on carpentry to bring their accommodation up to scratch.[1] These costs would not have needed repeating with every visit. But they give some idea of the level of upheaval a visit from the king and queen could bring.

There are, however, numerous occasions where Henry or Elizabeth were nearby. Could they have visited their boy discreetly, without creating the need for the full household to descend? Among the locations that the king and queen may have based themselves to be within a few hours' journey of Arthur, was Margaret Beaufort's palace at Woking. Journeys between the two could have easily been managed within the scope of the day. And such visits would not be captured by the paper trail that historians so readily rely on. As Arthur grew older, it was his turn to become the visitor. Trips to join his family at court became increasingly frequent. A modern-day adolescent may use their maturity to strike out away from their parents. But for Arthur, getting older probably meant he saw more of his mother and father.

In August 1497, Arthur was summoned to court at Woodstock, where he and his father received two Italian ambassadors. Both were clearly taken with the boy, whom they found to be "of remarkable beauty and grace and very ready in speaking Latin."[2] The Milanese ambassador correctly guessed Arthur's age at 11 (he was a month shy of his eleventh birthday), though noted that he was "taller than his years would warrant".[3] The Venetian ambassador mistook him for a 12-year-old.[4]

Arthur accompanied his father, the ambassadors, and other great men of the realm, such as the Duke of Buckingham and the chancellor, Cardinal Morton. Both ambassadors were then invited to a conversation with the queen and the king's mother.[5] Clearly, despite still being a young man, he could be trusted to carry himself well with the great men of the European stage. The Italian ambassadors wrote up their meeting with the prince and sent news back home. Had it not been for their letters, we would know nothing of the fact that Arthur was with his parents during the summer of 1497. The only clues would be a series of grants by the king to the prince's entertainers a few weeks later.

In September, 'My lorde prince mynystrelx' were rewarded 20 shillings, and his organ player was given 26 shillings and 8 pennies.[6] Later than month, Arthur's trumpeters were also granted a gift of 20 shillings.[7] The most obvious explanation for this is that Arthur had been responsible for providing the entertainment at court for some of his stay and that the king was pleased with what he heard.

This raises an intriguing possibility. If these grants indicate Arthur's recent presence at court, could other similar rewards from the king to the prince's servants provide hints as to when father and son were together? A similar pattern of grants to Arthur's minstrels and organ player are found a year earlier. This could suggest that Arthur had similarly been present at court at some stage during that summer of 1496. Given that this was the time when negotiations for his marriage were at their height, it's tempting to speculate that this impressive young man had been summoned to win over the ambassadors and secure a favourable report. If so, it shows just what a valuable asset the king believed his son was becoming. The evidence is fragmented at best. But from what we can see, from about the age of 10, Arthur was present at court during the big occasions. Especially if they had an international element. Given that, in both 1496 and 1497, the rewards were granted during or just after the summer months, it's even possible that Arthur was a regular visitor to court during that season.

Thanks again to the writings of the Italian ambassadors, we also know that Prince Henry was with his family in August 1497. It is highly likely that the Royal daughters, Princesses Margaret, and Mary were also present. The early months of 1497 had been gruelling ones for the King. The Scottish had threatened English security in the north and the Cornish had risen in the southwest. It may be that the king and queen sought to centre themselves by bringing their scattered family together. But it's also possible that such gatherings were more common, even if records of them simply don't survive.

Arthur was undoubtedly remote from his family. He certainly enjoyed less time with his parents than his siblings were treated to. But he may not have been the isolated and lonely figure that we so often imagine. As we stitch together the fragments of evidence available, bonds of warmth, love, and affection among the first Tudor Royal family gradually emerge.

From Arthur's youngest years, Henry VII must have been impressed on the prince's mind as a figure of awe and majesty. Even as an infant, the king's coats of arms were draped across Arthur's cradle. Tales of the great king's victory would surely have been recounted to the impressionable infant. When the patriarch paid a visit, those charged with the prince's care would have impressed the importance of "best behaviour" on the boy. They no doubt used every means of cohesion and discipline to do so.

Arthur would have been raised to be in constant wonder at his father's brilliance. After all, if Henry Tudor's story is told in the right way, his achievements do seem outlandishly remarkable. Arthur was likely encouraged to aspire to the childhood prowess of his father, which according to Bernard André had been remarkable:

> 'After he reached the age of understanding, he was handed over to the best and most upright instructors to be taught the first principles of literature. He was endowed with such sharp mental powers and such great natural vigour and comprehension that even as a young boy he learned everything pertaining to religious instructions rapidly and thoroughly, with little effort from his teachers, Indeed, at this time the highest disposition for virtue shone forth in the boy, and he was so attentive in reading and listening to the divine office that all who watched him saw signs of his future goodness and success. When as a young man he was initiated into the first principles of literature, he surpassed his peers with the same quick intellect he had displayed as a boy. For my part, I remember that his learned teacher, Master Andreas Scotus (may his soul rest with the blessed), then Master of Sacred letters at Oxford, used to say to me that he had never heard of a boy at that age with such great mental quickness and capacity for learning. He possessed such becoming noble manners, such charmful grace of royal expression, and such great beauty that, like a peace-making Solomon, he increased his stature before all mortals of his time.'[8]

These are the words of a sycophant, who had never known Henry Tudor as a child. But that same sycophant was also Arthur's tutor. André's words give us some sense as to the cult of wonder around the king that must have been cultivated in the prince's household. Nevertheless, if those raising Arthur were destined to do their job properly, they could not allow him to be totally consumed by narratives of flattery and sycophancy. A Prince must be raised to understand the brutal realities of Kingship. He would have known from a young age that his father was not universally popular. Aspects of his education, including the study of ancient texts and great polemics, would have taught him that a wise ruler must see through flattery and understand the intentions that lurked beneath it.

As his childhood progressed, Arthur would have played closer attention to public affairs. He himself was nominally involved in apprehending the goods of the traitorous William Stanley in 1495. He would have gained some grasp of the Perkin Warbeck crisis. Perhaps, as he developed more critical thinking as the recipient of what we would call a world-class education, he began to ponder whether some of the king's own actions might have contributed to elements of his problems, as they surely had in 1497. If so, he would also have quickly learnt the wisdom of keeping his own counsel in regard to such concerns.

We cannot know how much time Arthur spent with his father, but we can assume that at least some of their moments together would have been spent discussing the intricacies of kingship. At first glance, this would hardly seem likely to set the scene for an affectionate relationship. Yet there are signs that beneath the austere pretences, a more loving father and son bond existed between them.

Henry and his son may have cherished a shared love of music. The King was known for his passion for the art and, as we have seen, he often made rewards to Arthur's musicians who had clearly impressed him. When the king praised Arthur's performers, the prince must have been delighted. Did he work hard to cultivate minstrels and trumpeters whom he knew would impress the king? Is it possible that he saw this as a means of connection to his father beyond the business of government? We simply don't have the evidence to know for sure.

Thanks to his cutting-edge education, Arthur would also have been able to dazzle his father with poetry from the ancient Greeks and epic tales from antiquity. Henry VII was an enthusiast for the "new learning" and had promoted the cult of humanism in England. But thanks to the king's own championing of it in the education of his children, Arthur may even have been able to excel his father in learning. It certainly would have given them much to talk about.

Henry VII's ever-meticulous accounts also reveal a more relaxed side to their relationship. Ahead of Arthur's tenth birthday, Henry sent him some money so that he could play cards. Other records show that the king played his second son at cards and probably let him win. It's entirely possible that he did the same with Arthur.

Arthur's mother was an even warmer figure still. Almost universally praised for her grace and charm, it's quite possible that any time she spent with her son were among the happiest of the prince's life. Circumstances meant that the queen was able to enjoy far more time with her younger children than with Arthur. But we should be cautious before assuming that this represents any lack of interest or affection.

As we have already seen, Arthur was almost certainly premature. Elizabeth had to part with him when he was just a few weeks old. Both circumstances and protocol made it difficult to visit, though it's possible that she overcame such barriers far more frequently than records suggest.

Drawing on the latest research on the relationship between mothers and premature babies, Alison Weir has speculated that, given Arthur and Elizabeth's early separation, "this disruption to the bonding process may have affected the relationship between mother and son. A substantial body of modern research has shown that mothers show limited maternal responsiveness towards premature babies when there has been a prolonged period of separation after birth."[9]

Clearly, we would be wise to consider this as a serious possibility in this case. Even by the standards of Royal relationships, Arthur and Elizabeth's circumstances might have made it difficult to bond. But this picture must be held in tension with the acts of maternal love that Elizabeth displayed as often as she was realistically able.

After Arthur was deposited at Farnham, his mother visited him as soon as she was able. She appointed Arthur's lady mistress, and she clearly chose a woman she knew beyond doubt she could trust. At the first sign of trouble for the Tudor dynasty, Elizabeth fled to her son and plotted his protection. He was never far from her thoughts and when action was required to protect him, it was Arthur's mother that took the initiative.

Given the time that Elizabeth was able to enjoy with her younger children, a popular perception has arisen that while Arthur was the focus of his father's attentions, the future Henry VIII was the apple of his mother's eye. Previously, I had dismissed this as something of a lazy trope. The human brain loves to organise complicated scenarios into binary categories. I feared that analysis of the relationships within the first Tudor Royal family had fallen victim to such reductive thinking.

As we have seen, such a clear-cut distinction cannot be the full story. Arthur's safety and wellbeing were major concerns for Elizabeth. And Henry too, seemed to enjoy an affectionate and perhaps even indulgent relationship with his younger son and namesake. However, thanks to the robust research of David Starkey, I have become convinced that there is more evidence to this approach than I had previously given credit.

As we have seen, in August 1497, Arthur was present at court and met with a Venetian ambassador. After this meeting, the ambassador had an audience with the queen in the presence of the king's mother and Elizabeth's "son the prince." In the

English translation, it reads as if the "prince" in both meetings was Arthur and that he had joined first his father and later his mother. However, thanks to Dr Starkey's efforts to obtain a translation of the Italian original, it is now clear that the second prince refers not to Arthur, but the young Henry, Duke of York. Here, for the first time we have a clear parallel of the elder brother working with his father, and the younger staying close to his mother.

Dr Starkey's research also reveals that Elizabeth likely had a much more direct role in Henry's education and early life than would have been expected of her. He argues that, with no signs of a tutor appointed until the Duke of York was older, it could well have been his mother that taught him to read and write. He highlights a similarity in handwriting between the queen, Henry, and Princess Mary. Each of their hands are distinct from that of any known tutors of the Royal children. It is likely Elizabeth who inspired their style.[10]

What we can't assume from any of this is that Henry's closeness to their mother, inspired jealousy or resentment in Arthur. Of course, it's possible. But it's equally likely that Arthur thought his brother pampered or emasculated by such closeness to his mother. Arthur, the heir to the throne, was being raised to be a man. From the age of 6 he was in an almost exclusively male world. He might have thought it embarrassing for Henry to be dispatched with their mother and grandmother during an ambassadorial visit. He, Arthur, had met these dignitaries in the presence of the king and the chancellor. We'll never know if he resented or revelled in his more intense and masculine upbringing. But he probably never questioned it.

At Arthur's christening, his grandmother, Elizabeth Woodville had stood as godmother. It must have seemed to many, and perhaps Elizabeth herself, that she was destined to play a starring role in the upbringing of her grandson. But this was not to be. After the fiasco of the Simnel conspiracy in 1487, the dowager Queen retired to Bermondsey Abbey. She died just four years later. Arthur would hardly have known her. However, his paternal grandmother, Lady Margaret Beaufort, was to play a far greater role in shaping his early years. She may have been overlooked for Arthur's godmother in the earliest days of his life. But this moment of subservience disguised the leading role she was truly being primed to play.

Lady Margaret Beaufort is a mysterious and elusive figure. She has spent centuries being largely ignored by historians. Despite the fact that contemporary and near-contemporary accounts credit her with a central role in establishing the Tudor dynasty, scholars have either tended to focus more on her extensive patronage of education or sidestepped her altogether. Happily, more recent years have witnessed a surge of interest in the lives and influence of medieval and Tudor women. It is now far more widely recognised that Margaret was essential to the Tudor's early success and played a central political role during the reign of her son, Henry VII.

Inevitably, this has risked the pendulum swinging too far in the other direction. There can be a temptation to over-estimate Margaret's influence. Some popular fiction portrayals have even, inexplicably, chosen to portray her as a sinister character. And it is often far too widely assumed that Margaret emerged as a major influence in the lives of her grandchildren, without much evidence offered to substantiate such assertions.

When I began researching this book, I feared that this was a lazy narrative. I assumed I would quickly find evidence to rebut it. Or at least expose that there was little evidence in its favour. But as I started delving more into every aspect of Arthur's life – his household, his council and even his geography – the web of his grandmother's influence became difficult to escape.

As we have already seen, two men with very strong connections to Margaret Beaufort were prominent in Arthur's household. Sir Richard Pole, Arthur's chamberlain was her nephew and probably the most central figure in Arthur's upbringing after the age of six. Maurice St John, Margaret's great-nephew, was a more intimate servant of the prince's from about the time that Arthur turned 10.

These appointments alone do not necessarily suggest the hand of Margaret Beaufort at work. After all, her family were her son's only real family. Henry VII had very few men he could trust personally. His maternal relations, who were only related to Margaret in the half-blood, were the perfect choice for sensitive roles. While from respectable backgrounds, they posed no threat to the Tudors, and it was entirely in their interest to see the new dynasty prosper.

But at least one prominent member of Arthur's council was entirely Margaret's creature. William Smith, Bishop of Lincoln, was appointed to Arthur's council in 1493 and had taken charge of it by the mid-1490s. Smith's origins are obscure, but he seems to have obtained Margaret's patronage in the 1470s when they were near neighbours in Lancashire. When Margaret's son won the crown, Smith was immediately drawn into the Tudor circle of trust, being granted crucial church appointments and roles within government.[11]

Despite his proximity to Arthur, there are signs that Smith's ultimate loyalty lay with Margaret. By 1501, Arthur was beginning to flex his muscle and seeking to influence patronage and appointments. He attempted to secure a prestigious post at Oxford University for one of his servants.[12] Smith was chancellor of the university, and the prince naturally sought his support. The scholars of Oxford either ignored their chancellor or, more likely, Smith never truly championed Arthur's nominee. Instead, the position was given to Margaret Beaufort's preferred candidate. Could it be that Arthur's grandmother had more influence over some of his servants and officers than the young prince himself? Either way, Arthur must have learnt a powerful lesson. Future king he may be. But if he chose to go up against his grandmother, there was no guarantee that he would win.

Margaret may also have played a much more direct role in the life and care of her eldest grandson. As we have already seen, her palace at Woking gave her easy access to Farnham Castle, where Arthur probably spent the first six years of his life. Sean Cunningham's research also reveals that Margaret and her husband, the Earl of Derby, regularly travelled between Surrey and their home in Lancashire.[13] Ludlow or Bewdley would have both made perfect pit stops.

While we will never know what the relationship between Margaret and Arthur was like, it's tempting to imagine that she took this opportunity to make up for what she had missed with her own son. Henry VII, though devoted to his mother, scarcely saw her between the ages of 4 and 28. It's quite possible that her stored-up maternal affections were liberally showered on Arthur. If so, the image of the prince, as an isolated, joyless, and highly regimented child, once again deserves to be questioned.

By the time of Arthur's marriage, he was the elder brother to three siblings that had survived the perilous passage of infancy. Two sisters, Margaret and Mary, and his brother, Henry. Arthur would not have known his sister Mary well. He was 10 years her senior, making the Princess just 5 years old when her brother died. Records from Mary's childhood suggest that money was regularly spent on medication for her, indicating some vulnerabilities to her health. If Arthur was aware of this, it may have given him cause for concern, especially given the fragility of the first few years of life. But for most of the year, Mary and her health would have seemed far from the prince's world on the Marches.

It is far more likely that Arthur felt a much greater sense of connection to Margaret, the oldest daughter of Henry VII and Elizabeth of York. As we have seen, Margaret was born on the same day that Arthur was created Prince of Wales. He would almost certainly have met her early in her life. Perhaps to his young, 3-year-old mind, the two great occasions were somehow connected. It's tempting to believe that becoming a Prince and big brother on the same day, were two events that conspired to make him feel very grown up. They surely left a lasting impression.

Arthur and Margaret also shared a destiny when it came to their marriages. As we have seen, Arthur's in-laws Ferdinand and Isabella, were perennially keen to build a European alliance that could contain the ambitions of the French King and prevent him threatening Spanish dominance in Italy. Their children were useful assets to locking in their key allies, England, Burgundy, and the Holy Roman Empire. Scotland too, had an importance for Spain, albeit a reduced one. Yet, Ferdinand and Isabella were not able to offer the sweetener that might have won around the Scottish King to their cause: a marriage. They had, quite simply, run out of daughters. However, if their new ally Henry VII could offer one of his daughters to the King of Scots, the affinity across the three kingdoms could still be strengthened.

Negotiations for Margaret's marriage to the Scottish King, therefore, began in 1496, though they would not conclude until after Arthur's death. These negotiations were a direct offshoot of his own marriage negotiations. Just as he had begun to involve himself more in his own marital destiny as he approached adolescence, it is possible that he showed an active interest in Margaret's future. In 1498, both the queen and the king's mother had intervened to ensure that the young Margaret was not married too early, believing that the King of Scots would not wait before commencing sexual relations and damaging the girl. While these specific concerns were probably not at the top of the mind of a boy of 12, Arthur too would likely have been concerned for his sister's general welfare.

Such concerns for his sister may have increased over the years, as the first Tudor family endured their share of tragedies. Elizabeth of York gave birth to a child named for herself in 1492 but the poor girl perished just three years later. A brother, Edmund, died after little more than a year in 1500. Such tragedies were common in the fifteenth century, even among Royalty. But there is not a shred of evidence that the frequency of such fatalities made them any easier to bear.

Arthur's relationship with his younger brother Henry, is one of the most intriguing questions about the prince's short life. Sadly, it is also one that is impossible to answer. What we don't know is how well the two boys ever really knew each other. If it is correct, as this book suggests, that Arthur was more integrated into his family than is usually supposed, then the two boys may have spent significant periods of time in each other's company. Though what they thought of each other is anyone's guess.

Discussions around Arthur and Henry often assume that the two princes must have been of contrasting personalities. This is a well-rehearsed sibling trope. Parents today typically talk about which of their children is the 'clever one', the 'creative one', or the 'sporty one' as if to assume that one cannot be all or that all cannot be none.

Yet, while we must be careful to avoid falling into the trap of lazy stereotypes, there is some evidence that Arthur and Henry were cut from a slightly different cloth. While Arthurs may have been a little uneasy on the public stage, Henry loved to perform. Arthur's upbringing was serious and intense, but Henry was treated to a more serene start to life with his sisters and under the care of their mother. While Arthur's accomplishments were intellectual, Henry would later thrive as an athlete.

But such differences are too easily exaggerated. Arthur may not have thrived on attention as his brother did, but he completed all his public tasks admirably from a young age. Henry's early years were more relaxed than Arthur's, but he still received the rigorous knightly upbringing common amongst the upper class. Henry too, would later demonstrate significant intellectual interest and reasonable intellectual ability.

Ultimately, whatever their differences or similarities, the age gap between the two brothers meant that such things were unlikely to have mattered much. Arthur was five years older than Henry. There could have been little by way of personal competition between them. Even if Henry were the superior athlete, this is unlikely to have been clear in Arthur's lifetime. Had the elder Prince outperformed his brother intellectually, it would have been nothing more than what was expected of the older brother.

We don't know how often, if at all, Henry visited Arthur at Farnham, Ludlow or Bewdley. But if he did, he would have been well aware that he was entering his brother's dominion. Arthur was the centre of gravity in his own household. At the times he visited court or the Royal nursery that cared for his siblings, attention probably switched to him for the duration of his visit. Was Henry jealous of this or in awe of it? Maybe both. But it's unlikely that they were ever close enough, in age or geography, to be rivals.

However, had Arthur lived, this would almost certainly have changed. For reasons entirely beyond the control of either brother, it is likely that relations between the Prince of Wales and the Duke of York would one day have been strained. Because of the actions of their great-uncle, Richard III, Arthur may have grown to harbour an implicit mistrust of his sibling.

Regardless of the truth of the matter, Arthur would have been raised to believe that Richard III had betrayed the legacy of everything his brother, Edward IV had built to achieve. When the first Yorkist King left a child ruler to succeed him, he put his faith in his brother to ensure a smooth transition. Richard had demonstrated impeccable loyalty to date and could surely be trusted to protect the Yorkist inheritance. According to the narrative Arthur would have received, Richard responded to this trust with brutal betrayal. André, Arthur's tutor, would later write that Richard 'ordered that his unprotected nephews secretly be dispatched with the sword,' and that 'the entire land was convulsed with sobbing and anguish.'[14] It doesn't matter whether this was the true story. Arthur believed it was.

However well Arthur and Henry got on, this recent history would surely have been close to Arthur's thoughts as he grew older. Richard had been a demonstrably loyal brother to Edward IV. Yet, before the late King's body was cold, the man who should have ensured the crown descended to the next generation, snatched it for himself. Worse still, he even had the boys he was charged to protect brutally murdered.

This disturbing precedent may also have plagued the mind of Henry VII. It may even have influenced his decision not to raise Arthur and Henry together. Henry was probably being prepared to become a significant landed magnate in the north of England. Playing that role effectively could significantly bolster Arthur's rule. But perhaps their father, and even Arthur himself, believed that a healthy distance, leading to a degree of mistrust, could help prevent Arthur from following in the naïve and too-trusting footsteps of his grandfather, Edward IV. Had Arthur lived, a great relationship with his brother was probably unlikely. He was not the isolated and lonely prince of popular imagination. But he almost certainly was being brought up to believe that no one should be trusted entirely. Perhaps the blood of his blood and flesh of his flesh was to be no exception.

Chapter 11

The Spanish Princess

Before she was even old enough to remember, Katherine of Aragon had been saturated in Spanish culture. At her first public appearance, aged just 3, her mother held her up high to witness the spectacle of a ceremonial bull fight. She studied Spanish dancing and wore the Iberian fashions which would one day fascinate English commentators. From her infancy, Katherine toured the newly forged kingdom with her parents as they squashed rebellions and secured their rule. She even adopted a pomegranate, representing her parents' conquest of Grenada, as her own personal emblem.

But the Infanta's destiny was not to embody Spain's traditions. It was to secure Spain's ambitions. Katherine's parents, the high and mighty Ferdinand and Isabella had both inherited middle-ranking powers, isolated from the European stage. They were determined to forge them together and create a Spanish powerhouse to dominate the continent. Their daughters each had a role to play in this master vision. And it was in a quest to fulfil her own small piece of this destiny that the infant Infanta acquired the most un-Spanish of sobriquets: the Princess of Wales.

As we have seen, it was Henry VII that had initiated negotiations for a marriage between Katherine and Arthur. The Tudor dynasty was in its perilous infancy. Just the year before discussions began, the King had been forced to defend his crown in battle. Over sixty years had passed since an English king had successfully passed the throne to his son and Henry knew full well that Arthur would one day need all the help he could get. With a continental princess by his side, and progeny that were the grandchildren of the Spanish monarchs, men might think twice before casting their loyalty aside.

Yet whatever skill Henry or his team displayed in negotiations, the signing of the treaty of Medina del Campo, which agreed Arthur and Katherine's future marriage, owed little to English diplomacy. The die was cast for one simple reason: at that moment in time, it suited Spanish interests. Ferdinand and Isabella were rulers with a clearly considered foreign policy and a logical list of priorities. The first, was to secure their joint rule and to pass on a united kingdom to their heir. The second, to secure this legacy by dominating or neutralising the rest of Iberia. And the third, to bring Spain out from the shadows and onto the centre stage of European affairs. The Spanish monarchs, much like the Tudors, were great believers in their destiny. But they were also critical realists. Transforming their vision into a reality was dependent on containing the one European power that could stop them in their tracks. The kingdom of France. And it was this imperative that caused them to turn their attention to the fractious politics of Northern Europe.

The most pressing plan was to seal an alliance with the house of Habsburg, which through a series of inheritance and marriages had come to dominate much of the low countries and a series of territories that we call Germany. A deal would later be sealed through a double marriage alliance. The Spanish Prince Juan would marry the Habsburg Margaret of Austria. The heir to his father's vast territories, Philip, was betrothed to the Infanta Juana. Next on the list was to form a partnership with France's ancient enemy England. It was this master plan, and the fact that Ferdinand and Isabella had enough daughters to spare, that caused them to smile upon Henry's initial advances.

Arthur's engagement, therefore, was entirely political. And politics then, like politics today, had a habit of changing quickly. The Spanish Infanta's glaringly British title of Princess of Wales had probably always jarred a bit. It soon became a source of embarrassment to her parents. After the fall out of the Breton affair, both England and Spain made peace with France. The French King, Charles VIII was evidently keen to break apart the coalition against him. To do so, he was prepared to offer Ferdinand a sweetener that he couldn't resist.

Years previously, France had snatched away two counties from the Kingdom of Aragon: Roussillon and Cerdaña. Their loss was humiliating for Aragon and Ferdinand was desperate to reclaim them. Charles offered him both on a plate. But as ever, there were strings attached. The Spanish must swear to never conduct a marriage alliance with the 'old foes of France'.[1] And there was no confusion as to who these 'old foes' were.

This was a deal that the duplicitous Ferdinand could happily live with. On the 8 January 1493, he and Isabella signed a treaty agreeing to 'engage their royal word and faith as Christians not to conclude, or permit to be concluded, any marriage of their children with any member of the Royal family of England.'[2] With the stroke of a Spanish pen, Arthur's engagement was broken.

But Arthur's father, who had fought for everything he ever had, was not prepared to give up. He knew full well that Ferdinand would be tempted to betray France before the ink was dry on the treaty. Once his possessions were safely back in Spanish hands, it wouldn't be worth the piece of paper it was written on. On 10 March Henry commissioned his diplomats to 'treat with the ambassadors of the King and Queen of Spain, and to conclude a treaty of alliance and marriage between Prince Arthur and the Princess Katherine.' The Spanish could cast Arthur aside, if they wanted to. But England was not going to go quietly.

Despite his optimism, Henry must have known that his embassy would receive short shrift in Spain. Ferdinand's desire to reclaim his lost possessions may have been the trigger for the break in Arthur's engagement, but anyone observing the political scene in Europe knew that something far more fundamental had changed since the signing of the treaty of Medina del Campo. Much to the chagrin of Henry, at least one of the major European powers claimed to believe that Richard, Duke of York, the rightful King of England, was still alive. Ferdinand and Isabella were never going to marry their youngest child to an impostor.

Before the English could get their hands on him, Perkin Warbeck had fled France and sought refuge in Mechelen. The Dowager Duchess of Burgundy, Margaret of York had quickly recognised the boy as her nephew. Despairingly for Henry, she quickly set about trying to achieve international recognition for the man who she perhaps genuinely hoped was a resurrected York Prince. Most plucky pretenders would go about building support for their cause by appealing to the military men of Europe. But, probably at Margaret's suggestion, Warbeck realised that his tale of a young boy, wandering abandoned across the continent, might appeal more to the only powerful ruler who was also a mother. He soon dispatched a letter to Isabella claiming that he was the true heir to England who had escaped the Tower of London and was now finally in a position to reclaim his identity.

The Spanish Queen never replied. She likely didn't believe that this 'Prince Richard' was genuine. She probably didn't care. But his presence at the court of the dowager duchess created a major diplomatic obstacle to a marriage alliance with England. The dowager duchess of Burgundy was the step mother-in-law of Maximillian, King of the Romans. It was he who had joined Spain and England in opposing France's advance into Brittany and it was he who was essential to Ferdinand and Isabella's plan for Spanish supremacy.

Through first his wife, and later his son, Philip, Maximillian was the effective ruler of Burgundy, a duchy that encompassed modern-day Holland, Belgium, Luxembourg, and parts of France. As titular ruler of the Holy Roman Empire, he had influence that extended across the continent. To put it bluntly, his friendship was more important to Spain than England's. The Spanish monarchs would ultimately wed two of their children to Maximilian's progeny.

Unfortunately for Henry and for Arthur, Margaret soon converted her son-in-law to Warbeck's cause. While it was Margaret's wealth that supported the boy and his band of supporters, Maximillian treated him like a Prince. To all intents and purposes, he was harbouring a rival to Henry VII's throne making any kind of friendship between England and Burgundy impossible. Ferdinand and Isabella ultimately knew where their bread was buttered. If it came down to a straight choice between England and Burgundy, they would stick with their nearer neighbours. They were reluctant to put their youngest child in a situation where she would effectively be at war with her siblings. Nor were they keen to marry her to a prince that might not ever make it to the throne. But for all these obstacles, they knew well enough that the political wind could soon blow in another direction. They were determined to keep their options open.

Toward the end of 1494, the Spanish monarchs casually commented that they were 'not declined' to form a new alliance with England. Early the next year they again dispatched Doctor De Puebla to represent them at Henry's court.[3] The Spanish openness to resume negotiations with England were, once again, motivated by wider political factors. By 1495, relations with France had totally broken down. The French King had turned his ambitions toward building an empire in Italy and the Spanish were determined to clip his wings. They set about forming an anti-French league, ostensibly to protect the Pope, consisting of Spain, the King of the Romans, and the Italian states of Venice and Milan.

England's entry into the league would be a strategic coup for the Spanish. While Henry VII was never likely to dispatch troops to far-flung Italy, England would be perfectly placed to provide distraction at crucial moments. Yet, with Warbeck still at large, Ferdinand and Isabella could not offer Henry the one thing that could have enticed him into the league: a Spanish marriage for his son.

By 1495, Arthur was Prince of Wales, Earl of Chester, Duke of Cornwall and a Knight of both the Bath and the Garter. He was already ruling over his own regional government. Despite his youth, he was one of the richest men in England. But as far as Ferdinand and Isabella were concerned, his prospects simply didn't ring as strong in reality as they did on paper. Thanks to the tumultuous decades of the Wars of the Roses, the English throne had gained a reputation across Europe as being inherently unstable. With a credible pretender at large, history looked destined to repeat itself. There was no way on earth that the mightiest monarchs in Europe would abandon their daughter to such unfettered uncertainty.

Prince Arthur would never be as lucky as his father. Yet, on 3 June 1495 his luck changed decisively. Perkin Warbeck finally raised a fleet and attempted to land at deal in Kent. And he failed spectacularly.

De Puebla wrote to Ferdinand and Isabella that:

> 'the so-called Duke of York came to England with all the ships and troops he had been able to obtain from the Duchess Margaret, the Archduke, and Flanders. A portion of his troops disembarked, but the people rose up in arms against them without the intervention of a single soldier of the King. The peasants of the adjacent villages made great havock on the troops who had disembarked, and if the vessels had not been at hand not a single man of them would have escaped alive.'[4]

Despite his claims to be the genuine son of Edward IV, Warbeck had attracted no support on England's shores. His attempt at landing was repelled by locals without even the need to assemble a Royal army. Unlike in 1487, Henry VII had seen off a pretender without even needing to fight for it. All of a sudden, he seemed more secure on his throne. A throne that he now looked likely to pass to his son.

More significantly still, Warbeck's departure from Burgundy meant that he was no longer in Maximillian's custody. Whatever Margaret of York's hopes for the boy, the wider political community had no desire to see him return. The door for a reconciliation between Henry and the King of the Romans was finally open. Ferdinand and Isabella wrote to De Puebla, authorising him to tell Henry that they were "very pleased" to consider a marriage between their daughter Katherine and the Prince of Wales. They conceded that there was no need for negotiations to take long. Much of the terms had been set by the previous treaty. But they were clear on one thing: nothing could be finally agreed until there was peace between England and Burgundy.[5]

The renegotiations did not begin in earnest until early the next year. While there was a mutual understanding that the treaty of Medina del Campo would serve as a good basis for the discussion, much had changed since then. On 5 March, Henry established a commission of Thomas, Bishop of Rochester, John Dynham, William Warham, Robert Middleton, Richard Guildford, and John Rysley to:

> 'treat with Doctor De Puebla about the marriage between Prince Arthur and the Princess Katherine, her marriage portion and dowry, the time of her coming to England, the time and mode of the payment of the marriage portion, &c.'[6]

Ferdinand and Isabella had asked that the negotiations be conducted in secret. Ever keen to give themselves maximum room for manoeuvre, they were reluctant for either of the Kings of Romans or Scots to became privy to these discussions, as it might hinder their negotiations elsewhere. But for Henry VII, the reopening of discussions showed that he was well and truly back at the top table of Europe. He had absolutely no intention of keeping it quiet.

Negotiations began at De Puebla's lodgings in the monastery of the Augustine Friars, which he called "the most public place in the whole of England". There they were observed by 'sharp spies'. This, he informed his masters, was deliberately engineered by the English to 'cause more fear and suspicion to the King of France.'[7]

As with the negotiations of 1488, money was the early sticking point. The English heavily implied that the Spanish were in their debt. Without their efforts in invading France in 1492, Ferdinand would never have reclaimed Roussillon and Cerdaña. Such loyalty should be rewarded. Now that these possessions were back in his hands, surely Ferdinand could afford to reflect his newfound wealth in Katherine's marriage portion?

De Puebla firmly rebutted this. The restoration of these two counties had come from Spain's negotiations with Charles VIII. Even if England had dispatched 20,000 horsemen to Ferdinand's aid, it would be 'impossible to yield to their pretensions'. But despite the posturing so common of such negotiations, both sides seemed to agree that nothing significantly need differ from the previous treaty.[8]

The King seemed reluctant to entrust Arthur's marriage entirely to his negotiators. Unlike in 1488, he himself leant more heavily on the ambassador. At some stage in June, the two spent eight days together in 'a park twenty-five miles distant from London' where the King 'opened his heart to De Puebla.' He confided his sorrow that the Spanish were investing so much in their children's marriages to Maximillian's family but seemed too reluctant to conclude negotiations with him. He conveyed that there was nowhere in Christendom that Princess Katherine was more beloved than in England. And he reminded the ambassador that a marriage alliance would be a major blow to France. Once their children were married, Henry would be obliged to follow Ferdinand and Isabella in all things.

Henry's charm offensive seemed to do the trick. From this point on, De Puebla started to become more interested in doing Henry's bidding than that of his masters. He urged Ferdinand and Isabella to conclude the marriage treaty as soon as possible, even if the other treaties, such as England's entry into the league, would have to wait. After all, he reminded the Spanish monarchs, while the King was faithful to their cause, the English Parliament were extremely fickle. They could soon lose interest if a treaty was not quickly agreed. But despite De Puebla's best attempts, Henry fully understood that to obtain the desire of his heart, he would need to give Spain what they wanted most. That summer, he made formal moves to join the league.

From Arthur's perspective, one crucial thing had changed since his marriage was last up for negotiation: at almost 10 years of age, he was able to follow the discussions. There are signs that he did just that. On 2 July, the King granted a servant of Arthur's a reward of 20 shillings.[9] A few months later, he granted similar awards to Arthur's minstrels and lute player. It's possible that Henry had heard tale of their good work and decided to reward them. But it's more likely that the King had recently seen them in action. Arthur had probably been with the king in the early summer, exactly when negotiations for his marriage were at their height.

There can be no pretence that the prince was a significant decision maker in the proceedings. Even if had been 20 years old, his father's will would still have been paramount. Nor would he have had much to offer around the more technical haggling around the size of Katherine's marriage portion, how much of it could be offset by ornaments and what all of this meant for the King's military commitments. But his presence may have been crucial from a PR perspective. Henry had spent much of the summer trying to convince the Spanish that Katherine and Arthur should marry by proxy straight away, even though they were, strictly speaking, too young to commit. He then wanted the princess to depart from Spain as soon as was possible. Just a year later, Italian ambassadors would comment on how tall Arthur looked for his age. Perhaps his presence at court served to convince the ambassadors that Arthur, though young, was ready for marriage.

This is an analysis, that we need to treat with caution. We have no firm evidence that Arthur was present at court in the summer of 1496. De Puebla never mentions an encounter with the prince at this stage, though he was lazy in his communications and much of it doesn't survive. Yet, the strong suggestion that Arthur's servants were in the King's presence at exactly the time that the Spanish marriage negotiations were reaching their peak is too tempting a possibility to ignore.

Negotiations proceeded throughout the summer. And while Arthur had certainly left court by August, payments to messengers between him and his father could suggest that he continued to be kept up to date on their progress. On 22 September, Henry instructed the Bishop of London to agree final terms with the Spanish ambassador. For the second time in his young life, negotiations for Arthur's marriage were coming into land.

On 1 October, the English and Spanish negotiators finally agreed the binding clauses. Arthur and Katherine were to marry as soon as the boy reached his fourteenth birthday. Or sooner if it could be arranged and the Pope gave his consent. The marriage portion – the payment of which would later become a bone of such contention – was set at 200,000 scudos. In return, upon her marriage, Katherine would be entitled to one third of the revenues of Wales, Cornwall, and Chester. Her income would be augmented further still when she eventually became Queen. The princess was to lose all her Spanish inheritance but remain in line to the Spanish throne. Three years after their original agreement was dissolved, Arthur and Katherine were back together again. It would be another five years before the prince would fix his eyes on her. Whatever joy or excitement Arthur felt about the glittering prospect of a great marriage must have been tempered by moments of anxiety. After all, he had come this far before. He was old enough now to understand that fortune's wheel was capable of rapidly spinning in the opposite direction.

The prince was also old enough, and educated enough, to understand that treaty was no betrothal. It was nothing but a diplomatic agreement. And he may even have been worldly-wise enough to know that an agreement with a man like Ferdinand could count for precious little.

The English pushed quickly for the young prince and princess to be formally betrothed. Such an act would give their union some status in the eyes of the Church, creating a degree of "public honesty" between the two young Royals, making an actual marriage in the future, increasingly likely. The Spanish were quick to pay lip service to the idea, and Katherine signed a document which even authorised Du Puebla to act on her behalf in a proxy ceremony.

Both a formal betrothal and a marriage by proxy would help fasten the chains on the Spanish and lock them in to their commitment. But Arthur's father knew full well that until a marriage was consummated, it was dissolvable under church law. It would not be until they had custody of the princess that the English could be confident that Katherine's destiny lay with Arthur.

Katherine's parents seemed in no hurry to part with her. In fact, they were still insisting that their agreement be kept secret from the King of Scots. This may have actually been in England's best interests. While they dangled the possibility of a Spanish marriage in front of Scotland, they had a degree of influence over James IV, who was currently playing host to Perkin Warbeck. Once it became clear that Ferdinand had pledged his last legitimate daughter to Arthur, his influence with the Scots might evaporate. Nevertheless, this continued secrecy was surely unnerving to Arthur. His father-in-law had already cast him aside under the shadow of secrecy once before.

It would soon become clear, even for Henry, that 1497 was never going to be the year that Katherine made her voyage to England. This was the year that the Scots raided the north and the Cornish rebelled in the southwest. The Tudor King was facing the greatest security challenge of his reign. The Spanish were hardly likely to deposit Katherine into the midst of such instability.

Yet, despite these hazards and hinderances, arrangements for the betrothal trickled on slowly. Spain and England ratified various clauses as the year progressed. Finally, according to the Venetian ambassador on the 14 July there had been firmly concluded and published the marriage of the 'daughter of the King of Spain to the eldest son of the King of England'. Katherine, apparently, was to travel to her new land the following spring.[10]

The 'following spring' was a convenient commitment for the Spanish. It was both far away and sufficiently vague. Henry, and probably Arthur, were seasoned enough to draw little hope from it. Happily, for the King, that spectacular Tudor luck was about to strike again. After a second attempt at an uprising, led by the pretender himself, the Cornish rebels were decisively defeated, and Perkin Warbeck was finally captured. The man who had hovered like a black cloud over Arthur's future, marriage and destiny was finally in his father's custody. Surely his betrothed could finally join him.

Earlier that year, Henry had played hardball in his attempts to quicken Katherine's arrival. He had heavily hinted that there would be no easing of duties on Spanish merchants until Katherine set foot on English soil. Now it was time for a charm offensive. And for that, it was finally time to deploy his not-so-secret weapon: the charming and gentle queen, Elizabeth of York. At the end of the year, the English queen wrote to her Spanish counterpart, talking of the very great "friendship subsisting between them." A friendship that could only increase with the marriage of their children. She begged Isabella to write often about herself and the princess. She, Elizabeth, would do likewise with news about Arthur. The queen's words were dripping with maternal warmth, and the inference is clear. Henry, by defeating Warbeck had provided for Katherine's physical safety. Elizabeth would be on hand to provide for Katherine's emotional security.

Elizabeth would soon have the chance to demonstrate her charms in person to a new Spanish embassy. Ferdinand and Isabella had been growing frustrated with the patchy and tardy communications from De Puebla. With some justification, they worried that he was not giving them a true picture of life in England and was failing to work in the best interests of Spain. In the summer of 1498, they despatched two great men, the Knight Commander Londono and the Sub-prior of Santa Cruz, to give them the true lay of the land. Henry and Elizabeth knew that this was a crucial moment. It was time to dress to impress. With lavish enthusiasm, they reacted to the letters from Ferdinand and Isabella that the ambassadors had brought with them. According to De Puebla, 'to hear what they spoke of your highness and the Princess of Wales was like hearing the praise of God.'

The ambassador presented the Queen with two copies of a letter from Katherine and Elizabeth quickly dispatched the first copy to Arthur. The king and queen, in what we might consider an award-winning performance, then staged a mock quarrel around which of them would retain the second. The King – who had earlier declared that the letters from Spain meant more to him than memories of his late victory – insisted that the queen surrender the remaining copy to him. He wanted one to 'carry continually about him.' But Elizabeth refused. She had already sent one to Arthur and could not bear to be parted from the other. Both were clearly being absurd. The letters were in Spanish, which neither of them could read. But the Spanish were impressed and wrote with enthusiasm about the queen's many qualities. This touching little charade had done the trick.

Arthur was not present to witness his parents' performance. Curiously, he was in Calais and was not summoned back for the occasion despite the fact there seems to have been ample time to do so. Nevertheless, he may have seen his parents work so well together on previous occasions. If he had, it may have given him hope for his own marriage. After all, his parents, like he and Katherine were two people that had been put together for dynastic purposes. Perhaps he and his princess would one day form the kind of connection that his parents so clearly enjoyed.

After the success of the ambassadors visit, the Royal family finally seemed to hope that Katherine's arrival could be imminent. For the first time they began to discuss practical matters about her life in England. The queen and the king's mother sent word that Katherine should speak French as much as possible as neither of them spoke Spanish or Latin. They also requested that Katherine grew accustomed to drinking wine. The water in England was not drinkable.

By early 1499, there was still no sign of the Princess. The Spanish were now refusing to send Katherine until September 1500, when Arthur reached the age of 14. This was some eighteen months later than what the wily Ferdinand had agreed the year before. For the first time, we get a sense of Arthur's anxiety with the constant delays as he entered his adolescence. By way of De Puebla, the prince pleaded for 'a few lines from the Princess of Wales his wife.' Even if he could not yet see his bride, he longed to hear from her.

Clearly, any comparison between Arthur's experience and that of a modern youth, who fears that his girlfriend is 'ghosting' him, are severely limited. But the sense of adolescent anxiety may have felt similar. If so, his hopes may soon have been raised by an exciting development. While Katherine was still not ready to set sail, the couple were to be married in the spring. To us, the notion that two people who have never met can be married is absurd. But to the powerful families of early-modern Europe it was an accepted tradition. 'Proxy weddings', whereby a ceremony literally took place, with a nominated representative acting for the absent party, were fully valid in the eyes of both church and state.

On 19 May, many of the great men of the realm assembled at Bewdley Manor. It was probably the place that Arthur considered his home. As we have already seen, unlike the fortress of Ludlow Castle, Bewdley was purpose built for comfort. Given that the Spanish ambassador was in attendance, he would be able to relay to Spain the delights of the home comforts that Katherine could enjoy when she finally crossed the seas. Katherine had given her permission for De Puebla to stand proxy. Now aged 12 and a half, Arthur must have been full of pre-teen awkwardness as he took the hand of the old man, and confessed his 'deep and sincere love, for the said Princess, his wife.' In a deep voice, Arthur confirmed that he was making his nuptials *per verba de præsenti*, meaning that the union was indissoluble.

Sir Richard Pole, by this stage probably the most trusted figure in Arthur's life, held both the Prince's and De Puebla's hands in his as Arthur declared that he "accepted De Puebla in the name and as the proxy of the Princess Katherine, and the Princess Katherine in his person as his lawful and undoubted wife."[11]

Arthur had once again been tested in a court of public performance. Once again, he had excelled. By the laws of the church, he was wedded to Katherine of Aragon. But, on an even deeper level, he knew that he was wedded to the cause of the English alliance with Spain. The next crucial stage was to secure the presence of his own bride in England. Arthur knew that it was now his duty to make that English dream a reality.

Chapter 12

Secure in His Kingdom

England and Spain were united by treaty. Arthur and Katherine were bound together by church and law. But all concerned – including Arthur himself – were worldly wise enough to know that this was not enough. There was only one way that Henry and Arthur knew they could secure the marriage. And that was to take secure custody of Katherine herself.

On 5 October 1499, some six months after Katherine had once been expected to arrive, but a year before she was now due, Arthur appealed directly to his wife. The prince had been writing to his bride since at least the summer of 1498, but this letter, written at Ludlow Castle, is the only epistle that survives:

> 'Most illustrious and most excellent lady, my dearest spouse, I wish you very much health, with my hearty commendation.
>
> 'I have read the most sweet letters of your Highness lately given to me, from which I have easily perceived your most entire love to me. Truly, your letters, traced by your own hand, have so delighted me, and have rendered me so cheerful and jocund, that I fancied I beheld your Highness and conversed with and embraced my dearest wife. I cannot tell you what an earnest desire I feel to see your Highness, and how vexatious to me is this procrastination about your coming. I owe eternal thanks to your excellence that you so lovingly correspond to this my so ardent love. Let it continue, I entreat, as it has begun; and, like I cherish your sweet remembrance night and day, do you preserve my name ever fresh in your breast. And let your coming to me be hastened, that instead of being absent we may be present with each other, and the love conceived between us, and the wished-for joys may reap their proper fruit.
>
> Moreover, I have done as your illustrious Highness enjoined me, that is to say, in commending you to the most serene lord and lady King and Queen my parents, and in declaring your filial regard toward them, which to them was most pleasing to hear especially from my lips. I also beseech your Highness that it may please you to exercise a similar good office for me and to commend me with hearty

goodwill to my most serene lord and lady your parents; for I greatly value, venerate and esteem them, even as though they were my own, and wish them all happiness and prosperity.

May your Highness be ever fortunate and happy, and be kept safe and joyful, and let me know it often and speedily by your letters, which will be to me most joyous.

'Your Highness' loving spouse, Arthur, Prince of Wales, Duke of Cornwall, eldest son of the King.[1]

These words are carefully crafted poetry, composed in flawless Latin. They are not the sole work of a 13-year-old boy. Arthur was not writing alone. Nor would the decision to put pen to paper be one that had sprung from his heart. It may read like a love letter. But it was a carefully crafted communiqué of foreign policy.

The English were firing every arrow in their quiver in their bid to quicken Katherine's coming. The king had raised the stakes earlier in the negotiations. The queen had turned on the charm. And now Arthur himself was attempting to draw his wife to him with the language of a lover. Yet, his earnest plea that the princess's coming 'should be hastened', fell on deaf Spanish ears.

One last obstacle remained. A barrier that, in one form or another had lurked beneath the surface of the negotiations since the early 1490s. Just how safe would Katherine be when she came to England? And, when the time came, just how able would her husband be to fulfil his destiny and ascend the throne? Ferdinand and Isabella had long been nervous about Henry and Arthur's long-term prospects. The emergence of Perkin Warbeck as the Duke of York, with the credible backing of his Yorkist 'aunt' the Duchess of Burgundy, helped untangle Arthur and Katherine's first engagement. Only when it became clear that he enjoyed no significant support in England after his botched invasion of 1495 did negotiations begin again in earnest. But while Warbeck was now safely in the King's custody, the Spanish Kings knew full well that he was not the only threat to Arthur's succession.

In early 1499, a young Londoner named Ralph Wilford, raised a rebellion against the king. In a moment of fantasy, he claimed to be Edward, Earl of Warwick. He was quickly apprehended and ruthlessly executed. But it reminded many – including Ferdinand and Isabella – that there had long been a boy lingering in the Tower of London, with a much better claim to the throne than the king himself. That boy had since become a man. With the discrediting of Warbeck, he now represented the greatest hope of a Yorkist revival.

In the last two years, the Spanish monarchs had lost their two eldest children. Prince Juan, their heir, who had perished in 1497, and Isabella, who had succumbed the next year. It is no surprise that they now treated the destiny of their remaining children with even greater caution. Ferdinand and Isabella knew that they must one day part with Katherine. But they would never send her into the lion's den. And while Edward Plantagenet himself may not have been much of a lion, there were many Yorkist dissidents who were prepared to roar for him. If Katherine was going to leave the safety of Spain and embrace a future in England, something had to happen. And, either by luck or by design, something certainly did.

Perkin Warbeck had been treated relatively well since his surrender toward the end of 1497. The King kept him close at court but provided for his needs, giving over the pretender's wife to the care of the Queen. No doubt the King's inevitable temptation to parade the captive pretender as widely as possible was humiliating for the lad, but it did seem that Henry was committed to sparing Perkin's life.

Yet for Warbeck, only a life of freedom was one worth living. He had spent years as an adventurer and captivity, however comfortable, was not his style. In June 1498, he made a break for it. But this time, his luck had run out. He was quickly apprehended and placed in the stocks before being locked in the Tower of London. The King clearly had no intention of ever again permitting him any freedom. Yet he was still not planning his rival's destruction.

All that changed in the summer of 1499. A group of men loyal to both Warbeck and Warwick joined together to hatch a plot. The details are clouded in confusion, but the plan clearly involved freeing both men from the tower, raising a rebellion against the king, and placing one of them on the throne. The plotters seemed to find a means to communicate with both men in the tower, who consented to the plan. Warwick and Warbeck also seem to have communicated between themselves.

It was only after both men had supposedly given their explicit consent to the plan that they were rumbled by the authorities. Trials for treason quickly followed. No longer would Henry VII show clemency to those who threatened his throne. Warwick was executed on Tower Hill on 28 November. A few days previously, Warbeck had been hanged after repeating his confession that he was not Richard of York. Perkin Warbeck's death, though brutal, can have come as little surprise to contemporaries. The man had spent almost a decade undermining the King's position and stirring rebellion against him. He had made the sparing of his life a condition of his surrender, but it is hardly surprising that any future bad behaviour would be met with his death.

The Earl of Warwick is a different story. The young man had never before lifted a finger in rebellion. While his very existence represented a threat to the Tudor dynasty, there is nothing to suggest that he ever encouraged such attentions. After languishing in the tower for more than half his life, it's hardly a surprise that he jumped for a taste of freedom. It is also possible, though we cannot be clear, that he lived with some sort of mental deficiency, perhaps making him an easy target for plotters.

By the standards of the day, his execution may have been necessary. Henry VII's overwhelming priority was the security of his throne and his ability to pass on the crown to Arthur. It also illustrates the ruthlessness required to keep hold of power. Henry VII was never a King famed for a blood-thirsty nature. Yet even he could be capable of savage acts of cruelty when the circumstances required. It must have been one lesson that Arthur himself would never forget.

There is much about this botched rebellion that simply doesn't make sense. Why on earth were two such high-security prisoners as Warbeck and Warwick allowed to communicate? How did the men so easily manage to get messages to the prisoners? Why was the whole plot only rumbled once both men had given it their consent?

For most historians, these questions, along with the sheer timing of the event, make it inconceivable that there was no government involvement in the plot. That Warwick and Warbeck should implicate themselves in an act of treason at exactly the time Henry had to put concerns about the succession to bed, is far too convenient a coincidence. Was one of the conspirators a double agent for the King? Was the plot discovered in the early stages and allowed to proceed until such a time as the men implicated themselves? Could misinformation have been deliberately spread to give the plotters the impression that things might be easier to pull off than they really were? Unfortunately, we will never know.

The most likely interpretation of these events is that the Spanish monarchs had informed Henry VII that their daughter would not be sent to England until they were convinced the succession was secure. The fact that, in August 1498, De Puebla had written to his masters to assure them that, "he [Perkin] is so changed that I, and all other persons here, believe his life will be very short" suggests that the presence of live pretenders was a source of concern in Spain.[2]

Furthermore, De Puebla – who was often slack at writing, even with important news – was quick to write after the executions that:

> 'Now that Perkin and the son of the Duke of Clarence have been executed, there does not remain 'a drop of doubtful Royal blood,' the only Royal blood being the true blood of the King, the Queen, and, above all, of the Prince of Wales.'[3]

The best evidence that the lives of Warwick and Warbeck were a condition of Katherine's coming, is that Katherine herself seems to have believed it. Writing some 50 years after the event, Edward of Warwick's nephew, Cardinal Reginald Pole said:

> 'I will tell you of the grievous trouble and remorse which his Majesty's aunt, the most Serene Queen Katherine, had to endure, as frequently alluded to by herself, always thinking of this, namely, that a great part of her troubles emanated from God, not through

any fault of her own, but for the salvation of her soul; and that the Divine justice thus punished the sin of her father King Ferdinand, for when he commenced negotiating her marriage with Prince Arthur, the eldest son of the King of England, some disturbances took place at the time, owing to the favour and goodwill borne by the people to my mother's brother the Earl of Warwick, of whom we have made mention above, who being the son of the Duke of Clarence, brother of King Edward, became, by the death of that King's sons, next heir to the English crown. King Ferdinand, having by the agreements to conclude his daughter's marriage at that time, made a difficulty about it, saying he would not give her to one who was not secure in his own kingdom; and thus, by inciting the King to do what he already desired spontaneously, he was the cause of the death of that innocent Earl, who had no more blame in those commotions, nor could anything else be laid to his charge, save the danger which the King in Council alleged had already befallen him in part, through the existence of the said Earl; and in addition to this having heard the opinion of the King of Spain, he did that deed, of winch (as I have already said) he so greatly repented on his death-bed.'[4]

Pole was writing years after the event. He himself was not even born until a year after his uncle's execution. Nevertheless, his sources were impeccable. His father, Richard, had been Arthur's chamberlain. His mother, Margaret was Warwick's sister and later, a close confidante of Katherine's. His words should be taken seriously.

It is certainly true that no record of Ferdinand or Isabella making such a request survives. But as the long-drawn-out negotiations for the marriage proves, emissaries were often darting between England and Spain. They could have quite easily got a message to the king without committing it to writing for posterity. And for obvious reasons, it would be better for all if no proof of such a desire existed. The available evidence, largely circumstantial though it may be, points to Pole's statements being correct. Innocent blood was shed so that Arthur's long-drawn out marriage could finally become a reality. The future Kingship of Arthur Tudor had claimed its first casualty.

We should pause for a moment to reflect on what role – if any – the young Arthur may have had in the downfall of Warwick and Warbeck. This will evidently be challenging. Details of the plot and the precise role of the government in it simply don't exist. What we can see however, is how this whole episode fits into the context of Arthur's gradual emergence into public affairs.

Prince Arthur turned 13 in September 1499. Children certainly grew up faster in Tudor England than they did today and while 13 was generally considered too young to wield significant power, it was only so by a whisker. Arthur's grandfather, Edward IV, had won the crown in battle at the age of 18. His brother, Henry VIII, took charge at 17, and his nephew, Edward VI, started to wield influence over policy as a 15-year-old. In other words, Arthur was on the cusp of the age of influence. To that end, Prince Arthur had gradually started to play a more public role as he approached adolescence. As we have already seen, he was present at court for many of the big occasions. He had attended Parliaments since the age of 9 and begun to undertake tours of the country independently of either of his parents, which would have at least exposed him to some of the machinations of policy making. As we have also seen, Arthur was increasingly involved in negotiations and discussions surrounding his marriage. And the older he got the more important his involvement became. In early 1500, De Puebla was chastised by Ferdinand for the time it was taking him to secure amendments to the treaty of alliance between England and Spain. The ambassador's excuse was that the key decision makers were absent rendering him unable to agree anything. The king and queen were in Calais. And Arthur was in Wales, which he dramatically described as 'the distant depths of the Kingdom.' When it came to big decisions about Arthur's relationship with Spain, Arthur was now part of the sign-off process.

Another intriguing episode also gives us a hint that Arthur was emerging as a real figure of influence. Doctor De Puebla had long been frustrated by the presence in England of another Spanish ambassador, Don Pedro de Ayala. Ayala had previously served as Ferdinand and Isabella's representative in Scotland but, by his own election, had relocated to England in 1497. Perhaps because negotiations for a treaty of alliance between England, Spain and Scotland were underway, his presence was deemed useful. Both Henry VII and Ferdinand and Isabella were happy for him to stay. De Puebla felt differently. The two men clearly loathed each other, and Don Pedro wasted no time in undermining his rival at any opportunity. Once the negotiations with Scotland were concluded, De Puebla clearly believed his enemy should return to Spain. He took every opportunity to remind their mutual masters of the strength of this conviction.

In late 1500, about a year after the Warbeck and Warwick incident, someone informed De Puebla that Don Pedro has sought protection from the king and the Prince of Wales. He had supposedly asked both of them to write to Ferdinand and Isabella, beseeching the Spanish monarchs to let Don Pedro remain in England until at least the arrival of Princess Katherine.

Henry VII wrote accordingly. No such letter survives to prove that Arthur did likewise, but neither do most of his communications to Spain. Nevertheless, whether Arthur wrote or not scarcely matters. Nor is it important whether Don Pedro really did petition him to do so. What matters is that De Puebla clearly thought that it was credible that such a request had been made. This strongly suggests that Arthur was a figure to whom people at court were now making their petitions. They expected him to have the power and influence over people that mattered. Even the King and Queen of Spain.

By the age of about 12 or 13, Arthur was a man of influence. He was consulted on negotiations around his marriage and, at least nominally, gave his consent to some of the issues regarding England's relationship with Spain. He was petitioned by courtiers and increasingly drawn into the big decisions of the day. Is it too big a leap to go from all of that, to suppose that Arthur might have been involved with the decision to end the threat that Warbeck and Warwick represented? Perhaps. But this was an issue that touched him greatly. And while he was still young he was being raised to be a King that understood the need to be ruthless.

We will never know whether Arthur had any influence in the decision to frame these two young men and pave the way for his wife's arrival. But, at the very least, he would have understood what was happening. The path to power was hazardous and treacherous. And Arthur's, like so many of his forebears, would be paved with blood.

As the sixteenth century dawned, the path looked set for Katherine of Aragon to depart from Spain and join her husband in England. Ferdinand and Isabella quickly instructed Katherine to ratify the marriage. They themselves confirmed that they were content with the substance of the alliance and praised Henry for 'the extraordinary love which he has shown them in all things.'[5]

Yet, as the weeks passed Arthur's hopes of setting eyes on his princess must have started to fade. On 24 March, Don Pedro wrote to his masters informing them that Henry was sad to have heard nothing. He reminds them that "the English are suspicious and changeable" and hints that Henry may be considering pulling out of the marriage altogether and forming an alliance with France.[6]

Henry was surely not serious about abandoning the Spanish alliance. He had invested so much in it. But it must have been beyond frustrating for Arthur and his father that there was still no sign of Katherine's departure. They had moved heaven and earth to make this marriage happen. Blood – probably innocent blood – had been spilt. And yet, Arthur's in-laws remained as intransigent as ever.

The King was prepared to take desperate measures to unite his son with his Spanish bride. Earlier in the negotiations he had played hard ball by withholding many of the trade benefits of the treaty until Katherine arrived. In the first half of 1500 there are hints that he resorted to skulduggery. Not only were there rumours that Henry was considering marrying Arthur to a French bride, but there was also talk that Arthur had already cast the Infanta aside in favour of another continental princess: Margaret of Austria, the widow of Katherine's own brother.

Ferdinand and Isabella's son had tragically died in 1497, soon after his marriage to Margaret. Since then, relations between Spain and the King of the Romans had all but collapsed. The idea that England and Burgundy, whom Spain had done so much to reconcile, were now teaming up against up against them was humiliating to Ferdinand and Isabella.

Clearly, there was not an iota of truth in these rumours. How they surfaced remains a mystery. Could they have been circulated by Margaret's father, Maximillian, with the sole purpose of disconcerting the Spanish? Or had the English proactively encouraged such talk in order to spur the Spanish into action? Katherine's parents had been genuinely distracted by affairs closer to home. Moorish rebellion had broken out in Grenada and Ferdinand was forced to mobilise troops to restore order. An ambitious undertaking that occupied much of the early months of the year. But there were likely more personal considerations that motivated the Spanish Queen's retention of her daughter.

In the last three years, Ferdinand and Isabella had lost their eldest daughter, Isabella, and their son, Juan. The heiress to their joint-Kingdom was now their married and absent daughter Juna, cruelly nicknamed 'Juana la Loca' due to concerns about her mental health. Despite their promising progress of the 1480s and 90s, the turn of the century was witnessing the collapse of their dynasty and tarnishing them with tragedy. Is it any wonder that they wanted to hold on to their youngest child for just a little bit longer?

Eventually, a date was tentatively agreed for the summer. With a cautious optimism, Henry authorised the Earls of Suffolk and Essex, along with Lord Harrington, Lord William Courtney, Sir John Peche and William De La Pencre to:

> 'hold royal jousts and tournaments, and to perform other feats of arms at Westminster, in honour of the marriage between the Prince of Wales and the Princess Katherine of Spain, which is expected to take place towards the end of August next. Challenge all gentlemen, of whatever nation they may be, and whatever weapon they may use, to answer them in the lists on the fifth day after the solemnization of the said glorious marriage'[7]

Now it was time for the real planning to begin. Discussions opened around who Katherine should bring with her. Henry VII, no doubt nervous about the possibility of funding a myriad of foreign dignitaries *ad infinitum*, stressed that the princess would be well served by English officers and servants. There was no need for her to come mob-handed.

But Spanish pride was not so easily satisfied. Katherine's almoner responded, somewhat provocatively, by enclosing a list that showed just how large the princess's entourage was to be. The English saw no need whatsoever for Katherine to bring many senior male officers. English men could perform those roles proficiently. And while they conceded that Katherine would of course bring Spanish ladies with her, they insisted that each must be from good families and beautiful. Or at least, "not ugly."[8] The marriage was, after all, about keeping up appearances.

Such niggles in negotiations were expected. None of these issues were ever likely to become major sticking points. But unfortunately for the ever-anxious Arthur, in the spring of 1500, Katherine's parents experienced a total collapse of confidence in the alliance with England. They finally realised that their ambassador had been lying to them.

On 25 May, the Spanish monarchs ordered their trusted secretary, Ferdinand Alvarez to send them "all documents and papers in his keeping which relate to the treaty of marriage between Princess Katherine and Prince Arthur concluded at Medina del Campo."[9] De Puebla had constantly assured them that he had secured a better deal than the one they had signed in 1489. Now it was time to cross-reference both treaties and discover whether their once-trusted ambassador was as good as his word.

They were horrified with what they discovered. Upon examining the latest treaty in light of the first, they found that 'the second treaty does only not contain any improvement, but, in the contrary, much less favourable to them than the first'. They took issue with almost every clause De Puebla had negotiated. Not enough of Katherine's marriage portion could be offset against her ornaments and jewels. The final payment of it was now due after solemnisation rather than the likely later consummation. No fixed sum had been agreed for the Princess's jointure nor had a date been fixed for a marriage ceremony after Katherine's arrival. After years of suspicion, the Spanish monarch's trust in their ambassador had finally evaporated. The treaty must be renegotiated, and it was finally time they received a true account of life in England. Yet another Spanish ambassador must be sent to English shores.

Ferdinand and Isabella dispatched Gutierre Gomez de Fuensalida, Knight Commander of Haro to finally establish the truth. In Fuensalida, who arrived in England in June, the Spanish had finally found an envoy who was more interested in reporting the truth than trying to outwit his ambassadorial rivals. His visit was incredibly significant. As we shall explore later, it is also from his words that we gain our most insightful hint about the state of Arthur's health during his adolescence. But for now, what matters is that the ambassador managed to get negotiations back on track and restore his masters' confidence in the commitments of the English. Nevertheless, Ferdinand and Isabella insisted on further delay. Katherine could not possibly set sail until Arthur achieved his fourteenth birthday in the autumn.

Earlier in the year, Henry VII had been pleading with the Spanish to dispatch Katherine straight away. He may even have resorted to trickery to try and force their hand. Yet, remarkably, he not only consented to this new delay but suggested a further one. If Katherine could not come in the summer, he said, she should delay her voyage until next Spring. She should not travel in the autumn "on account of the great perils by the sea."[10] It was a remarkable turnaround. We shall later explore what may have triggered Henry's change of heart. Despite this further delay, the direction of travel was finally clear. Arthur, at his in-law's insistence, repeated the proxy marriage ceremony once he turned 14 and was legally old enough to commit. Negotiations about exactly who, and how many Katherine should bring with her from Spain continued. But as 1500 drew to a close, there was finally a sense that Katherine's coming was imminent, though she would not finally set sail until the next autumn. After endless negotiations that had lasted for most of his life, Arthur was finally destined to behold his bride. Little did either of them know how much stormy weather, both literally and figuratively, lay on the horizon.

Chapter 13

The Condition of Wedlock

On a cold, crisp November afternoon, Arthur sat perched on his horse outside the village of Dogmersfield. No doubt brimming with adolescent anxiety, he awaited a crucial order from his father. When he received word, he was to ride into the village, enter the manor house and come face to face with the woman he had been destined to marry since before his third birthday. Katherine of Aragon had landed in England about a week before. Senior members of the nobility had been stationed along the path from Southampton to London to ensure that she could be received in style at each stage of her journey. There was just one problem. She had sailed to the wrong port.

The Infanta's journey had been treacherous. 'Thympacient wiendes of that coostis' had not seen fit to grant her smooth passage. Her first attempt to leave Spanish waters was aborted after the storms proved too strong. Eventually, Henry dispatched a skilled English captain to escort her. But instead of arriving in Southampton, as had long been planned, she docked at Plymouth on 2 October, 'fer in the contreth of the West'[1] She was over 150 miles from where she was supposed to be and from where her grand reception awaited.

The people of Plymouth had rarely played host to a member of the high nobility. Let alone a foreign princess. Now, without warning, they were responsible for giving their future Queen her first welcome to England. As soon as they realised what had happened, 'with goodlie maner and haste' they prepared the most extravagant gifts they could muster and set her on her journey to the 'aunciant Citie of London' The king had to dispatch a carrier to transport the princess's belongings from Plymouth to her new home of Ludlow at a cost of 10 shillings.[2]

Perhaps the surprise and spontaneous jubilation of the Plymouth gentry allowed their sentiments to seem all the more authentic. Katherine's confessor later wrote to Queen Isabella that the Princess 'could not have been received with greater rejoicings, if she had been the Saviour of the world'[3] Given Katherine's distance from London, there was no time to waste. A new plan to ensure she was received in proper estate was hastily thrown together. The King's steward set off immediately to intercept her, so that she and her party could be sufficiently provided for. The Earl of Surrey led a group of the nobility to greet her in style. Finally, the Duchess of Norfolk, along with 'a goodly companye with her of countesses, baronesses and meny other honourable gentylwomen' undertook a mad dash across the country to ensure women of sufficient rank were on hand to accompany the Infanta.

By this time, the king was bursting with anticipation. The marriage of his son to a foreign Princess had been the corner stone of his foreign policy. His great dream was finally coming into view. He could almost smell his victory. The question of how long Henry must wait before setting eyes on his daughter-in-law would prove an issue of great dispute between the English and Spanish. On 4 November, the king left Richmond with a company of Dukes, Earls and Barons and set course for Easthampstead in Berkshire. At the same time, Arthur set off from the Marches to rendezvous with his father. Here, amid the beams of winter sun, 'the true and loving Englisshe people pleasauntly perceive the pure and proper Prince Arthure, the heire of their lefull londes and successour by grace grantid of God, full solemnly to salute his sage father before their owne presens, the which was great gladnes to all trusty hertes '

King and prince, finally together, hastily arranged a meeting with the Spanish prothonotary, a legal officer that had accompanied the princess to England. Henry made his intentions clear. He required an immediate audience with Katherine. The king and his son had been waiting for the Infanta for over thirteen years. It was finally time for the Spanish to deliver.

The prothonotary refused to comply. He cited an 'injunction and commaundmnet of their soveraigne Lord of their lond that they should in noo maner of wise permytt ne sugger their ladie and Princess of Espayne, whom they had to guyde and in gouvernans, to have eny meting, ne use eny maner of communycacion neither company, unto theincepcion of the very daie of the solempnisacion of the marriage'.

This breakdown in communication resulted in part from cross-cultural confusion. But the Spanish officer may also have been over playing his orders. Technically speaking, Arthur and Katherine were already married. There was no canonical need for a further wedding ceremony at all. Consummation was all that was required to seal the deal and it is difficult to see how any meeting between Katherine and Arthur could be deemed improper.

But Ferdinand and Isabella had been adamant that consummation must not take place before a public ceremony. Their orders to their Spanish servants were probably aimed at ensuring there could be no suggestion of cohabitation between the prince and princess prior to such an event. The actions of Richard III in 1483 had given the English a bad reputation on the world stage. Ferdinand and Isabella knew that a once-valid marriage could be easily dispensed with. The Spanish too, were not averse to such machinations when politics required. The Infanta's marriage must be valid beyond doubt in order to ensure her protection for the future. It may have seemed like paranoia at the time. But Katherine's later treatment by Henry VIII shows that the Spanish caution was justified.

In reality, Henry VII was just as keen as them to mark the marriage of their children in style. This was a moment of triumph for the Tudors and a public wedding ceremony was exactly what the King had in mind. But even he was not prepared to dispatch his son down the aisle without even being allowed to see the bride's face. Appearance was a huge part of projecting a public image. And the King needed advance warning if Katherine's appearance needed careful management.

Henry quickly summoned his councillors together for an emergency summit on how to proceed. Unsurprisingly, each councillor believed that the king was in the right. He, Henry, was master within his empire and realm. Katherine and her servants were now so far into it, there could be no question that they were the king's to command. It was time for Henry to take his orders directly to the princess. The disruptions of recent days had no doubt been nerve-wracking to an already anxious Arthur. The King, no doubt mindful of the impact on his son, instructed the prince to await further instruction, while Henry proceeded to Katherine's lodgings at nearby Dogmersfield to prepare the way for his boy. He was greeted, perhaps reluctantly, by the senior Spanish dignitaries, the archbishop of Santiago, and the Count de Cabra.

Once again, the Spanish entourage resisted admitting the King to his daughter-in-law's presence. Katherine was at rest and could not possibly be disturbed. But this time, there was to be no more debate about it. The king had demanded an audience. His demands must be honoured. He would see Katherine, he insisted, even if she were in bed. That is why he had come, and he would not leave until he had got what he wanted. Eventually, the Spanish relented. In truth they had no choice. Katherine granted Henry 'an honourable metyng in her third chambre, where were perused the mooste goodly words and uttred of the langueges of bothe parties to as great joye and gladnes as in eny perones might ever covenably have ben had.' Henry would later tell the queen that the meeting with Katherine had gone well and that he 'lkyd hir person and behavour.'

Arthur's father had paved the way for his son. Now, it was the moment of truth for the boy himself. The prince was escorted by his father into Katherine's chamber. He had probably been thinking and perhaps dreaming about this moment since he was a small child. Now, under the flicker of candlelight, he finally came face to face with his bride. Arthur would later write to Katherine's parents that he had never felt such joy in his life as when he beheld the sweet face of his bride. There was no woman in the world, he claimed, that was more agreeable to him.[4] As with all Arthur's letters to Spain, the primary objective of this communiqué was diplomatic. It was sent to convey sentiments of friendship to Spain, not to serve as a record of his true feelings.

Yet, there is every reason to think that Arthur was overwhelmed by joy. Or at least relief. Katherine of Aragon was probably never a great beauty. But her early portraits show her to be handsome, presentable and, to a teenage boy, eminently desirable. The Princess was a wife who could help secure Arthur's throne and provide heirs with unquestionable Royal blood. Perhaps they could even be happy together.

What Katherine made of Arthur; we simply don't know. As we shall see later, there is evidence to suggest that the prince may have already been in some degree of physical decline by the time of his marriage. Did Katherine notice? Did she, remembering the tragic death of her brother Juan, begin to fear that history might repeat itself? If so, these were worries for another day. The Princess still had several mountains to climb before she faced the trials of the marriage bed.

The most immediate challenge for the young couple was how to communicate. They had both written beautiful Latin letters to each other, but their spoken Latin, probably under the siege of teenage tension, was failing to cut the mustard. The Archbishop of Santiago helped translate between the couple. Henry, anticipating this problem, had also brought a talented linguist, Lady Guildford, to help the couple converse. The young couple, the king and Katherine's household all ate together before Arthur and Katherine were finally granted their first private conversation. It would have been more awkward than it was passionate, but mercifully it would not last for long. Minstrels were summoned and dancing began. It was still too soon, however, for the young couple to dance together. Instead, Arthur danced with Lady Guildford, 'right plesand and honouralby.' It had been a tense, awkward and emotionally exhausting day. Both prince and princess must have been relieved when it was over.

A detailed herald's account, written by an eyewitness to much of the festivities, chronicles Katherine's arrival into London and the spectacle of her wedding. The herald, however, is largely silent about Arthur's movements in between his meeting with the Princess and the day of the nuptials. Then, like now, the focus of a wedding was the bride. Even when the groom was the Prince of Wales. It is Katherine's movements that are chronicled in detail.

After her introduction to her husband and father-in-law, Katherine and her household began their journey toward Lambeth, where rich lodgings had been carefully crafted for her. On her way, she passed through Kingston upon Thames. The village – as it then was – was the place that the ancient Saxon Kings had been crowned and was loaded with historical significance. At Kingston, Katherine was greeted in some style by the 'richly beseyn' Duke of Buckingham and his brother Lord Henry Stafford. They were surrounded by 300 yeoman, dressed in the black and red livery of the Stafford family. This marked the first real planned spectacle since Katherine's arrival.

After Arthur and his brother Henry, Edward Stafford, Duke of Buckingham, was the premier nobleman of England. His mother, Catharine Woodville had been Arthur's great aunt making the duke and his brother two of the prince's closest relatives. They also descended from Edward III and had a dubious history when it came to loyalty to the crown. Edward IV had kept the Staffords at arm's length. Richard III had drawn them to the centre of his regime with devastating consequences. The Tudors had kept both boys cautiously close. By 1485, they were fatherless, and the new Henry VII had placed them in the care of his own mother, Margaret Beaufort. The vast Stafford fortune had, in part, been used to fund Arthur's household as a child. Sean Cunningham has speculated that, the fact the duke refused to take some of Arthur's servants into his household after the Prince's death, may suggest a lingering resentment.[5]

But whatever their intrinsic distrust of the Staffords, men of their stature could not easily be side-lines. The younger brother Henry was already on track to be created Earl of Wiltshire and their prominence at Arthur's wedding suggests that they were being well and truly brought in from the cold. Katherine, of course, would have known none of this. She lodged with them overnight at Kingston, but we have no knowledge of what interaction – if any – she had with them. The next morning, the Staffords escorted Katherine to Lambeth where she seems to have been afforded a chance to rest. She would certainly need it. For the next day would begin a series of pageants and spectacles not witnessed since the queen's coronation.

On 12 November, Katherine gathered her Spanish retinue and rode to St George's Field, about a mile and-a-half away from her lodgings at Lambeth. Here they were greeted by "a right seemly company" of senior nobleman and churchmen. Many of the great men of the realm, including some to whom Katherine was already familiar, such as the Duke of Buckingham and the Earl of Surrey had assembled to meet her along with the great men of the Church. Katherine had met her first husband just days before. Now, for the first time, she set eyes on her second. The 10-year-old Prince Henry, Duke of York had joined Katherine's escort. This would have been a significant moment for both of them; even now they knew their destinies were to be inter-woven. But neither could have imagined how big a part they would play in each other's futures. He was still, after all, just a little boy. With her retinue from Spain, and her mighty English escort, Katherine now stood at the head of an army of splendour. They led the princess over London Bridge and into the city, where four spectacular pageants had been lavishly prepared to receive her. A Tudor pageant consisted of a lavish display that served as a stage for actors dressed as characters from history, theology, and mythology to perform. Over the rest of the day, Katherine was to see both English craftsmanship and Tudor propaganda at their finest. Her arrival into the already ancient city of London was met with six spectacular pageants.

As she crossed London Bridge, she was greeted by a 'tabernacle' consisting of two stages designed like flowers beneath a picture of the Trinity. When she reached Gracechurch Street, she beheld a mighty castle of three to four feet rising out of the water. At Cornhill a great moon-like sphere surrounded by astrological symbols rested atop three great pillars. A wheel like the sun shone at Cheapside, surrounded by candles and with an image of Arthur at its centre. Eventually, she came face to face with the 'Temple of God' at the Standard in the Cheap. It consisted of four great pillars, and on each stood a man, 'with marvelous hoods, and sum with hats, and their robys set full of peryls, and we semblaunt unto the prophets.'

Each of these pageants was loaded with heraldic and dynastic imagery. There were red and white roses, Beaufort portcullises, Welsh red dragons, and the greyhounds from Henry VII's personal coat of arms. At this stage, Katherine probably knew little about the significance of these symbols. A lack of any attempt to teach the princess English suggests that future preparation for life in England was not a great priority for her parents. But they would come to be at the centre of her destiny and identity. Katherine was to become far more closely associated with the imagery of Tudor rule than fate would ever allow Arthur to be.

At each pageant, the princess was greeted by figures from fantasy, astrology, and history. Each had words of wisdom to impart. At London Bridge, her namesake, St Katherine, reminded her not to forget God, her first husband as she prepared to embrace Arthur, her second. Men outside the castle called "Policy", "Virtue" and "Nobility" informed her of the personal qualities she would need to guide her. Her ancestor, King Alfonso, appeared to remind her of her destiny. Even God himself found time for a few words. The almighty impressed upon Katherine the importance of loving and defending mother church: something that Katherine would hold true to until her dying day.

To many onlookers, these series of pageants must have seemed like a collection of disjointed, though magnificent, displays. But to those educated in the finer points of astrology, it would have been clear that the princess was being guided through a celestial journey that appraised her of her heritage and pointed to her destiny. At the first pageant, the tabernacle at London Bridge, Katherine is addressed by St Ursula. Given the content of her speech, informed spectators would have understood this as a coded reference to Ursa Minor, the constellation which was believed to reside next to the star 'Arcturus'. Throughout the pageants both the prince and princess would be alluded to through this celestial code.[6] The inference is unmissable: the union of Katherine and Arthur was, quite literally, written in the stars.

What Katherine made of any of this is a mystery. At this stage, she still spoke little English and while the pageants boasted the odd Latin inscription, these would hardly have been enough to grasp the meaning of each presentation. Nevertheless, the sheer scale of the spectacle must have conveyed an unambiguous message. This was where Katherine was meant to be. England was her destiny. In years to come, when memories of these pageants had faded, both Arthur's father and his brother would force Katherine to endure isolation and hardship. Yet she never lost her sense of loyalty to her adopted country. A loyalty that may even have started to grow amid the pageantry of London.

As so often in Tudor pageantry, the creators had not shielded away from comparing the Royal family to figures of awe and wonder. Henry VII had been alluded to as God the father, and Arthur, God the son. So, it is no great surprise that when Katherine was being addressed by God himself, this was the moment that people first became aware of the King's presence. During this pageant the King had 'conveyed himself sumwhat prevy and secretly and stode in a merchauntes chambre.' Arthur and the many of the great men of the realm were with him. In a nearby chamber, the Queen assembled the great ladies. As the pageant drew to a close, many of Arthur's servants began to line the streets. It would still be another day before the prince and princess would appear together in public but for the first time, Katherine may have begun to sense he was close.

Then, in a sight that was 'the moost goodly wise that ever was seen in Englond' the servants of the great men of the realm, along with the 'strangers' from Spain, rode over the bridge and into the city. They saluted the princess and, along with the senior officers of the city and proceeded to the furthest end of the Cheap and the entrance of St Paul's Cathedral. By this stage Katherine must have been exhausted. But she still had another pageant to endure. At its centre was a great pier of stairs, one each for the seven virtues: faith, hope, charity, justice, temperance, prudence, and fortitude of strength. At the top of the stairs were two thrones – one of the prince and one for the Princess - each with a sceptre and crown of gold. The message was clear: Katherine's marriage to Arthur would rest upon virtue.

*

On Sunday 14 November, the day of the wedding, St Paul's Cathedral was decked out with 'the moost excellent ornementes apperteynynyng unto the worship of God and honour of this joyefull maryage and union of the moost reverent prince and princes.' Jewels, relics, and plates of 'wonderful riches and precyousnes' filled the church from the altar to the choir.

Today, we are used to Royal weddings being a grand affair. But this was typically not the case in Arthur's time. His parents had enjoyed a low-key wedding and Katherine's later marriage to Henry VIII was no great event. Arthur's nuptials, however, were to be the greatest Royal wedding that Tudor England would ever witness. It was vital that this moment of triumph was visible. At Arthur's baptism, the font had been placed on steps so that all could witness his welcome into the Christian faith. Now, years later, at the heart of St Paul's, a round stage 'covered in red say' was raised where the Prince and Princess might 'conveniently stond' as the sacrament of marriage was administered. Henry VII had taken the crown in battle, defended it twice and seen off two pretenders. He had now secured a great international marriage for his son. This was his greatest moment of triumph. Everyone was going to witness it.

The conventions of Royalty had forced the king and queen to be absent from Arthur's christening, fifteen years previously. Strictly speaking, the same rules should have applied to Arthur's wedding. The bride and groom were meant to be the stars of the show. They should not be overshadowed or outranked by the sovereign. But for Henry and Elizabeth, this was a day they simply couldn't miss. A closet was prepared above the vault, where the Royal couple could watch the ceremony through a window, beaming with parental pride and dynastic delight.

Between 9 and 10 that morning, Arthur departed his lodgings at the King's wardrobe, surrounded by attendants. He headed for the south door of the cathedral, entered the church, and made his devotions. He was then led to a secret chamber within the Bishop of London's palace where 'he chaungid his vesture and induyd himself the ryall and comfortable apparel of weddyng spousage.'

Little attention is given to what Arthur was wearing. All we know is that he donned a garment of white satin. Once again, it was clear that he was merely a supporting character. The day belonged to the bride. Katherine's arrival certainly didn't disappoint. Ahead of her entry, processed the Spanish nobility and "a right goodly multitude of estatis the lordes and gentilmen in their araye and ordre" walking two by two and arm in arm. In a moment of irony, Katherine was accompanied into the church by her future husband, Henry, Duke of York. Despite being just a boy of 10, he was already showing his confidence in public and his love of performing. Princess Cecily, Arthur's aunt, bore her train, followed by Katherine's ladies and gentlewomen.

Even the court herald, usually so preoccupied with order and precedence, had to concede that Katherine looked beautiful. She too was dressed in white satin, with a coif on her head of white silk and a border of gold, pearl and precious stone. An elegant veil fell from the coif to her middle, covering 'great parte of hir visage' Katherine was every inch a fairy tale princess. Yet despite the romantic flavour of the decor and ceremony, no one would be allowed to forget that this marriage was a business deal. Before the ceremony could proceed any further, the king's councillors assembled to publicly proclaim that this union was the will of the King of England and the King of Spain. They then publicly stated the amount that was due to Henry for the marriage portion, and they surrendered to Katherine letters patent, that confirmed her jointure.

Frustratingly, the herald's account says little about the ceremony itself. Simply that the Archbishop of Canterbury did 'conjoyne their noble persons toguyder as the custom and sacrament in this bhealve doeth require and aske.' Then, in a moment of publicity worthy of the House of Windsor, Arthur, with Katherine on his right side, exited the church first from the south, and then from the north. The multitudes that had gathered could finally witness the triumph of the Tudors and 'behold their persones'. The people were overcome with the joy of the occasion. They shouted 'King Henry' and cried 'Prince Arthur.' Never must the Tudor succession have felt more secure.

For the young couple, the day was far from over. After receiving the applause of their people, the Princess and Princess returned to the altar for the mass of the Trinity. They then exited the church to the west door, encountering the seventh great pageant of the occasion: a green mountain covered in trees and herbs and flowing with wine. Eventually, they passed into the palace of the Bishop of London. A chamber had been fabulously decorated with 'every annowrement that might belonge to so noble estate'. The great men and women of England and Spain began a great feast of venison, fish, and plenty of wine. At about four or five o'clock in the afternoon, the Earl of Oxford, as great chamberlain sent for the Duchess of Norfolk, the highest-ranking lady in England outside the immediate Royal family. She, together with the Spanish Countess of Cambria, were dispatched to prepare the marital bed that the prince and princess would take to after 'the condicion of wedlock.'

After two or three hours, the Earl of Oxford, inspected the chamber, tested both sides of the bed and certified that it was ready for the couple. Katherine was taken to the chamber and ceremoniously laid out on the bed while Arthur was left to dance with 'pleasure, myrthe, and solas'. Eventually, the Prince was brought to join his wife. The bed was blessed by the bishops and wine and spices were prepared for the young couple's refreshment. Finally, man and wife were left alone. To the herald that wrote the account on which this chapter is based, there is little doubt what happened next. These 'worthy persones' concluded their marriage by the act of consummation. It was certainly what people expected them to do. However, years later, Katherine was to strenuously deny that sexual relations had ever taken place between her and Arthur. And, as we shall see, there is every reason to believe that she was telling the truth.

Chapter 14

Portrait of a Prince

The image of Henry VIII is the most recognised of any King of England. Immortalised by Hans Holbein the younger and the flourishing portraiture of the sixteenth century, Henry's projected stature, strength and regal bearing have become almost synonymous with England's history. Had his elder brother lived to become king, no doubt a cult of portraiture would have flourished around Arthur. It may have been his face, and not Henry's, that became a symbol of English kingship that was instantly recognised by people around the world.

Inevitably, Arthur's premature death makes his face significantly harder to find. Mercifully, however, Arthur's image survives. Five representations of the prince which are either contemporary to his life or were produced in the decades that followed it help us begin our quest to piece together the image of the first Tudor prince. Two of these five tell us little of what Arthur actually looked like but do provide hints around how his status was perceived. The first is an image from a book of ordinances located on a manuscript in Christ Church Oxford. Here, Arthur, his parents and his siblings kneel before the scene of the meeting of Joachim and Anne, the parents of the virgin Mary. The second, is another scene of Arthur's family kneeling, this time against the backdrop of St George, England's patron saint, slaying a dragon. The inclusion of Princess Katherine, not born until 1503, in both works suggests they were not completed until after Arthur's death, but they may have commenced in his lifetime. In both images, Arthur kneels behind his father. His younger brothers, Henry, and Edmund, kneel behind him. Opposite the men is the queen, with her four daughters – Margaret, Mary, Elizabeth, and Katherine, kneeling behind her. The fact that the three children who had died as infants are depicted as adults – a common practice in such portrayals – shows that the images cannot be an attempt at portraiture. Various inaccuracies in Royal dress may also suggest that they were not produced under commission from the court.

Perhaps more promising, is an image of Arthur within a magnificent stained-glass window at the priory Church at Great Malvern, Worcestershire. In the image, which we can date as between 1499 and April 1502, Arthur is every inch the pious prince of chivalry. He wears his rich armour as Prince of Wales, including his coronet, with long blonde hair flowing beneath it. He kneels at prayer within a canopy, a tented structure that the high nobility regularly used for privacy within churches. Depictions in stained-glass are rarely an attempt at portraiture. We can take no confidence that the artists were even trying to represent Arthur accurately, or even that they had ever laid eyes on him. In fact, it's possible to identify similar facial features across the works of the company that created the display at Great Malvern, which suggests such designs were used widely.

Nevertheless, there are similarities between Arthur's depiction here, when he was probably a teenager, with another painting of him at a similar age. Great Malvern was not far from Arthur's base on the Welsh Marches. It's quite possible that people viewing this masterpiece may have previously clapped eyes on him or at least seen an accurate likeness. Furthermore, the window was almost certainly commissioned by Sir Reginald Bray, a councillor of Arthur's father who, along with two other knights, appeared in the original. Bray would certainly have known what Arthur looked like and may have wanted the stained-glass window to capture him properly.

Until recent decades, there was no definitive likeness of Arthur that scholars could be confident in. But in 1993, an art dealer called Philip Mould, researcher Piers Davies and picture restorer Simon Gillespie, managed to accurately identify a portrait of Arthur as dating to the early Tudor period. It had once belonged in the collection of the Earls of Granard and is now in the collection at Hever Castle. It is probably the same portrait that was listed in the Royal Collection in the time of Charles I.

In this portrait, Arthur is on the brink of adolescence and is dressed in expensive robes, a velvet cap and boasts long sleeves of cloth of gold. He is holding a white carnation which is a symbol of betrothal. The portrait was almost certainly based on an original created for Katherine of Aragon and her parents. It probably dates from 1497, when the young couple were formally betrothed and when Arthur would have been on the verge of his eleventh birthday. He wears a spectacular jewel around his neck in a cross-like shape. This was probably designed to allude to the crucifixion, becoming a subtle means of conveying his piety to the 'Catholic Kings' who would soon be his in-laws.

One further image, which sits today in the Royal Collection, illuminates what Arthur may have looked like around the time of his actual marriage in 1501. It is clearly in the same style as the Hever portrait and was probably based on an original that was designed to show his progression and be dispatched back to Spain with the dignitaries that returned after Katherine of Aragon was settled. Some have reasonably questioned the identification as the sitter is wearing dress that was popular in the decades after Arthur's death. A sophisticated red cap featuring a gold broach, a cloth of gold shirt beneath glorious red robes, covered by a magnificent chain of white and red roses. Arthur would never have dressed like this. Could it be that the real sitter was his younger brother Henry VIII?

But the best evidence strongly suggests that this is an image of a teenage Arthur. The portrait is almost certainly the same as the one recorded in Henry VIII's inventory as, 'Prince Arthure wering like a rede cappe with a broche upon it and a collor of red and white roses.' It was also listed in the inventory next to a portrait of a young Henry VIII. As Frederick Hepburn correctly argues, this, 'indicates that the compilers of the inventories recognized two different sitters in these paintings.' It is most likely that this painting was based on a contemporary portrait of a teenager Arthur and that his dress had been modified in a later version. If so, this gives us two reliable likenesses of the prince at the ages of about 11 and about 15. We can start to build a picture of what the adolescent Arthur may really have looked like. In both portraits, Arthur has pleasantly pale skin. His hair is brunette with a hint of red. His eyes are hooded, bagged and slightly weary. He has inherited the long, sloping nose of his father and his grandmother, Margaret Beaufort. But that doesn't mean that Arthur's features were entirely Lancastrian. While he is clearly of slim build, he already shows signs of the double chin common among the house of York. Depending on his future lifestyle, he could well have one day grown as fat as his brother Henry VIII. And he certainly bears a resemblance to his grandfather, Edward IV. The gaunt physique of the Beauforts would perhaps not be so easily maintained for Arthur.

In both portraits, Arthur's face sports a certain seriousness. This will partly be due to the nature of the medium and the need to position the prince appropriately to his audience. But in as much as eyes can ever serve as windows to the soul, Arthur's hint at a boy not yet entirely at ease with himself. Yet, he is clearly handsome and well suited to the expensive attire that he adorned. If these portraits were designed to impress his young bride and his indomitable in-laws, it is surely likely that they achieved their purpose.[1]

Through robust and relatively recent research, we gain a real sense of what Arthur may have looked like. Sadly, no amount of research can reveal much about his personality, character, or even his interests. The accounts of his father, Henry VII may provide a scattering of hints. The King's early gift of an expensive bow may suggest that Arthur was athletic in his childhood and eager to pursue his interests. Henry was clearly impressed by Arthur's minstrels and trumpeters, whom he regularly rewarded. It's possible that father and son shared a passion for music. While there are genuinely signs that he was intellectually gifted, evidence that he played cards for money and enjoyed moments of boisterousness with his friends show that he had a lighter, more jovial side. Though with the heavy responsibilities that he knew rested on his shoulders from a young age, it's difficult to imagine that he was ever carefree.

What we do know, is that Arthur's premature death was devastating to the people that served him. As we shall see, emotions ran very high at his funeral and the herald who wrote the account clearly believed they were genuine. In part, that will be because those closest to Arthur were mourning their lost futures. Had he lived to become King, they would have expected to rise further still. But there are indications that it went much deeper than that. Arthur's great friend, Gruffydd ap Rhys, even chose to be buried with the prince.

We'll never know what aspects of Arthur's character inspired such loyalty. Was he already showing signs of inspirational leadership? After all, his father found it hard to instil much affection among his followers, but Arthur was from a line of charismatic Yorkists for whom popularity came much more easily. Was he good company? Did he have a wicked sense of humour? Or was it clear signs of vulnerability that caused people to grow protective and attached to him? Perhaps he was simply kind and measured at times when he could have elected to be haughty.

It is impossible for the biographer not to form an impression of their subject. But when that subject lived 500 years ago, and source material is sparse, that impression is inevitably subjective. The thoughts and reflections I have formed of the first Tudor Prince, should be understood in light of this crucial disclaimer. Yet, the further I have delved into each aspect of Arthur's life and every dimension of his character, one word has repeatedly leapt out to me: determination. For a number of reasons, the challenges that Arthur faced over his short life may not have come easily to him. But he constantly demonstrated resilience in the face of adversity.

This was true at the moment of Arthur's birth. He had arrived early and, while he does not seem to have been significantly ill, he must have fought hard to be the thriving, well-developed boy that the Spanish ambassadors inspected just eighteen months later. Aged just 3 years old, he faced a gruelling two-day event which saw him dubbed a knight and created Prince of Wales. While moments of fatigue or bad behaviour may have been redacted from the official accounts, the fact his father was prepared to present him to the entire nobility speaks to the scale of his progress during his infancy.

During his tenure on the Welsh Marches, Arthur undertook several tours and great occasions. He seems to have won the hearts of his people, despite not being a natural performer. When his bride Katherine finally came to England, it seems to have been Arthur himself that pushed for her to join him at Ludlow, perhaps hoping that her presence would increase his personal authority.

Finally, his determination can perhaps best be seen by his insistence of distributing alms on Maundy Thursday 1502, just days before he died. Some have taken this as evidence that his final illness must have been sudden. But as we are about to discover, there is significant reason to believe that Arthur, at least in his later years, was no longer the thriving physical specimen that had once delighted both Spanish and Italian ambassadors. At adolescence, his physical health and development seem to have taken a turn for the worse. If, as this section has conjected, he was a boy of great determination, then he would have needed every ounce of that resilience to see him through the responsibilities that sat on his shoulders as he knocked on the door of manhood.

The drama of Arthur's premature birth and the tragedy of his own untimely death has led many to believe that he was plagued by poor heath throughout his short life. It's possible that the early decision to settle Arthur at Farnham after his birth, rather than take him to a palace nearer London resulted from a desire not to move him too far from his birthplace at Winchester. Whatever fears existed soon seemed to subside. There is no evidence to suggest that Arthur was a sickly infant, And much to imply that he wasn't.

Given his high rank and importance to England, there were naturally always doctors in Arthur's household. Eyebrows have been raised about a payment to a doctor in 1488 for 'medical attendance upon Prince Arthur'. But as we have seen, such payments were perfectly normal where children of the high nobility are concerned. By the age of 22 months, Prince Arthur was clearly thriving. This is when, at the early stage of negotiations to marry Arthur to Katherine of Aragon, Spanish ambassadors were invited to inspect the child naked.

Had there been any concerns about Arthur's health, or around his development, Arthur's parents would never have extended such an invitation. If Arthur's physique had represented any kind of embarrassment, the boy could easily have been dispatched to an outpost too far away for the Spaniards to visit. Instead, he was presented with pride. And the Spanish were clearly impressed with what they saw. They wrote to Ferdinand and Isabella that:

> 'He appeared to us so admirable that, whatever praise, commendation, or flattery anyone might be capable of speaking or writing would only be truth in this case. As he (the King) was aware of this, he wished that Sepulveda should take his figure, image, and appearance to Spain...'[2]

Arthur continued to make at least satisfactory progress into his childhood. By the time he was 3 he was deemed ready to present to the realm's elite when he was dubbed a knight and created Prince of Wales. The first three years of life were particularly perilous in the fifteenth century. The fact Arthur had survived them would have given his parents confidence that it was time to show him off.

During these gruelling ceremonies he handled all the physical aspects adequately, riding into Westminster Hall. After his creation, his physical training probably increased with the appointment of a marshal to his household. By the age of 6, the King felt confident enough in his son to dispatch him to the Welsh borders to form a regional government. When he was almost 11 years old, two Italian ambassadors commented on his impressive height. One even mistook him for being a year older than he actually was.

More recent historians have tended to assume that this trajectory of good health and flourishing development continued into Arthur's adolescence. David Starkey boldly asserts that Arthur's 'physical progress fully matched his educational achievement.'[3] Frederick Hepburn concludes that 'Arthur's physical health seems to have been perfectly normal up to the time when he succumbed to what was probably some form of plague.'[4]

But, for many years, English historians have been making one crucial mistake: they've been looking at the wrong sources. Or at least, the wrong version of the right ones. When understood correctly, correspondence around Arthur's marriage negotiations hint at a more fragile and vulnerable Prince as the boy entered his adolescence. Much of the source material for this period of Arthur's life can be found in the letters exchanged between Ferdinand and Isabella and the various ambassadors that they had posted to England. These sources fell into the hands of English historians during the Victorian era, when scholars travelled to Spain, translated the correspondence, created summaries, and compiled them into a calendar. It is these summaries, to be found in a publication called *The Calendar of State Papers: Spain*, which most British scholars draw from.

But summaries, for entirely innocent reasons, often omit crucial facts. In recent years, Professor Patrick Williams has explored and translated the letters themselves. And it is from these translations that we gain some insight into Arthur's limited development and failing health as he reached his teenage years.

In May 1500, Ferdinand and Isabella's confidence in their feckless ambassador De Puebla finally collapsed. Suspicious that he had not negotiated the marriage treaty to Spanish advantage, they decided to compare the agreement, clause by clause, with that which had been negotiated over ten years before. They soon found that despite his claim to have secured big improvement on the treaty negotiated in 1489, a number of the clauses were decidedly disadvantageous. One of the many clauses they queried gives us a valuable insight. In 1489, the two parties had agreed that Ferdinand and Isabella would only be compelled to hand over the final instalment of the dowry once the marriage was consummated. However, in the version that had emerged in the second agreement, this instalment was due once the marriage was solemnised. The Spanish monarchs quickly spotted that this was far from an improvement in terms. According to the English summary found in the Calendar of State Papers, they wrote to their ambassador that:

> 'The second treaty settles that the first instalment of the marriage portion should be paid ten days before, or after, the solemnization of

the marriage. This clause must be altered. It must be said, instead of ten days after the solemnization "ten days after the consummation of the marriage" for some time might still intervene between the solemnization and the consummation of the said marriage. At all events one half of the first instalment must be made payable only after the consummation of the marriage.'[5]

Even this is interesting. Teenagers may have married young. But this shows there was not always an expectation that sexual relations would immediately follow. However, William's translation of the Spanish original is more revealing still. In this more accurate version, Ferdinand and Isabella do not write passively that 'some time might still intervene between the solemnization and the consummation.' Instead, they more pointedly state that they 'now understood that some time might intervene between the solemnisation of the marriage and its consummation.'[6]

This strongly suggests that Ferdinand and Isabella had recently become aware of new information about their son-in-law. By this stage, Arthur was three months away from his fourteenth birthday and soon to be of age to consummate a marriage. Just three years before, the Italian ambassadors had commented on his height and implied that he looked old for his age. But something appears to have changed. On its own, this reference would not be enough to convince us that either Arthur's health was in question or that his development had been stunted. Though it's not obvious what, perhaps there could be some other way to understand the Spanish monarchs' words. However, Ferdinand and Isabella's statements coincide with evidence that Arthur's own father was growing increasingly concerned about his son's readiness for marriage.

In the early months of 1500, Henry VII had been growing increasingly impatient with constant Spanish delays. By this stage, Arthur and Katherine had conducted a proxy marriage. The King had even arranged for the death of two young men in order to appease Spanish concerns about the succession. But even now, the Spanish monarchs seemed in no hurry to dispatch their youngest daughter. Henry started to play hard ball. According to reports by Spanish ambassadors, he was beginning to question whether the Spanish marriage was the right path for Arthur. Could a French alliance prove more fruitful? In February, Don Pedro de Ayala first expressed his nervousness about Henry's renewed warmth to the French. He begged Ferdinand and Isabella to write soon, warning them that: 'the English are changeable. They observe that the King of France, who is not a relative of Henry, writes to him oftener, and gives more detailed accounts of all that occurs to him, good or bad.'[7] By April, he had heard that the English and French may even be in discussions about an alternative match for Arthur, writing that that King of France had 'offered them the sister of Monsieur d'Angoulême in marriage to the Prince of Wales, with a marriage portion of 200,000 scudos.'[8]

It's highly unlikely that Henry was truly considering such a radical change of direction. But it's quite possible that the English were encouraging the rumours to circulate. The Spanish had pontificated for long enough. It was finally time to force their hand. Ferdinand and Isabella quickly set about to reassure Henry that their plans were serious. Yet even now they dithered. It's possible that they were trying to keep their options open until the last possible moment. Global affairs were certainly moving quickly. But it's more likely that, following a host of family tragedies over recent years, they simply wanted to keep their youngest child close for as long as possible.

By the summer of 1500, Ferdinand and Isabella had insisted on yet another delay before dispatching their daughter. We don't know what reasons they offered but they were clear that Katherine would not set sail before the autumn. Remarkably, Henry relented. Not only did he quickly accept their reasoning. He actually offered a further delay. Katherine's departure, he insisted, should be put off until next spring. She must not risk traveling in the winter or the autumn, lest bad weather hinder her passage or cause her harm.

From Henry's perspective, this was a remarkable turnaround. Just months before he had seemingly threatened to walk away from the Spanish marriage altogether. Now, he had made his peace with further delay and initiated an even further one. Yes, he may have had valid concerns about the princess travelling in the rougher months of the autumn. But given that is precisely that time of year that Katherine would eventually travel during in 1501, this can hardly be the real reason for his newfound patience.

Could it be that, by the summer of 1500, Henry VII had finally accepted his son was not yet ready to live as a married man? While children from powerful families married young in Tudor times, as we have seen, some believed that teenage sex could be dangerous to the male. To the Royal houses of Europe, this fear had doubtlessly been reawakened by the death, in 1497 of Ferdinand and Isabella's own son, Juan. Some blamed his cause of death on exertions in the marriage bed following his marriage to Margaret of Austria. Juan had been 18 years old. If Henry VII's original timescale had been followed, Arthur would be wedded and bedded at just 14.

Henry only saw Arthur sporadically. There is some evidence to suggest the Royal family spent parts of the summer together. It could be that he had recently come face to face with his son for the first time in months. If so, was he struck by how his once tall and thriving son suddenly seemed weaker or frailer? Or, given the lapse in time since he had seen Arthur, was he expected to be presented with a towering young man, only to find a Prince that still looked young and boyish?

Alternatively, it could be that the prince had recently fallen ill. We know that there had been disease in London earlier in the year. Could it be that Arthur had been struck down quickly and taken longer than usual to recover?

Of course, it's possible that the reasons for Henry's insistence on a delay were about something else altogether. Perhaps he was simply sick of protesting and recognised that the princess would come when she comes. But yet another source suggests that, at about this time, the King was growing concerned for the health of his son. As we have already seen, in the early summer of 1500 there was yet another Spanish ambassador present in England. Having suffered a long-overdue collapse of confidence in De Puebla, the Spanish monarchs had dispatched Gomez de Fuensalida to provide real account of what was going on in England. At the end of June, he posted a wide-ranging letter. This passage, translated by Professor Williams is the clearest contemporary evidence that fears around Arthur's fragility existed in England:

> 'I have understood from a reliable source that the king has decided that the prince will know his wife sexually on the day of the wedding and then separate himself from her or two of three years because it is said that in some way the prince is frail, and the king told me that he wanted to have them [Arthur and Katherine] with him for the first three years so that the prince should mature in strength.'[9]

Ambassadors are not always reliable. But in this instance, de Fuensalida's words can be trusted. After Arthur and Katherine were eventually married, a letter from the king to the Spanish monarchs confirms that the Henry had deep concerns about Arthur and Katherine's living arrangements and the fragility of his son. He had agonised about sending the princess to Ludlow and the tenderness of his son had been his primary consideration.[10]

Arthur was no longer the strapping boy he had promised to be when he stood on the brink of adolescence. Something had either caused him to grow frail or stunted his development. Such were the strength of his concerns that Henry VII was prepared to consent to a delay in the princess coming to England. And even, when she did, he would consider taking measures to ensure that teenage sex was kept to a minimum. What then, can we say about these health concerns that plagued Arthur or affected his development? In truth, very little.

Years later, the nephew of Katherine of Aragon's doctor, would claim that his uncle had believed Arthur was suffering with *tisis* at the time of his marriage. As Giles Tremlett explains, this was 'a Spanish catch-all word covering everything from pulmonary tuberculosis to any wasting, feverish disease that produced ulceration of some bodily organ.'[11] This is the only near-contemporary account of Arthur's health in his teenage years that provides any degree of detail. But it is difficult to take it seriously. The evidence was given thirty years after the event, second-hand and in the most highly charged of political circumstances. It was designed to prove that Arthur and Katherine had never consummated their relationship and needs to be cautiously understood in that light. It also seems that, had Arthur's decline been quite so stark and dramatic, there would be more surviving evidence of it. English writers might have been circumspect in what they wrote but it's unlikely that contemporary Spaniards would have felt the need to hold back. That Arthur endured some kind of physical decline is highly likely. What it looked like is harder to fathom. But, with all the usual caveats in play, it might be possible to offer three credible points of speculation.

At the heart of Arthur's fragility may have been a slowness to enter puberty or to develop at the rate of most boys his age. Years later, many of the men who served him were quizzed as to his age when he married. Some confidently knew his age, having read his date of birth in the Royal book. But others remembered him as 14, a year younger than he actually was and the minimum age for a man to enter wedlock. One, albeit a highly biased witness, claimed to believe that Katherine of Aragon was years older than her husband. In reality, the princess was just nine months senior. But it's possible that she looked every inch the woman when next to her childlike husband.

It's also possible that Arthur's parents became aware of their son's declining development before he was even 12. As we have seen, at age 11, Arthur was brought to court to meet with two Italian ambassadors. Both were impressed with his height, intellect, and beauty. But just one year later, in July 1498, Ferdinand and Isabella dispatched a crucial Spanish embassy to give an account of life in England. This was the embassy that Henry and Elizabeth pulled out all the stops to impress. They staged a fake row over which of them retained custody of the Spanish letters and bent over backwards to express their love for Ferdinand and Isabella. Curiously, Arthur himself was nowhere to be seen. The official reason given was that Arthur was in Calais, though on what business isn't clear. Yet, despite it involving traversing the channel, the king and queen did have sufficient time to call their son back to meet with the emissaries of his future in-laws. Were he still such a prized visual asset, is it not likely that they would have done so? Is it too far-fetched to suppose that he was proactively dispatched to Calais in order to ensure that a meeting with the Spanish ambassadors was impossible?

While there is no doubt that Arthur undertook gruelling public routines in his role as heir to the throne, it's possible that he tired easily. His absence from accounts of the festivities surrounding his own wedding is notable. That's partly because Katherine, not he, was the star of the show. But short of presiding with his father over one gathering, and attending the ceremony itself, his role is a minor one.

He attends feasts and jousts, but, with the exception of one dance, he is rarely the centre of attention. Could it be that his loving father, concerned about his tendency for fatigue, had built time to rest into his programme? If so, this is a luxury that was scarcely afforded to Katherine. It's also possible that Arthur's immunity was lower than other teenagers his age. As we shall see, there is evidence of sickness at Ludlow around the time of his death. But there is nothing to suggest that any member of his household was significantly ill. It could be that the boy was susceptible to infection and took longer than expected to recover. It may have been an episode such as this that first alerted the King to his son's fragility in 1500.

Explicit descriptions of Arthur's health, or conversely his lost vigour, do not emerge until 30 years after his death. Historians tend to over-examine these sources, which all depend on testimony offered in highly contentious circumstances. But as this account has shown, there is significant evidence from accounts written in the prince's own lifetime that suggest a degree of decline as he entered his teenage years. As to what that looked like, we can only speculate. But it is a reality we must continue to grapple with as we explore the one question which is perennially associated with Arthur's story: what exactly took place between prince and princess on the night of their wedding.

Chapter 15

A Night in Spain

The questions of what passed between two young people on the night of their wedding and in the duration of their short marriage are intensely personal. In normal circumstances, even the biographer should be circumspect about such an intimate discussion. Yes, the consummation of Arthur's marriage was a matter of international significance to contemporaries: but ordinarily, it need not fascinate historians to the extent that it has.

Yet the question of whether or not Arthur ever consummated his marriage to Katherine of Aragon has become the one most commonly associated with him. And the blame for that lies squarely with his brother, Henry VIII, who made the question of Arthur's sex life a matter of constitutional, legal, and canonical significance 25 years after the prince's demise. Seven years after Arthur's death, his widow, Katherine married the newly crowned Henry VIII. For the first years of their marriage, they presided over a glorious court. They convinced ambassadors of their extravagant love for one another and seemed like an equally-yoked match at the dawn of a golden era.

Katherine would soon blossom into the perfect renaissance queen. She presided at tournaments. Led a household with high moral standards. She gave wise counsel to her husband the king and even ruled England while he made war on their mutual enemy of France. But she failed in the one domain that mattered most and over which she had no control: providing her husband with a son and heir. After 15 years or marriage, it was clear that she never would.

If Henry had ever been in love with Katherine, he was well and truly out of it by the mid-1520s. He needed a new wife to give him, and England, a Prince. Happily, in the form of one of Katherine's own ladies, Anne Boleyn, he had the perfect candidate in mind. Just one problem remained: what on earth was he going to do with Katherine? The King quickly alighted on a solution. Katherine, he decided, had never really been his wife at all. After all, she had been married to his brother Arthur. The book of Leviticus was clear: if a man married his brother's wife, they would remain childless. For Henry, this matched his circumstances perfectly. He and Katherine may have been blessed with a thriving daughter, Mary. But as far as he was concerned, 'sonless' was as bad as 'childless'.

Henry quickly set a legal train of events in motion to separate himself from his queen. But Katherine was able to halt proceedings in their tracks. Henry had violated scripture in no way, she maintained. Because she had never been Arthur's wife in the truest, biblical sense. The marriage had never been consummated. Or to put it simply, the couple had never had sex.

Both the governments of England and Spain set about trying to establish the facts. Many that had served Arthur and Katherine at their wedding and lived with them at Ludlow were still alive. Perhaps the truth of the matter would lie in their testimony. Yet, it quickly became apparent that the consensus in England differed widely to opinion in Spain. According to those that had known Arthur well, he had claimed his marital rights with vigour on the night of his nuptials. And he wasn't afraid to boast about it. According to Arthur's friend and servant, Sir Antony Willoughby, after his first night with Katherine, Arthur said:

> 'Willoughby, bring me a cup of ale, for I have been this night in the midst of Spain;' and afterward said openly, 'Masters, it is a good pastime to have a wife.'[1]

Accounts by Maurice St John and other servants, suggests a similar story. Memories in Spain however, differed significantly. A male servant of Katherine's would testify many years later that:

> 'Francisca de Cacerces, who was in charge of dressing and undressing the queen and whom she liked and confided in a lot, was looking sad and telling the other ladies that nothing had passed between Prince Arthur and his wife, which surprised everyone and made them laugh at him.'[2]

These sources must be handled with extreme care and caution. They were all gathered almost 30 years after Arthur's death and in the most highly charged of political circumstances. We can't dismiss them altogether. But they are hardly a good place to begin our discussion. Ideally, we would begin by examining the contemporary evidence. Sadly, little exists. We know that Arthur and Katherine were put to bed together after their wedding and that they spent the next day apart. We are clear that they were sent to Ludlow together but that there is a strong suggestion that, while at the Welsh border, it was the King's will that they would not share sleeping arrangements. Beyond that we know nothing. The months after Arthur's death, however, reveal much more. And it is likely in these letters and communications between the Spanish and English that we find the truth.

By 10 May 1502, news of their son-in-law's death had reached Ferdinand and Isabella. Although they would later claim great sorrow for the occasion, stating that 'affliction caused by all their former losses has been revived by'.[3] However, their real concerns, as parents, were for Katherine's welfare and, as monarchs, to salvage the alliance with England that Arthur and Katherine's marriage had represented.

Throughout most of the protracted negotiations around the marriage, England had been the chaser. While the match always contained advantages for both nations, the benefits had always leaned more in England's favour. But over recent months, the scales had tipped. Following a number of personal and diplomatic tragedies, the Spanish monarchs were struggling to secure their two most fundamental objectives: the future of a united Spain, and dominance over the French. They needed English support now more than ever. The best way to secure that for the medium term was the tried and tested mechanism that had forged the alliance in the first place: marriage.

Almost immediately, Ferdinand and Isabella dispatched a new ambassador to England. There were already two Spanish ambassadors at Henry VII's court. But what would come next was far too delicate and high-pressured to entrust to either of them. The mighty Ferdinand, Duke of Estrada was to take charge of affairs in England. And the feckless De Puebla was instructed in no uncertain terms to obey him. Estrada was sent with two conflicting instructions. The first was clear: Katherine was to return to Spain immediately. After conveying Spanish sympathies to the English king and queen, he was to insist upon the princess's repatriation. But a separate set of instructions reveal that this was nothing more than a bluff. His real mission was to negotiate a marriage between Katherine of Aragon, and Prince Henry, the second son of Henry VII. The 11-year-old boy that would become heir to the throne once it was clear that Katherine wasn't pregnant.

It was not until the July of that year that Isabella wrote to her ambassador, asking him to establish whether Katherine and Arthur's marriage had ever been consummated. This is revealing. The fact she asked shows that Isabella thought such information was important. But the tardiness with which she did so hints that it was not the preeminent consideration. Isabella would have known that the path would be smoother if Katherine remained 'as she was'. If Katherine had been married to Arthur in the fullest sense, then she would be related to the young Henry in the first degree of affinity. As far as the church was concerned, they were as good as brother and sister and, theoretically, marriage was forbidden.

But Isabella knew full well that such restrictions were eminently surmountable. Provided the political circumstances were right, the Pope could be persuaded to issue a bull of dispensation: a powerful canonical document which would authorise the marriage despite these considerations of affinity. After all, he had already made allowances for Katherine's sister, Maria who had married their sister's widower

Manuel of Portugal. In that case, there had been no question that consummation had occurred. Isabella had given Manuel a child.

The fact Isabella was seeking to establish the facts proves that she thought it was perfectly credible that, despite five months of cohabitation as man and wife, Arthur and Katherine might never have consummated their union. We can't be sure *why* she thought that possible. But it shows that a young couple instantly consummating their union was not always universally expected. Initially, Isabella received a conflicting response. Katherine's confessor Alessandro Giraldini believed that the marriage had been consummated. Katherine's mistress, Dona Elvira Manuel, insisted on the contrary. Frustratingly, neither of their letters survive and we cannot know what evidence either of them cited to support their claim.

Of all people in England, after Katherine and Arthur themselves, Dona Manuel was the best placed authority on the subject. In Spain, it was customary to inspect the bed sheets the morning after the marriage to check for signs of consummation. While this was not standard practice in England, it is likely that the Spanish lady acted in the ways of her culture. If she did not discover what she was expecting to find, this would almost certainly have precipitated a conversation with Katherine who is likely to have confided in her mistress. It could be that Katherine herself did not understand exactly what had or hadn't passed between herself and her young husband. But Dona Manuel would have been left in no doubt whatsoever. Unsurprisingly, it was Dona Manuel's account that Isabella believed.

Isabella quickly passed on this information to the ambassador who was in turn to convey it to the King. The path to a union between Katherine and Henry would have to be slow. Henry was still three years away from marital age. With this information, it could now be reasonably smooth. It is very unlikely that Dona Manuel was lying to her queen or that Isabella was being less than truthful to her own ambassador. This is not because either was above deception. The evidence suggests quite the contrary. But in this instance, they had very little reason to lie. The case of Katherine's sister had proven that consummation was a barrier that could be quickly overcome. Lying about it then, could have jeopardised Katherine in the future.

It is possible that Isabella believed that, while consummation could be overcome, things would be easier if everyone pretended it had never taken place. She may even have felt there was some merit in tricking the English King. But in this instance, she would almost certainly have brought her ambassador into the deception with her. The Spanish monarchs were quite used to briefing their envoys to be blatantly dishonest. If that had been Estrada's mission, his queen would have appraised him of the facts.

Henry VII was soon won around to the prospect of a second Spanish marriage. He committed his new heir, Henry to marry his brother's widow when of age and a new treaty was quickly negotiated. However, unlike the Spanish, Henry was insistent that Katherine's marriage to Arthur was treated as if it was consummated and that papal dispensation was sought accordingly. If Isabella had been insincere in her belief around Katherine's virginity, there was no need to maintain the pretence now. The English clearly did not see consummation with one brother as an insurmountable barrier to a union with another.

The Spanish monarchs, keen to cement the support of the English, quickly signed the treaty. Papal dispensation was sought on the basis that the marriage between Arthur and Katherine had been consummated. Yet Isabella never seems to have fully made her peace with this state of affairs. There was no political advantage to Isabella in pretending that her daughter remained a virgin. The fact she did so simply suggests that she believed it to be the truth. The most important consideration for Isabella was that validity of Katherine's second marriage would be beyond challenge in the future. If the papal dispensation stated that the marriage to Arthur had been consummated, when no such consummation had taken place, could even *that* call the legitimacy of her union, and the children of it, into question?

Isabella was quite the prophetess. Decades later, Katherine faced exactly this conundrum. Early in the divorce proceedings initiated by Henry VIII she declared that she had come to her second marriage a virgin. Thomas Wolsey, Henry's ever-clever minister was the first to spot that Katherine had laid a trap for herself. The Papal dispensation had been clear that her marriage to Arthur was consummated, before authorising her to marry Henry. If that had never been the case, surely neither the bull, nor Katherine's marriage to the King could be deemed valid.

Katherine, herself as clever and sharp minded as many lawyers, was not to be outdone. She quickly produced a copy of a bull of dispensation secured by her mother and dispatched to Spain. This dispensation said that 'perhaps' her marriage to Arthur had been consummated. It covered all the bases. It also contained less errors than the copy in England and was altogether more robust. Given the convenience of this bull, many in England thought it a forgery. No record of it was found on the Vatican rolls, though that does not itself argue against its authenticity. Unsurprisingly, the Spanish authorities would not surrender the bull to the English, though they allowed Henry's envoys to inspect it. Despite these critiques however, the dispensation was much later inspected by twentieth century palaeographic experts. They judged it to be 'unquestionably authentic.'[4]

The status of Katherine's virginity was proving no issue in negotiating a marriage with Prince Henry. Yet, Isabella simply couldn't let the matter lie. So convinced was she that her daughter's first marriage had never been consummated that she obtained extra protection from the Pope. She knew that any inaccuracy in information could come back to haunt her daughter. And as the decades that followed were to prove, her suspicions were justified.

The Spanish believed that Arthur and Katherine had never consummated their marriage. They had access to the best witnesses, and they maintained this position even when there was no political advantage to doing so. Even when it was clear that England saw the issue of consummation as no major barrier to progress, Isabella went to the extra trouble of securing an additional Papal dispensation which she felt more accurately reflected the status quo.

The historian cannot share Isabella's certainty. There is too much room for ambiguity, and we simply don't know what information we are missing. But the available evidence in the weeks and months after Arthur's death suggests that the Spanish Queen was correct. The best assessment of the available evidence leads us to the conclusion that Arthur went to his grave with his marriage unconsummated. Even if it's a conclusion that we must hold with a degree of caution.

This leaves us with two crucial questions. Why, if Isabella was correct, did the English maintain otherwise? And why, given that Arthur and Katherine were of appropriate age for consummation, did they fail to do the deed. As we shall see, the answers to both questions are probably intricately connected.

According to Ferdinand, the English knew full well that Katherine remained a virgin. Their desire to treat the marriage as consummated was simply a case of being 'belt and braces'. As he wrote to his ambassador in Rome:

> 'In the clause of the treaty which mentions the dispensation of the Pope, it is stated that the Princess Katherine consummated her marriage with Prince Arthur. The fact, however, is, that although they were wedded, Prince Arthur and the Princess Katherine never consummated the marriage. It is well known in England that the Princess is still a virgin. But as the English are much disposed to cavil, it has seemed to be more prudent to provide for the case as though the marriage had been consummated, and the dispensation of the Pope must be in perfect keeping with the said clause of the treaty. The right of succession depends on the undoubted legitimacy of the marriage.'[5]

Ferdinand had a point. The English were certainly keen to get the legalities right. It had been less than 20 years since Richard III had used the questionable circumstances surrounding this brother's marriage to declare the young Edward V illegitimate and seize his throne. Despite having previously assured the Spanish monarchs that there remained 'not a drop of doubtful Royal blood" in the Kingdom, outside of his own family, Henry knew full well that this was a fiction. In a scenario where the English King's second son, Henry, had perished like Arthur, leaving his child to take the throne, there must have been no question of that child's legitimacy. There were many in England who might have fancied their chances as ruler. The

A Night in Spain

Duke of Buckingham for one, not to mention the Plantagenet-blooded children of the queen's sisters. If the marriage between Henry and Katherine was to go ahead, everything must be by the book.

But the problem with Ferdinand's analysis is that it is inherently contradictory. If Henry VII really believed that Katherine and Arthur had never slept together, then obtaining a dispensation that stated that they had was hardly a 'by the book' approach. As Henry VIII's wily minister Thomas Wolsey was later to point out, in that scenario, it would be far wiser to secure a dispensation that dealt with the 'public honesty' of Katherine's betrothal to Arthur. This would have dispensed with the complications arising from the very public way that the young couple had married and lived together as husband and wife.

Henry VII was anything but stupid. Nor was he casual when it came to the detail. If Isabella had foreseen that any problem with accuracy could present Katherine with trouble in the future, why hadn't the King? He, of course, wouldn't have been as concerned about the princess's destiny as her own mother would. But he would have cared passionately about the legitimacy of his future descendants by her. Besides, as Isabella was to prove, the Pope was happy to issue an "all bases covered" dispensation. Why did the English King not insist on seeking that? There is a chance that Henry had been motivated to maintain that the marriage had been consummated in order to secure the remaining instalments of Katherine's dowry. The marriage treaty had – after some negotiation – stated that the final payment would not be surrendered until after the union was fully sealed. If Arthur had never slept with the princess, the Spanish monarchs owed the English King nothing.

But for Henry VII, there were financial considerations on both sides of the scenario. Yes, if the marriage had not been consummated, he would not be entitled to the remainder of the dowry. But he would also have come under far less pressure to deliver Katherine her jointure, amounting to a third of the revenue of Wales, Chester, and Cornwall. Besides, it's unlikely that even as fiscally prudent a monarch as Henry VII would risk undermining the legitimacy of the heirs of his dynasty just to get his hands on Spanish treasure.

The most logical explanation is that Ferdinand was wrong on one crucial point. It was not the case, that Katherine was widely thought of as a virgin in England. The King believed that his son had been able to consummate the marriage. And there's probably an obvious reason why: Arthur, or people close to Arthur, had told him that this is precisely what had happened. As we have already seen, many in Tudor times believed that sex could be dangerous for teenage boys. These fears had almost certainly been exasperated by the death of the Spanish Prince Juan soon after his marriage. Henry was not shy about talking to his son about such matters. He had instructed Arthur not to sleep with Katherine after the wedding night as concerns about the boy's health continued to manifest. However, he had still told his son that the marriage should be consummated on the night of the ceremony. A marriage was not truly set in stone until this act took place. Without it, the alliance with Spain could be broken. And Henry VII would be unable to secure the remaining instalments of Katherine's dowry.

Arthur and Katherine spent the day after their wedding apart. It was on this day that the prince supposedly made his bragging and bawdy comments about his sexual prowess to his slightly older gentlemen servants. During the course of this day, he almost certainly spent time with his father. The question of whether he had consummated his union, while intimately personal, was also one of diplomatic significance. His father almost certainly asked the question. Arthur probably gave an answer that was not altogether accurate. Does this then, make Arthur a liar? After all, Dona Elvira had likely checked the bedsheets, spoke with Katherine, and determined the truth of the matter. Or could it be, more generously, that the events of that night were more ambiguous than is often supposed?

As we have already seen, by the time Arthur was entering adolescence, there were concerns about his health and development. It is unlikely that these were physically striking, other than the fact he looked young for his age. However, those that spent time with him may have noticed clear signs of problems. While we simply don't have the evidence to diagnose, it seems likely that he may have tired easily and was slow to recover from illness.

By anyone's standards, by the night of his wedding, Arthur had endured a big day. He would have been drinking from early in the afternoon and may have been exhausted come the evening. Is it possible that, after being put to bed, he had every intention of making the Princess his wife in deed as well as law? But is it also possible that his energy could not match his ambitions? If he was an exhausted, under-developed teenage boy of dubious stamina, this would hardly be surprising. Especially when he knew that the eyes of the world were metaphorically upon him.

If this scenario, or one that resembles it is true, we will never know exactly how far Arthur was able to satisfy expectations. It could be that some sexual activity took place but that things had not progressed far enough for Katherine to consider it a consummation. After all, if today's popular culture is to be believed, it's quite possible for twenty-first century teenagers to share a disagreement around whether they "did it" on their first attempt. How much more might that have been the case for the young of the sixteenth century?

This perspective, though impossible to prove, helps make sense of everything that followed. If Arthur had been bashful about his sexual performance, doesn't that make it even more likely that he would brag about his prowess? After all, his gentlemen ushers were roughly half a decade older than him. Despite his superior status, when it came to manly antics, he would have been keen to impress and win their masculine approval. And of course, for Arthur himself, it would have seemed no major deception. While there would not be immediate opportunities to right the wrongs of the night before – if, as seems likely, his father had arranged for them to keep a distance at Ludlow – he was not expecting to drop dead. One day, he and his Katherine would truly live together. He would be older, stronger and lustier. There was plenty of time to make a wife out of her yet.

Katherine herself may have initially been unsure about what had passed between her and her husband. After all, years later, the hapless Anne of Cleves – fourth wife of Henry VIII – claimed to believe that a good night kiss was enough to consummate a marriage. While it seems unlikely that Katherine would ever have been that naïve, she was a young woman. And she was entering a very confusing world.

Once Katherine shared the events of the night with her mistress, she would instantly have known that whatever had happened was not enough to constitute consummation. Whether or not she relayed this to the princess we cannot be sure. But it would help explain her conviction to Isabella that Katherine remained "as she was". And of course, years later, when Katherine married Henry VIII, she would have learnt just what it meant to consummate a union with a lusty partner. Drawing upon the contrasting experiences of her two wedding nights, Katherine could testify with conviction in 1528 that she had never known Arthur as her husband. A conviction that this long-suffering woman was to take to her grave.

To what extent Arthur believed he had failed in his duties, remains a mystery. But if he did, it's likely that he was eager to right his wrong. As we have seen in the previous chapter, Arthur was a boy of great resilience and determination. And it may have been this determination which convinced him that Katherine must return to Ludlow with him. But as Arthur was about to discover, his plan to keep his wife by his side was yet another conviction that the prince would have to fight for.

Chapter 16

Righteous Order and Wisdom

Whatever happened the night of Arthur and Katherine's wedding, one thing is beyond doubt: the princess deserved a rest. In recent weeks, Katherine had departed her home country and braved the storms of the sea before embarking on a cross-country trek across England. Upon her arrival in London, she had been subject to a day of dazzling but demanding ceremony before finally taking centre stage at her wedding. She had certainly earned some respite.

During the Monday, Katherine kept to her chamber, in the presence of her ladies. She had to tolerate just one visit, with the Earl of Oxford bringing a message and gift from the King. She was even spared the pressure of conversing with the Spanish nobility who had accompanied her. Margaret Beaufort threw a lavish reception for the foreign dignitaries at her palace of Coldharbour.

Both prince and princess had ample reason to recharge their batteries. The festivities were far from over. On the Tuesday, Arthur and Katherine attended a mass of offering at St Paul's in the presence of the nobility. On the Wednesday was the ceremonial dubbing of the new knights of the Bath. Thursday, saw the beginning of the jousts, the Duke of Buckingham leading for the challengers and the young Marquess of Dorset heading the defenders. Great banquets were held on the Thursday and the Sunday with the jousts continuing into the following week. Eventually, almost two weeks following their wedding, Arthur and Katherine could escape with the king and queen to Richmond. While they were still at the epicentre of the Royal court, a degree of tranquillity was finally on offer. The young couple were not due to depart for Ludlow until 21 December. They had six weeks to get to know each other among the rest of Arthur's family, granting the princess an opportunity to spend time with her in-laws. Katherine would later claim that she and her first husband spent just seven nights together over the course of their short marriage. Even if, as is likely, all of these nights of shared sleeping arrangements took place in London, they clearly had separate lodgings and the chance for a little bit of breathing space.

Details are scarce about how they spent their time. Was Arthur nervously avoiding his new bride? Or was he anxiously trying to impress this attractive and older woman? If the latter, then he was about to learn a lesson that has mortified teenagers throughout the ages: parents can be very embarrassing.

After the festivities were over, Henry VII wrote to Johan de Cuero, keeper of Katherine's wardrobe. The Princess had brought with her many beautiful jewels and ornaments. The King demanded that they were surrendered to him. The jewels that would adorn Katherine, and the splendid treasure she would bring with her from Spain, had been a sticking point between the two nations since the very beginning of the negotiations. Back in 1489, the treaty of Medina del Campo had agreed that a quarter of Katherine's marriage portion could be offset by ornaments and jewels belonging to the princess. This arrangement had been broadly retained in subsequent interactions, but the Spanish expressed concern about an inherent ambiguity. Would these precious jewels actually have to be surrendered to Henry? Or would it simply be acknowledged that they offset funds that the king would otherwise have to invest in ensuring that the Princess looked the part.[1]

De Cuero clearly believed that the understanding was the latter. And this is probably the most logical reading of what had been agreed in the treaty. He refused to surrender the jewels, claiming instead that his instructions were to have them weighed and valued so that Henry could provide a receipt for them.[2] This response infuriated the King. Why on earth should he issue a receipt for something he had not received? Henry made no bones about his frustration and Katherine, and probably Arthur, were quickly dragged into the furore.

Luckily for Arthur, the king's anger soon passed. In the presence of Katherine's mistress Dona Elvira Manuel, the King went to the princess to explain and apologise. The account of what passed between them comes to us from the ambassador Don Pedro De Ayala. It is clear that his account has been crafted to deliver a fatal blow to his rival ambassador, De Puebla. As such, we should treat it with some caution. However, when writing to Isabella about what had transpired, he believes that she will already have heard much of the tale from the princess. It is unlikely that De Ayala, at this stage in his relationship with Katherine, would have embroiled the princess in a conspiracy. We can broadly trust the thrust of his account.

Henry apologised to Katherine for what he claimed had been a monumental misunderstanding. Ahead of his first meeting with the princess, the king claimed that De Puebla, the original Spanish ambassador, had read him a letter from Ferdinand and Isabella that claimed Henry was within his rights to take possession of Katherine's jewels and ornaments. Because of the Spanish monarchs' insistence on writing in their native tongue rather than Latin, Henry had little choice but to trust the ambassador's translations.

But when Henry encountered resistance, he summoned De Puebla. Either he was being wilfully defied or there had been some kind of fatal miscommunication. De Puebla now came clean with the king about his plan. He had devised a means whereby Katherine could keep her jewels and the King could cash in at the expense of Ferdinand and Isabella. If the jewels and ornaments were not surrendered,

Katherine would clearly use them. Henry could then justifiably refuse to accept used goods. So ashamed would Katherine's parents be, that they would allow the princess to retain her soiled possessions and send funds to the king to cover his loss. Katherine would win. Henry would win. The only losers would be the Spanish monarchs.

Henry, however, could not go along with this plan. He was, he claimed unconvincingly, simply unable to obtain any advantage at the expense of Katherine's parents. The princess must keep her jewels. And the last thing that Henry would want is for anyone to think him poor. He could spend a million of gold without going into debt.[3] De Puebla was probably not quite as villainous in all this as De Ayala portrayed him. Ferdinand and Isabella did not recall him from his post. It seems unlikely that they thought him guilty of orchestrating a scheme against them.

It is more likely that the plan was the brainchild of Henry himself. The payment of Katherine's marriage portion had always been – and would continue to be – a sore point. Perhaps he reasoned that, given the chance, Ferdinand and Isabella would have been only too happy to cross him for financial gain. If so, he was probably right. But eventually he had come to his senses. Perhaps those that he listened to, such as the queen, had convinced him that this was hardly the best way to kick off relations with Katherine and her family. It could even be that Arthur himself had summoned up the courage to intervene.

The letter of De Ayala to Ferdinand and Isabella also sheds light on Henry VII's lingering fears about the consequences of sending Katherine back to Ludlow with Arthur. As we have seen, teenage sex was thought to be dangerous for the male. While Henry had instructed Arthur not to maintain a sexual relationship with Katherine after consummation for the first few years of their marriage, he would have known that with both Prince and Princess of Wales far away at Ludlow, this edict would be hard to police.

It could be that the gruelling days and weeks surrounding the wedding had demonstrably taken their toll on Arthur. While Katherine's role had been unyielding, Arthur had almost been conspicuous by his absence from much of the festivities. He had stood at his father's side at Baynard's Castle, presiding over a gathering of English and Spanish before the wedding. Then of course, there was the day itself. But beyond that the Prince's role is notably muted.

That's partly, of course, because Katherine was the real star of the show. Not only was she the beautiful bride, but she was also the symbol of England's new international status. Yet, there could be more to it than that. It's possible that concerns continued about how well-suited Arthur was to such a gruelling schedule of activities. Space and rest could have been carved out for him.

It could also be that, seeing him next to his new bride, it really struck the king that Arthur looked young, childlike, and underdeveloped. Katherine was only nine months older than her husband, but years later, many of Arthur's servants incorrectly remembered the age gap as being much greater. This may suggest that she looked very much like an adult woman wed to a child. If so, this would surely have unsettled Arthur's father. The king summoned Don Pedro De Ayala to discuss the dilemma. His counsellors, and Arthur's counsellors had disagreed about what to do for the best. There were, he told the ambassador, strong arguments both for and against sending Katherine to Ludlow.

What these arguments were are not recorded. But it is not hard for us to take a guess at them. If Arthur returned to Ludlow with a wife, it would be abundantly clear that he was now a man. It would strengthen his authority immensely and help him take the next step in establishing himself as a regional leader, accelerating his preparation for Kingship. But on the flip side, there was Arthur's age, fragility, and health to consider. To De Ayala, Henry's hesitation was all part of a grand deception. Despite his feigned indecision, he was determined that the princess travel with Arthur to Ludlow. Should she do so, she would take her jewels and ornaments with her. This would then give Henry grounds to protest to her parents that the instalment of the marriage portion that these artefacts represent can hardly have been considered to be paid. He would require compensation.[4]

But De Ayala was being ungenerous. While a financial motivation can never be ruled out when it comes to Henry VII, on this occasion the King was acting as a loving and agonised parent. A letter, signed by Henry himself, to Ferdinand and Isabella proves that Henry was concerned about Arthur's fragility and the consequences of sending Katherine to Ludlow. While De Ayala claimed that Ferdinand and Isabella were relaxed as to whether Katherine cohabited with her husband, Henry's letter makes it clear that he believed that the Spanish monarchs desired their daughter to go to Ludlow with Arthur.[5] This explains, in part, why he may have felt under some pressure.

Eventually, the question was put to Katherine herself. Would she like to take up residence at Ludlow with Arthur? Or should she remain behind in the care of the king and queen? The Princess answered tactfully. Perhaps she too suspected that this was part of a ploy to extract additional funds from her parents. In this matter, nor in any other matter did she have any will other than the king's. The king continued to press her for a view. After all, he would hate to make any decision that gave her annoyance.

Such an impasse continued for four days. Eventually the King asked Arthur to try and discover his wife's wishes. According to De Ayala, the prince was under orders to persuade Katherine to join him at Ludlow. But realistically, it is likely that this was always Arthur's preferred option. Whatever the state of his health, he surely believed the time had come for him to be recognised as the prince and man that he was. And real men, he would surely have believed, lived with their wives.

He and Katherine had been apart for long enough. Yet even her husband could not extract an answer from Katherine. Finally, perhaps giving into petitions from Arthur and believing it be the will of the Spanish, the King agreed that both prince and princess should be sent to the Welsh border. It may have been a decision that he regretted for the rest of his life.

Before the Prince and Princess departed, Henry was determined to recover his reputation with Katherine after the shambolic display of greed over her jewels. His entire policy centred around the creation of a solvent monarchy. Now, he, after decades of trying to impress Ferdinand and Isabella, had risked making himself look like a scrambling pauper in the eyes of the Spanish. He was determined to find a chance to show his generous side. And fortunately for him, Katherine's homesickness soon presented a golden opportunity. After the great dignitaries that had escorted Katherine from her mother land returned to Spain, the Princess was overcome with melancholy. Arthur would surely have been among the first to notice any change in her character and it is entirely possible that it was he, who alerted his father to her condition.

Henry quickly invited Katherine and her ladies to his great library. He also assembled a number of English ladies, perhaps those not too much older than the princess, and showed them 'many goodly pleasaunt bokes of werkes full delitfull'. Many of the books were in Latin, meaning Katherine herself would have been able to appreciate their merits. Then, perhaps even more excitingly, he brought forth his jeweller, to show them rings, precious stones, and jewels of 'goodly fachion.' Each lady was told that they could pick a jewel to keep. Katherine, could pick first, followed by the Spanish ladies. The English ladies could quibble amongst themselves for the spoils that remained. Arthur must have prayed this event would impress his wife. And Henry must have dearly hoped that worlds of his generosity would reach Ferdinand and Isabella.

Toward the end of December, Arthur, 'departed from the Kinges Higness his father with his goodly Lady and wife, the Lady Kateryn of Hispayn, unto the seid conreth of Walys, governing the seid conreth moost discretly and aftir moost and righteous ordre and wisdam.' After the glitz and glamour of her time in the capital, taking up residence in the Welsh Marches must have come as quite a culture shock to Katherine. But to Arthur, it must have been the closest feeling he had ever experienced to going home. Arthur, as we have seen, had been the figure of an important administration in Wales and along its border since he was 6 years of age. As he returned with a wife by his side, he must have dearly hoped that his new, adult status, would usher in an era of his own personal rule.

The success of Arthur's council had depended on its ability to successfully manage relations between the mighty landowners in and around the principality. In this, Arthur was at a distinct advantage. The major landowner in South Wales was his great uncle Jasper Tudor, Duke of Bedford. His grandmother, Margaret Beaufort, through her marriage into the Stanley family and her wardship of the child Duke of Buckingham, was also a major figure of influence in the region.[6] Their support would have gone a long way to establishing the success of Arthur's rule. This great patriarch and matriarch of the house of Tudor had once collaborated to keep Arthur's father safe from harm. As the 1490s opened, they again worked together, in a very different way, to do the same for his son.

Given the need to ensure that all major landowners were represented in Arthur's government, it was initially the great men of the region that were given powers and responsibilities to administer justice on the prince's behalf. This included Jasper himself, Sir William Stanley, and the Earl of Arundel. However, it would not be long before the men of Arthur's household, closely associated with Arthur himself began to take the leading role on his council.

John Alcock, Bishop of Ely, initially headed Arthur's council. He was eminently qualified for the job, having acquired huge local knowledge as a former tutor to Edward V and as a previous Bishop of nearby Worcester. By the mid-1490s however, William Smith, Bishop of Coventry and Lichfield and a creature of Margaret Beaufort's, had taken the reins. Active also in Arthur's government were his chamberlain, Richard Pole, his comptroller Henry Vernon, and John Mourdant, Arthur's attorney. Later, William Uvedale, who would replace Vernon as comptroller and Richard Croft, who would take over as steward also became associated with the prince's administration.

As well as maintaining order and justice in Wales and along the border, Arthur's council was responsible for ensuring that his feudal rights were respected and claims in his name were pressed. And this, they did with zeal, across the whole of his vast estate. They investigated breaches of liberties in Chester, raised heavy taxation in Cheshire and fined tinners for infringements of the stannary laws in Cornwall. So enthusiastically were Arthur's rights pressed in North Wales that the council had to deal with armed insurrection against them in Meirionnydd in 1498.

For his first five years on the Welsh border, Arthur probably had little to do with the detail of his administration. While he sat at the bench in Hereford in 1493, aged just 6, this was primarily an opportunity to make it clear that the prince was now in situ on the border. However, he is next recorded as presiding directly over justice in 1498, the year that he turned 10 and seems to have started to play a more active role in his own affairs.

One area that he was perhaps allowed more direct input into was that of patronage. If he was the author of the fortunes of those around him, then it seemed that Arthur was disposed to reward loyalty. Many of the yeoman and grooms of his chamber that had been with him since he was small were rewarded with offices across his estate. Some of the servants closer in age to Arthur, who seem to have joined him around 1498, were bestowed with stewardships.

It's possible that Arthur's childlike inclination toward generosity to his friends became an issue of concern to his councillors. As Steven Gunn points out, "a number of his grants are carefully qualified with the provision that they were made by the advice of the lords and other members of his council."[7]

It's possible that Arthur, a determined young man, was growing weary on these restraints of his councillors. If, as this book has speculated, he was already in a position where he was now being drawn into matters of national policy, it must have grated that rule across his own principality was being so closely monitored. As we have already seen, Arthur seems to have been instrumental in persuading Katherine that she should join him in Ludlow, against the better instincts of his father. Could it be that Arthur hoped that by returning to his power base with a wife by his side would help him to finally be taken seriously as an adult lord and master?

Arthur's household had already undergone three significant shifts. The first – which he would have been too young to remember – was when his nurse was retired, and he was moved out of the nursery into a more masculine environment. The second, was his move to Ludlow and Bewdley which saw him come fully under the power of men like Pole, Vernon and Uvedale. And the third, when he was about ten in 1498, when he was appointed a new tutor. At the same time, a group of young men closer to his age were given posts as his servants and companions. It is quite possible that he believed Katherine's arrival would mark a fourth transition. The household would now be both male and female, headed by a married couple with Arthur as the senior figure. What right would anyone have to gainsay a married man?

If this is correct, then Arthur may not have been alone in eagerly anticipating Katherine's debut on the Marches. Despite his title and the remit of his government, it is possible that the prince never actually crossed over the border into Wales. While Spanish correspondence does refer to him being 'in Wales' and touring 'his principality' it is also clear from other letters that the Spanish ambassadors had a hard time distinguishing between Wales itself and the English counties that bordered it. But there is evidence of a number of churches and important buildings installing decorations of the Prince of Wales's feather and Katherine of Aragon's pomegranate at around the time of the marriage.[8] This may suggest that a grand tour of Wales was on the horizon.

Sadly, due to a lack of any real surviving evidence, almost nothing can be said of the five months that Arthur and Katherine spent together on the edge of their principality. There is no record of them residing anywhere other than Ludlow Castle, though it's possible they also spent time at the more comfortable manor of Bewdley. We also cannot know whether Arthur respected his father's wishes and ceased attempts at a sexual relationship. Years later, his servants would testify that they had often escorted him to Katherine's chamber, where it was presumed that they spent the night together as man and wife. This could be evidence of Arthur's attempts to consummate the marriage he had probably failed to on his wedding night. Or it might be a later invention designed to appeal to the perspective of Arthur's brother Henry, who was desperate to prove that Arthur and Katherine had been intimate.

Sadly, if this book is correct, and the last years and months of Arthur's life were subject to failing health, then it seems unlikely that the prince and princess's months of matrimony were a season of particular happiness. Katherine still couldn't speak the language. Whatever desire Arthur had to impress his wife; he probably lacked the energy. Not only would the Princess have surely battled with homesickness, but the dismal weather of that time of year would have made the beauty of the Welsh border impossible to enjoy. Arthur had returned to his principality with a princess by his side and high hopes for the future. Could he, that ever-determined prince, finally be allowed to assume control of his administration and be recognised for the married man that he was? However much these hopes were realised, and whatever the quality of their marriage, a cruel twist of fate would ensure that neither Arthur nor Katherine were to enjoy if for long.

Chapter 17

Le Morte d'Arthur

As the sun set on a wet, spring evening, a messenger galloped at breakneck speed from Ludlow to Greenwich. This was the second time in six months that a gallant rider had defied the usual expectations of travel time in order to bring vital news to the king. The first had been in the previous October when, in record time, the King received the chaotic, but fundamentally welcome news that Katherine of Aragon had arrived safely in England. Albeit some 150 miles from where she had been due to dock. This time, the news was of even greater consequence and offered no silver lining. Prince Arthur, the hope of the Tudors, had perished.

Just five months before, Henry VII, through the marriage of his treasured son, had celebrated his greatest moment of triumph. His family stood united with the most powerful dynasty in Europe. He had plotted a path to Tudor succession for the next generation. He had demonstrated his magnificence to the people of England and the watchers of the world. Now, or so it must have seemed, he was left with nothing but a broken heart and a wasted investment. How had the future been snatched from them so quickly and so decisively?

Arthur's final illness seems to have been sudden. Little more than a week before he died, he apparently distributed alms to poor men during a Maundy Thursday service. The courtier who chronicled Princess Katherine's arrival to England, is the only contemporary writer to give any comment on the disease that tragically took Arthur's life:

> 'At the which season grue and encreased upon his body, whethir it were by surfett or by cause naturall, a lamentable and ne, the pleasure of God wer hever to be paciently takyn and suffrid the moost petifull disease and sikenes, that with so sore and great violens hedde batillid and driven in the singler partise of him inward; that cruell and fervent enemye of nature, the dedly corupcion, did uttirly venquysshe and overcome the pure and frendfull blod, without almaner of phisicall help and remedy. Thus the lyvely spirites of this noble Prince finally mortified, oure Realme of Englond and all Cristente dolour, sorow, and great discomp fort.'[1]

The obscure reference to 'the singler partise' of Arthur being driven inwards had given rise to speculation that the prince had been suffering from testicular cancer. While that's plausible, it seems ambitious to alight on such a theory with any confidence given the paucity of information. And while 'singler partise of him' could be a coded reference to his testicles, there is certainly no guarantee that it is.

Too often, historians view the cause of Arthur's death through the lens of their existing theories. They analyse the available information through the prism of what they already believe about his health and the likelihood of him having consummated his marriage. Those that already believe Arthur's health was poor, rendering him unable to sleep with Katherine, tend to dismiss the possibility that there was any kind of pandemic or sickness sweeping through Ludlow. They find the cause solely located in Arthur's pre-existing vulnerabilities.

Commentators who think the prince likely of boasting vigorous health, and acting just as vigorously in the bedroom, tend to pin the blame on a wider and unexpected public health phenomenon. But the evidence, as it so often does, makes such a clear-cut or one-sided analysis difficult to sustain. Probate records from the Bishop of Hereford's consistory court show that 1502 had the third highest mortality rate of any year in the sixteenth century, with the deaneries of Ludlow and Leominster suffering more than any other area.[2] This does suggest some evidence of disease in the town and ties into the account of Arthur's funeral, which says that the men of the city had not attended because of 'the siknes that then reigned emonges them'.[3]

However, despite this significant evidence of some local sickness or disease, it does not seem to have dramatically impacted any other member of the prince's household. Those closest to Arthur, who would have most regularly been in proximity to him were able to discharge their onerous duties after his death perfectly adequately. Had any of them been ill, they were clearly quick to recover.

What we can't be sure of, is how this disease affected the Princess of Wales, if indeed it did at all. Months later, in the August of that year, Ferdinand and Isabella received word that their daughter was unwell. Reacting with understandable panic, they insisted that she was withdrawn from the 'unhealthy' place of Ludlow, if she had not been so already.[4]

But the Spanish monarchs were far away and receiving only dribs and drabs of information. And it is not clear from their communications whether they believed Katherine had been struck down at the same time as Arthur, or in shock of his death. Some thirty years later, the view in Spain was that Katherine had become ill in reaction to Arthur's death, though that information must be treated with a pinch of salt, as it was wrapped up in the debate around the validity of Katherine's second marriage. What we can say with certainly is that, even if Katherine had been afflicted by the same disease as her young husband, unlike Arthur she was to quickly recover.

Ludlow does, so the evidence suggests, seem to have been victim of a sickness around the time of Arthur's death. While it either caused or contributed to Arthur's demise, it seemed to create few problems for other members of his household. All of this leads us back to the most logical explanation: that Arthur, while not necessarily demonstrably weak and sickly, suffered from an underlying vulnerability. He was more susceptible to disease and infection. Ultimately, this vulnerability, potentially connected to his premature birth, contributed to his premature and tragic death. Beyond this analysis, all theories around the specific rely more on speculation than evidence.

The sweating sickness, which may have arrived in England with Henry Tudor's invading army in 1485, has often been blamed for the death of his son. This death, which appeared sporadically in England from 1485 to 1551, came on suddenly beginning with cold shivers, dizziness, headaches, body pain and exhaustion. The sickness lasted for about a day, after which the sufferer would either die or recover.

If this theory is correct, it would certainly explain how Arthur died so suddenly despite seemingly being active just a week before. It might also account for how many recovered quickly while Arthur perished, as different outcomes seem to have been a common feature of the disease. Nevertheless, there is no other evidence for an outbreak of the sweating sickness in 1502 and it would be bad luck indeed if Arthur were the only significant member of his household to succumb.

Others have maintained that Arthur likely died of tuberculosis. But other than that being the likely cause of his father's death and that of his nephew, Edward VI, little by way of evidence is offered to support the theory. Though if the Spanish descriptions of Arthur that emerged three decades later can be trusted, that would certainly add weight to the possibility.

Whatever the local sickness, Sean Cunningham intelligently speculates that the presence of Spanish officers and servants in the prince and princess's establishment, may have made the household at Ludlow more susceptible to it. In previous years, it might have been easier to protect Arthur from local diseases that were common in England. All of his household men would have developed a degree of immunity to them, and such sicknesses may not have even entered the castle walls. But the men and women from Spain would not have been used to local diseases, including the sweating sickness. While none of them seemed to become seriously ill from it, it could well have been they that brought it closer to Arthur's door. If, as seems likely, he possessed underlying vulnerabilities, it would likely have affected him more gravely than it impacted its carriers.

Ultimately, there remains insufficient evidence to determine the cause of Arthur's death. Even when medical records are more plentiful, attempting to diagnose at a distance of 500 years can be a fool's errand. Historians have naturally speculated about causes and it makes sense to capture those on these pages. But we perhaps do no justice to the victim by attempting to draw any firm conclusions about the precise nature of his demise which looks destined to remain a mystery.

Sir Richard Pole wrote immediately to the King to convey the grave tidings. Through his appointment as Arthur's chamberlain, and his marriage to the Queen's cousin, Pole had enjoyed huge social advancement in recent years. At times, he must have struggled to believe his luck. As he took charge of writing the words that no servant wishes to convey to his master, he must have morbidly reflected on how great promotion could come at a cost.

The messenger reached Greenwich in just two days and presented the bleak missive to the King's councillors. Immediately they sent for the King's confessor. On the morning of Tuesday, 5 April, the confessor knocked on the door of the King's chamber and was quickly granted entry. Kings were rarely afforded much privacy, and Henry was far from alone. But the confessor immediately dismissed all others present. It would have been at that moment, that Henry knew his spiritual father was the bearer of a tragic tale.

The moment needed no extra drama. Yet the confessor chose to add some for good measure. '*Si bona de manu dei suscipimus mala autem quare non sustineamus*', he said. These were words that Henry would have instantly recognised from the book of Job: "shall we receive good from God, and shall we not receive evil?" It was the darkest of tidings. He handed Henry the letter.

Perhaps to the confessor, the King should have replied to this devastating news with the courage of a true Christian. He too could have echoed the words of Job and cried: "the Lord gave and the Lord hath taken away; blessed be the name of the Lord." But Henry had no courage left. Instead, he did the only thing his heart could fathom and sent instantly for the queen. Ever since she was a child, Elizabeth of York had wielded relentless resilience in the face of constant tribulation. She had, not once but twice, fled to sanctuary when her family's fortunes were under threat. She had known three brothers perish and lost two infant children of her own. Now, in the face of her greatest trial yet, she once again transformed into a tower of strength. Henry, the queen said lovingly, must remember his own mother. She had begotten just one child. Yet God had kept him safe and lead him to the throne. And they were still blessed with one healthy son and two fair princesses. God was still with them and more than anything else, they were both young enough to have more children. The king thanked her for her comfort and Elizabeth retired to her chamber. She had focused all her thoughts on the future and, as she so often had, on the comfort of her husband. But when she reached her chamber, she ceased to be a queen or a wife and simply became a mother. A mother who had just learned that her firstborn had perished. She collapsed into a grief that she had never known before.

So 'sorrowfull to the heart' was the queen's grief, that those around her could think of nothing but to send for the King. Henry now knew it was his turn to be strong and he rushed to his wife's side. Here, he repeated the words of comfort that she had uttered to him. Even in the midst of tragedy, there had to be the glimmer of hope.

At first glance, the determination of both the king and queen to focus on the future of the dynasty strikes the modern reader as cold. Should their thoughts not have focused on their loss, rather than seeking a replacement for their son? But this is to misunderstand the tender emotions shared between the couple at the moment of their despair. Yes, Henry and Elizabeth had a dynasty to think of. But like so many in the throes of grief, they were trying to process and cope with it by grasping around for any practical action they could take. This account of their shared grief and mutual comfort speaks volumes of their love for Arthur. When their first son was born, this young couple may still have been unsure of each other. They were trying to navigate the dynamics of an arranged marriage, in its earliest days of existence. Fifteen years later, they had blossomed into a loving, caring and mutually supportive couple. Arthur's birth had united them. His death brought them closer than ever.

For several years, Arthur's closest servants had tended to his daily needs. Now, they were charged with preparing his body for its final rest. With great care, and perhaps some expert assistance, members of the prince's household washed and embalmed their master's body, before dressing it with spices and 'othir swete stuf such as thoes as bare the charge therof cowde purvey.' They placed Arthur's body in a chest or coffin, carefully covering it with a black cloth featuring a white cross. With rings of iron, they securely fastened the cloth to the chest and placed it under a table in his chamber, draped with cloth of gold. Atop the cloth stood several burning candles and lanterns. The chamber referred to here, was almost certainly his presence chamber, rather than the bed chamber in which he slept. It would have been in the presence chamber that Arthur had presided over his satellite court. Here, in the protection of his coffin, he could hold court one final time, as members of his household came to pay their respects. As the mourners came to pay tribute to their prince, the poor men to whom Arthur had so recently distributed his alms, stood vigil over the coffin for almost three weeks.

Ludlow, with the possible exception of Bewdley, was the place closest to Arthur's heart. And it seems that his heart never left it. According to a plaque discovered in St Mary Magdalene Chapel within the castle in 1684, Arthur had requested that his heart be buried there.[5] This is not mentioned in the contemporary account of his death and funeral. But it was a common practice among lords of great estates, who wanted at least a part of them to remain in places of significance. Arthur's 'lying in state' at Ludlow allowed his household time to mourn. But it also served a more practical purpose. His funeral, like that of other great lords and members of the Royal family, was to be a grand affair. It was to be anticipated by other moments of mourning, each of which would take time to plan. Surviving records show that £892 2s 1/2d was spent on Arthur's funeral.[6] This is about the same figure as the annual revenue of a Baron. On 23 April, Arthur's hall was emptied, and the yeoman of his chamber lifted the coffin unto a trestle table. Three bishops arrived to bless the body with holy water. Then the great men of Arthur's household and council, picked up the coffin to begin a solemn procession to St Laurence Ludlow, the local parish church.

The great men that comprised the procession were those that had orchestrated the prince's government. Sir Richard Pole, his chamberlain. Sir Richard Croft, his steward and Sir William Uvedale, his comptroller. These men had been crucial to the prince, but they were not truly his friends. It was men closer in age to Arthur, friends, companions, and servants, who bore the canopy over the corpse. Anthony Willoughby and Maurice St John, whom Arthur had supposedly bragged to of his sexual prowess after his wedding night, were joined by Robert Radcliffe and Edward Howard, son of the Earl of Surrey. Other younger men joined the procession. Lord Gerard, son of the Earl of Kildare and Arthur's cousin, Lord John Grey, a younger brother of the Marquess of Dorset, who had probably been raised in the prince's household.

At each corner of the canopy flew a banner, again carried by a man from Arthur's service. Thomas Troys carried a banner of the Trinity. Sir Thomas Blount, the banner of the Patible. The banner of our Lady was borne by Thomas Dudley with Edward Hungerford flying the banner of St George. Ahead of the corpse, walked Sir Gruffydd ap Rhys, Arthur's dear friend, carrying the prince's arms. On each side of them, was an officer of arms.

Throughout the morbid proceedings, the Earl of Surrey, acted as the chief mourner. Surrey was not the senior peer of the realm, being outranked by both the Duke of Buckingham and the Marquess of Dorset, both of whom had played a significant role at Arthur's wedding. But with the Tudor succession once again under threat, it seems like clouds of suspicion were once again forming over those with Plantagenet blood or loyalties to the house of York. Surrey was the most senior nobleman who did not risk reminding onlookers that many alternative claimants to the throne were lurking in the shadows.

Dressed in a foreboding black hood, the Earl walked behind the coffin. He was followed by the Earls of Shrewsbury and Kent, Lord Grey Ruthin, Lord Dudley and Lord Powis. Finally, walked Sir Richard Pole, who was accorded the precedence of a Baron for the proceedings. Each of these men would have been decked out in black cloth. Black, like it is today, was the common colour of mourning. Unlike today, it was extremely expensive. Money spent on black cloth accounted for forty per cent of the entire funeral costs.

Ahead of the coffin processed the many religious men connected with the life of the household, who were followed by two Spanish servants of the princess. Katherine herself does not seem to have attended any of the official mourning events, there being no official role for the deceased's spouse to play. The way of the entire procession was lit by many poor men – probably those that had stood vigil for the prince-carrying bright, burning torches.

Upon reaching the church, Arthur was deposited in the choir. The Bishop of Lincoln, who had known Arthur since he was a small boy, lead the assembled mourners in a dirge. The Bishops of Salisbury and of Chester both read a lesson before all departed to the castle. They returned to the church the next morning. Each of the Bishops led a mass – one of our Lady, one of the Trinity and finally, a requiem. The Earl of Surrey, as chief mourner, surrendered the first of many offerings that he would make over the next few days. After him followed the offerings of the other great men, in order of precedence. Finally, the poignant sermon was delivered by Doctor Edenham: 'blessed are the dead who die in the Lord'.

The service at Ludlow featured many of the hallmarks of a funeral. But it was not to be here, where Arthur had spent so much of his short life, that would serve as his final resting place. The prince was to be buried thirty miles away at Worcester Cathedral. Worcester was not the closest Cathedral to Ludlow, but it had two clear advantages over nearby Hereford. The first, was that another Royal had been buried there in 1216. Even if that Royal was the discredited King John. The second was that it afforded the opportunity to parade Arthur through much of his dominion as a powerful Marcher lord, as was a tradition for great magnates.

Throughout the great events of his life, the English weather had never been a friend to Arthur. A downpour had drenched the guests at his christening. Heavy storms had almost prevented the coming of his wife to England. Much of the ceremony surrounding his wedding had to be rearranged to account for the weather. Now, in the moment of his final journey, he was again confronted by the hazard of a spring downpour.

A solemn chariot had been prepared to carry Arthur through his dominion, departing on 25 April. It was meant to be drawn by six horses, each draped in expensive black cloth woven with gold. The chariot itself, driven by three men, was covered in black velvet featuring a white cross of gold. But the elements made such elegance impossible. As they attempted to set off the Ludlow to Bewdley, the heavy rain created 'the foulist, caulde, wyndy and rayny day' that the chronicler had ever seen. So severe were the conditions that it took oxen to draw the chariot.

Eventually, they reached Bewdley where Arthur was taken to the chapel – almost certainly of the manor house where he had spent so much of his childhood - for one, final goodbye. Less than three years earlier, Arthur had proudly stood in the chapel before many great men as he was wed, by proxy, to a Spanish Princess.

Now, he lay there lifeless as churchmen sang a dirge. The next morning, the mourning party returned for a mass of requiem where the Earl of Surrey gave the offering. In a final act of charity to the community that had hosted much of Arthur's childhood, a dole was distributed 'to every pore man and woman.'[7]

As the mourning party prepared to depart Bewdley, Croft and Uvedale rode ahead to Worcester. It was their job to ensure that Arthur's final arrival was not interrupted or delayed by any passing traffic. The controller and steward of the late prince's household, 'suffryd no man, malier, nor othir to entre the gate of that citye into the tyme the corps was come.' After a muddy and difficult journey to Bewedley, Arthur's chariot was in need of attention. 'Furst ffresshe scochions were sett on the chare [chariot] and draught horsis where nedid'. New men arrived to bear torches. Thankfully, the sun was finally shining. The gentlemen of the mourning party could progress toward Worcester unhindered.

When they reached the gates of Worcester they were greeted by 'the balliffes and the honest men of that citie on alonge a rowe in every side.' Churchmen and children were assembled in great number. The street from the town gate to the cathedral was filled with men standing on either side bearing burning torches. When they reached the gate, Arthur's corpse was removed from the chariot and incensed by the bishops. Then, as before, he was conveyed into the cathedral, under a canopy of estate and with great ceremony.

Just fifteen years before, Winchester Cathedral had been decked out in colourful splendour to mark Arthur's arrival into the world. Now, on this tragic counterpart of an occasion, Worcester Cathedral would be decorated with equal, if solemn splendour. There could be no doubt as to the status of the boy they had bought to bury. The banners of the king and queen hung alongside those of Arthur's in-laws, Ferdinand and Isabella. Next came Arthur's own banner, next to his wives, followed by that of Cadwaladr – the ancient British King whose arms Henry VII had laid down in thanks after his victory at Bosworth field. Their ancestors' arms had protected Henry that day. Yet somehow, they had failed his son.

All of these banners had been expected. As were the banners of Wales, Chester and Cornwall, the lordships over which Arthur had wielded dominion. But some may have raised an eyebrow over the inclusion of the arms of the French duchies which the English, somewhat fantastically, claimed sovereignty over. Henry VII had found little time or inclination for serious war with France to reclaim English possessions. Could this be the only surviving hint that he had hoped his son might one day reclaim the imperial mantle?[8]

As Arthur's body was incensed and prepared, nine abbots and priors read lessons. The vicar general led deacons and other secular priests in the singing of the dirge. After this there was a 'goodly watche of lordes, knightes, squyers, gentilment usshers, officers of armes, yemen, and many othir' that were left to stand vigil over the prince. Prince Arthur was never a man to be associated with military prowess. The events of his father's reign had given him no opportunity to lead or follow an army. Even by medieval standards he was slightly too young to have played a direct role in putting down rebellions. It's also likely that, if there were concerns around Arthur's health, he may have been shielded from some of the more militaristic aspects of knightly training in his later years. Nevertheless, Arthur had been Prince of Wales, a great lord and a knight of both the Bath and the Garter. His knightly arms would act as the centre point of his final march.

The men who had served Arthur loyally, now took up the arms that the prince could no longer bear. The officers of arms delivered Arthur's crest, shield and sword to his faithful mourners. Then, in a spectacular display, which only took place in the funerals of great lords, Lord Gerard, acting as Arthur's man of arms, rode into the choir on a great horse, decked in a caparison sporting Arthur's arm. He carried Arthur's poleaxe, the head downward, and surrendered it to the Abbot of Tewskesbury, the gospeller at the mass.

The herald that recorded these events had a formal task to complete. As ever, he gave due attention to the precedence and position of the men involved. He focused much of his writing on the form and process, noting that the coat of arms was given to the senior Earls of Kent and Shrewsbury before the shield was passed to Lord Grey Ruthin, an heir to an Earldom. Finally, the sword, pommel down, and the shield were given to the baronial Lord Powis and Sir Richard Pole.

But even the heraldic writer, with his eye on precedence and protocol, simply could not ignore the sheer emotion of the event. Carrying Arthur's arms, witnessing the final march of his horse, and being surrounded by his imagery and symbolism must have been overwhelming. As the writer notes, to have seen the weeping after the offering was done, 'he had a herd hert that wept not.'[9]

Each man knew that following weeks of extended mourning, the final moment was upon them. Like many mourners today, the act of organising a funeral had perhaps provided a welcome distraction from grief. The plans were elaborate and hastily assembled and there had been much to occupy their minds. But soon it would all be over. The floodgates of emotions finally opened.

The Earls – Surrey, Shrewsbury, and Kent – who had known Arthur the least, performed their task with composure. They each draped a pall of cloth of gold over the coffin. Arthur's great friend, Gruffydd ap Rhys offered the deacon the rich embroidered banner of the prince's arms. For the final time, the bishops incensed the body. Arthur's gentlemen servants lifted the coffin and marched it to the south end of the high altar where the grave had been dug. They had served him, laughed with him, guided him, and planned their future around him. As they lowered the body into the grave, their tears fell with him. The Bishop of Lincoln set the cross over the chest and scattered holy water and earth upon it. He had been the president of Arthur's council. Commissioned by the king and the king's mother to keep their prodigy safe. Through no fault of his own, he had failed. He wept marvellously. Each of Arthur's men had performed their last act of service. A dead Prince had no further need of a household, servants, or almsmen. William Uvdale and Richard Cofte, in an act of great finality, broke their staffs of service and surrendered them to Arthur's grave. The gentlemen ushers did likewise with their rods. Each of these great men, despite their knightly status and mighty ambitions, sobbed like children. 'It was a pitious sight, who had sene it.'[10]

Chapter 18

King Arthur

The reign of Arthur's brother, Henry VIII, was one of the most remembered in English history. That's partly because, across four decades of drama, his rule was bathed in every colour of the rainbow. The accounts of his endless marriages, controversial divorces and spectacular beheadings are dripping with the stuff that thrillers are made of. If a fiction writer presented Henry's story to a publisher, they would probably be told to go away and tone it down. But all of these spectacles – colourful and enticing though they are – risk disguising the real consequences of his reign. A time in which the fabric of England was fundamentally changed forever.

The break with the church. A revolution in the role of Parliament. The placing of women in the succession. The construction of England's first real navy. Each of these would help shape the divisive destiny of the century that would follow and sowed the seeds of the imperial future that caused Britannia to emerge as the major world power of the eighteenth and nineteenth centuries. It might sound glorious. But most achievements attributed to Henry VIII were secured by accident, luck or brutal tyranny. Whether Henry was actually an effective king remains a subject of fierce debate.

It is because Henry's reign is seen as such a seismic shift, that Arthur's death is often billed as a major turning point in English history. Had Arthur lived, England would have been 'spared' the reign of the brutal tyrant and, for better or for worse, England's destiny may have assumed a very different shape. But how different would the reign of King Arthur have been? And what possible signs and indications can we search for to even begin attempting to answer an entirely speculative question? To Francis Bacon, Henry VII's seventeenth century biographer, the question was a non-starter. He argued that:

> 'Of this Prince, in respect he died so young and by reason of his father's manner of education, that did cast no great lustre upon his children, there is little particular memory. Only thus remaineth, that he was very studious and learned beyond his years and beyond the custom of great Princes.'[1]

While the question of what Arthur's Kingship might have looked like is fundamentally unanswerable, we can try and be a little more ambitious than Bacon.

Yes, we will never know what kind of man, let alone king, Arthur would have proved to be. But there are three areas we can explore that may help us imagine with credibility. The first, is to dismiss some of the lazy tropes that automatically assume that Arthur possessed a different temperament, worldview and set of priorities to his more famous brother. The second is to set what would have been Arthur's reign in the context of reforms to monarchy, government and society that began under his grandfather, were accelerated by his father and eventually, perhaps reluctantly – progressed by his brother. And thirdly, we can take what we know of Arthur's character, background, beliefs, and experiences and creatively speculate how he might have applied them to the challenges of the sixteenth century.

As we have already seen, there is legitimate reason to believe that Arthur was a fundamentally different character to his infamous brother. While Arthur was raised with a heavy burden upon him from a young age, Henry was nurtured in a more carefree environment. There may well be reason, as this book has argued, to suppose that Arthur spent more time in the bosom of his family than is often assumed. But Henry still had greater access to their parents. He almost certainly saw more of what we would call their 'fun sides'. This must have had a profound impact on the character development of both. Even if – strictly speaking – we lack the evidence to be sure of it. While their father was letting young Henry beat him at cards, Arthur was learning about Royal life the hard way. He was pressing his claim against rival lords, fighting for power among his councillors and even dispatching men to put down armed rebellion. Their approach to work, study, diligence, and festival would have been markedly different as a result. While Henry loved to perform to a crowd, Arthur seemed less comfortable in the spotlight. The younger brother was at ease with people and while Arthur may have enjoyed a bawdy joke with his friends, there was likely always a distance between prince and servant which was impossible to overcome.

Yet none of these differences make it more likely that Arthur would have been any less ruthless a ruler than his brother. In fact, without Henry's gregarious nature, Arthur's entire court and government might have seemed both more austere and severe than the one that Henry presided over. The contrasts between the fun-loving, show-off Henry and the serious, dutiful Arthur have led to more lazy contrasts being assumed in the public imagination. While spoilt Henry reacted to not getting his own way by finding a head to chop off, measured Arthur would have taken a calmer approach to the challenges that faced England in the decades of his reign.

Maybe. But probably not. Arthur was being brought up to be an effective ruler. But he was not being raised to be a nice man. He wasn't being raised to be a cruel one either. He certainly learnt about the concepts of charity, grace, mercy, and clemency that were essential in a renaissance prince. But it was pressed into him from a young age that his rights as a prince, and later a king must be respected and honoured.

In his regional government of Wales and the surrounding counties, this was a theory that Arthur was beginning to put into practice. His council ruthlessly pursued his own rights. They were remorseless in collecting debt and harvesting his feudal interests. They levied heavy taxes on Chester and clamped down on abuses of Stannary rights in Cornwall. He did forgive men that wronged him. But it usually came at a cost.

Perhaps Arthur had no real influence on any of these decisions. But while there is evidence that his councillors had to keep an eye on his commendable generosity to servants, there is nothing to suggest they had to reign in a natural desire for clemency. Maybe the evidence for his boyish protests for mercy simply doesn't survive. Or perhaps, more likely, he simply believed his councillors were doing a good job of defending Royal interest. By the time he was a teenager, he would certainly have known what they were up to.

It might well be that Arthur's reign would have proved less bloody than his brother's. Like his father, he would perhaps have been more likely to part a man from his money than his head. But like Henry, Arthur too was the grandson of the blood-thirsty Edward IV and the York tendency for brutality may well have raised its bloody head within Arthur. He too would have been seasoned by the challenges of kingship. He too would have learnt the necessity of brutality.

Arthur was certainly better prepared for the realities of rule. He may well have manipulated the levers of power to get what he wanted more effectively than his brother. He may have been less easily led by agenda-based courtiers and restrained some of the worst excesses of the need that all kings have for blood shed. But let's make no mistake. Arthur could be every bit as ruthless as a prince needed to be. We cannot say with any confidence that those that crossed him as king, be it wives that failed to produce sons, bishops that refused to obey or ministers that were unable to deliver, would have met any less ruthlessness than they did under his brother.

Had Arthur, rather than Henry, become King in 1509, he would have wielded one clear advantage: he would surely have held a much better grasp on the institutions of government. The ancient nobility was fundamental to the effective functioning of medieval England. The sixty or so families that held great estates, possessed grand titles, and inherited their right to sit in Parliament. The King's role was to maintain order among the nobles, policing their quarrels and enabling them to prosper. They, in turn, managed relations with the lower but crucial class of 'gentry' landowners. The nobility expected to be consulted on crucial aspects of policy. In return, they recruited men for the king's armies and enforced his laws across the Kingdom.

But this system, which had probably always owed more to theory than practice, had come under considerable strain during the Wars of the Roses. Order among the nobility had collapsed and the shockwaves echoed across the country. While Arthur's grandfather, Edward IV, had managed to rebuild a semblance of rule through the ancient blood of the realm, it was clear to the early Tudors that wider reforms were necessary.

By the end of Henry VII's reign, Kingship was emerging as a more structured and autocratic institution. The size of the Royal demesne – the land owned directly by the King – increased dramatically. This enabled Henry to build a great affinity among the gentry class, by appointing his own men to stewardships and offices across vast estates. They could enjoy the revenue of the land while Henry retained the ownership. In return for their bolstered fortunes, they would quickly array troops for the King at times of crisis. Never again would the king be so dependent on the dubious loyalty of the great lords of the realm. Such reforms strengthened the king's hand. But they also sent a clear message to the ambitious men of the Kingdom: if you want to progress, grow rich and gain influence, service to the king was the path to pursue.

Henry's more institutional approach to kingship can be seen across his government. He favoured diplomacy over war. Rather than rely on the nobility to maintain order across the country, he made greater use of the court system. And while he never grew to trust men of the old blood of the realm, he kept them in check through the threat of fines and limits to their freedom. Strictly speaking, few of Henry's tactics were new. They had all been used by various English kings before him, particularly Arthur's grandfather, Edward IV who had begun his own series of modifications. But the instruments and machinery of government grew significantly under Henry VII. It's an exaggeration to say that his reign sowed the seeds of the modern state. But not an outrageous one.

This style of Kingship did not suit the first Tudor's 17-year-old successor, Henry VIII. He made quick and public efforts to distance himself from his father's rule. Two of the elder Henry's counsellors were executed on trumped-up charges and the young king quickly began to draw the old blood of the realm into his trusted circle. Part of the reason for Henry VIII's change of direction was a sensitivity to the public mood. His father's policies had become more extreme in his later years as he grew ever more insecure and tyrannical. But it was probably deeper than that. Henry, unlike his father, was truly of the old, Plantagenet blood of England. He wanted to govern like a heroic king of chivalry. Not an old, boring bureaucrat.

To the nobility, Henry's ascension was a breath of fresh air. In the first decade of his reign, they were back in power. Margaret of Clarence, Yorkist princess and widow of Arthur's chamberlain, Richard Pole was granted her ancestral title as Countess of Salisbury. Thomas Howard was restored to the Dukedom of Norfolk.

Men such as Henry's first cousin, the Marquess of Dorset were given crucial military commands based on their blood status rather than their competence. It was, at least on the surface, just like the old days.

There was just one problem. It didn't work. Across two decades of reform, Henry VII had turned government into a big administrative machine. And that machine needed attention. The elder Henry had managed this by pouring over the finer detail of government. The younger, who hated writing and suffered from a short attention span, was never going to follow suit. Nor did anyone want him to. A King more interested in the pursuit of pleasure was far easier to control.

By the end of Henry VIII's first decade in power, an ambitious and highly talented churchman named Thomas Wolsey had emerged as the solution. He, with the king's blessing, had inserted himself at the centre of government. If the king was not a man to commit himself to the detail of business, he needed a servant that could. In the process, Henry and Wolsey effectively created the untitled but very real role of "chief minister" which was to dominate Henrician and Elizabethan politics.

The early years of Henry VIII's reign, therefore, represent a lost decade in the reform of government. High spending on entertainment bolstered the mood at court. Botched attempts at war with France may have provided fleeting moments of glory. But little progress was made in devising intelligent strategies to govern England effectively. Had it been Arthur, rather than Henry, that had succeeded their father, this decade would probably have been put to better use. Due to his training, experience - and probably his temperament - Arthur would have been much better placed to insert himself at the head of the kind of government that his father had constructed. While Henry VIII had needed to publicly distance himself from his father's policies, had Arthur survived in 1502, his father would probably never have grown so insecure and tyrannical. Arthur, while wanting to make his own mark, may not have seen the need for such a dramatic change of direction. In many respects, Arthur's administration at Ludlow was already a government in waiting. The men that served in his household and on his council could have expected an influential role and great reward. No wonder their tears fell so heavily as they cast their prince into the ground. Under Arthur, England may have entered the 1520s with a highly sophisticated system of government. As a man trained to master detail quickly, he may have felt no need for the 'chief minister' role that his brother so relied upon. Would he, as a result, have been less susceptible to faction than his brother, Henry VIII debatably grew to be?

What any of this would have meant for England, is difficult to say. It could have led to the creation of a more fair and balanced government. But it may have seen Arthur emerge as an even more autocratic ruler than his brother. He would almost certainly have managed the Royal coffers better. Though it's far from impossible that as the son-in-law of the Spanish King that Arthur too, would have been unable to resist the temptation for war with France.

Arthur had been named for a fabled ruler that personified medieval kingship. One that had ruled with knights around a table and forged his reign on valour, honour, and courage. But the real Arthur's inheritance would have been one of a growing institution and a burgeoning bureaucracy. Centralisation, administration, and the beginnings of meritocracy are the Tudor's governmental legacy. Arthur would likely have embraced them with enthusiasm. Despite his initial attempts to restore the medieval and chivalric kingship of old, Arthur's brother Henry would eventually emerge as another great reformer of government. Even today, historians furiously debate exactly what his legacy was, how much he strengthened the hand of Parliament and whether he, inadvertently, sowed the seeds for a clash between King and Commons that would cause the outbreak of the civil war of the seventeenth century. What isn't disputed however, is that Henry's lasting legacy was his decision to split with the Roman Catholic Church and declare himself head of the Church of England.

The early sixteenth century was a time of great religious upheaval across Christendom. A group of theological reformers, led by a German theologian called Martin Luther, had formed a powerful movement which was questioning fundamental Catholic doctrines around the nature of salvation, the Holy sacraments, and the power of the Pope.

Henry VIII's decision to break with the Pope were not motivated by these theological considerations. Earlier in his reign, he had even written a treaty that denounced them. But by the mid-1520s, it became clear that Katherine of Aragon, Arthur's widow, and Henry VIII's wife since 1509, was not going to provide the King with a son and heir. At around the same time, he fell in love with an English woman called Anne Boleyn. He was determined to put Katherine aside and make Anne his wife.

There was just one major problem: the Pope refused to grant an annulment. Katherine's nephew, Charles V, had emerged as the major powerhouse of Europe. Not only was he King of Spain and Duke of Burgundy, in 1519 he had replaced his father as Holy Roman Empire. And he was in no mind to see his aunt cast aside in favour of an English upstart. After years of negotiating, Henry finally had Parliament declare the king head of the Church in England. The Kingdom was now on a spiritual path distinct from the continent and it's king was the principal policy maker. Henry now ruled over the bodies and souls of his people. An increase to his power that defied magna carta and made him the most powerful man to ever wear the crown of England.

In today's 'emotionally intelligent' society we tend to downplay the wider political, economic, and religious considerations that shape great historical changes. Instead, we favour a more human and personal explanation. This can be exceedingly dangerous. But in the case of England's break with Rome, such an understanding is entirely correct. There were other factors at play; yet without Henry's desire to free himself from Katherine and make Anne his Queen, this monumental watershed in England's history simply would not have occurred.

As such, we can say with confidence that, had Arthur lived, it is highly unlikely that England would have so drastically parted ways with Rome in 1533. But this does not mean that there would have been no change in England's religious fabric. We know little of Arthur's own personal theological leanings. Yet, there is every reason to question the oft-cited notion that, had the prince lived, England would today be a Catholic country.

Arthur would have understood the importance of leaving a strong and stable succession as much as Henry VIII. To their worldview, that would have meant leaving a son, and preferably multiple sons, to succeed them. While there's no guarantee that Arthur and Katherine would have been able to "succeed" where Henry and Katherine had 'failed', they would certainly have had time on their side. Arthur would probably have begun a regular sexual relationship with his wife when they reached their late teens. They could have reaped the fruits of youth's fertility. And, even if Katherine and Arthur had not produced a boy, it seems unlikely that Arthur would ever have cast her aside. He could be just as ruthless as his brother. But he had also been invested in the Spanish marriage since he was old enough to remember.

The circumstances that created the independence of the Church of England simply don't exist in a scenario where Arthur lives. But how would Arthur have responded to the wider religious influences that were rippling across Europe? While little attention has been paid to this by historians, Prince Arthur had one major thing in common with Martin Luther, that infamous reformer. They were both, indirectly, students of St Augustine of Hippo.

St Augustine was a fifth-century theologian, widely regarded as one of the founding fathers of Christian thinking. Martin Luther had been an Augustine friar and it was Augustinian theology that helped shape the thinking that created reformed doctrine. It was Augustine who placed a strong emphasis on the sovereignty of God, the doctrine of predestination and a salvation that was not dependent on outward appearances. Today, some theologians argue - perhaps too simplistically – that the reformation was little more than a reassertion of Augustine's theology.

Arthur had been raised under Augustine's theological shadow. Like Luther, Arthur's tutor Bernard André was an Augustine friar. He and Arthur studied Augustine's seminal works and the ancient church father was probably the greatest intellectual influence on the young Arthur's theological development. Of course, we have no insight into how seriously Arthur took any of this. We know next to nothing about his devotional practices, his attitude to scripture or his interest in theology. And many, many of those discipled in the ways of Augustine never embraced reform, going to their graves as fierce Catholics. Nevertheless, such influences on the young Arthur should give us pause before assuming that he would have remained forever a faithful son of Rome.

Assuming that his reign had lasted into the 1540s, Arthur would have begun to face a number of financial challenges. However well he had managed the Royal coffers. When in crisis, the Tudor instinct was always to centralise: to draw more power to the king. Henry VIII, with the help of Cromwell, soon cottoned on to the fact that his own, peculiar reformation gave him license to take huge parcels of land from the monasteries to enrich himself and his servants.

Would such a potential windfall of resources have escaped Arthur's notice at a time when he was feeling the pinch? Would a Tudor centraliser, such as himself, resent the fact that the Church represented a sometimes-stubborn power block that remained free from the king's control?

We shall never know the answers to these questions. We certainly don't have sufficient evidence to articulate what Arthur's policy toward the church would have been. But there is sufficient room to doubt that the Catholic future of England would have been entirely safe in King Arthur's hands.

That Arthur's death changed the course of the sixteenth century makes for a good headline. But, as we have seen, an educated guess as to what the reign of a second King Arthur could have looked like makes such a claim difficult to substantiate with any certainty. While the circumstances of his reign would have been markedly different to that of his brother, Henry, many of the signature aspects of his rule may not. A shift toward autocracy, a ruthless approach to dealing with enemies, and further reforms of government. Under Arthur, it's even possible that religious reform may still have found its way to English shores and into the hearts of policymakers.

However, for the individuals who would dominate the English court in the early sixteenth century, life would have been radically difficult under the rule of King Arthur. It is difficult to see how either Wolsey or Cromwell – Henry VIII's influential ministers – would have grasped hold of as much power. Men who had served Arthur faithfully, such as Willoughby and St John would probably have secured positions of prominence. And if Henry VIII had never come to the throne, six women in particular would have lived very different lives. Katherine Parr, the sixth wife of Henry VIII, would never have been Queen of England. After the death of her second husband in 1543, she would have been a reasonably comfortable widow and could perhaps take a husband more of her choosing. Katheryn Howard, the wife that Henry had put to death at just 21 years of age for a misjudged dalliance, might have lived to become an old woman. With her mixed fortunes of no money but good connections, she may have made a decent, gentry marriage. Anne of Cleves would likely never have left Germany. Through either a marriage to a German Prince, or an honourable spinsterhood, she would have been spared the public humiliation of rejection.

Jane Seymour may have escaped death in childbirth. Though that was a common risk for women of the day. Anne Boleyn, with her clear charisma and obvious ability, would perhaps have made an advantageous match. But more than anyone else however, it is the destiny of his wife and almost life-long fiancé that would have been most transformed by Arthur's survival.

The years following Arthur's death were turbulent and traumatic for Katherine of Aragon. Her initial expectation might have been to be sent home to Spain, which would surely be of some comfort. But at that precise moment in international affairs her parents, the Spanish monarchs needed European allies. The friendship of the English would be better secured if the princess remained in situ and be pledged in marriage to Henry, the new Prince of Wales and heir to the throne.

Henry, however, was just 11 years of age. He could not marry Katherine for at least three years, creating plenty of time for political uncertainty to unsettle her position. At one stage Henry VII even threatened to marry the girl himself. A suggestion that must have horrified Katherine as much as it scandalised her parents. When Katherine's mother died in 1504, the princess lost a powerful protector. Her father, Ferdinand, quickly fell out with Henry VII. Katherine was then consigned to a long limbo where she was neither married to her prince nor permitted to return to Spain. Neither father nor father-in-law provided for her adequately, forcing her to embrace the struggles of genteel poverty.

In 1507, Katherine, lonely and isolated, received a glimmer of hope. Her father finally honoured her wishes and dispatched a Spanish confessor to take charge of her spiritual wellbeing. Katherine herself was delighted by the arrival of her spiritual father, Fray Diego Fernandez. But others close to her had significant concerns. No doubt sensing the vulnerability of the princess, the confessor quickly became a controlling figure in her life. According to Gutierre Gomez de Fuensalida, who returned to England as Spanish ambassador, Fernandez's influence over the princess was creating a scandal. He would admonish her over the pettiest of sins. Eventually, Fuensalid wrote to Ferdinand to report a highly concerning incident:

> 'Lately he [Fernandez] made her [Katherine] do a thing which much grieved the King. It was this, that whilst staying in a lonely house which is in a park, the King of England wished to go to Richmond, and sent to say to the Princess that next day her Highness and Madame Mary his daughter should be at Richmond, where he would go before or after them.

'The Princess obeyed the order, but next day when she was about to start, and Madame Mary was waiting for her with the company deputed to go with them, the friar came and said to the Princess, "You shall not go to-day." It is true that the princess had vomited that night. The princess said, "I am well; I do not wish to stay here alone." He said, "I tell you that upon pain of mortal sin you do not go to-day."

The Princess contended that she was well, and that she did not wish to stay there alone. The friar, however, persevered so much that the Princess, not to displease him, determined to remain. When Madame Mary had been waiting for more than two hours she sent to tell Madame Mary to go, but that she did not feel well. The English who witnessed this and had seen the Princess at mass and at table, rode off with Madame Mary and went away, whilst the Princess remained alone with her women and only the Maestre Sala and her chamberlain, who had been absent and came by chance. The distance was at the utmost less than one league.

There is no need to speak of the provisions the Princess had that night, for as the contingency was not expected it was not provided for, nor did they give themselves much trouble to provide for it. Next day the King of England did not again give an order to send for the Princess, as though she had been staying in such company as suited her, and they tell me that the King was very much vexed at her remaining there. The following day the Princess went [to Richmond] accompanied by no other living creature than three women on horseback, the Maestre Sala, the chamberlain, and the friar, a numerous [company]! These and other things of a thousand times worse kind the friar makes her do. It is more than 20 days since the King last saw the Princess, nor has he, since her staying away, sent to know how she is, although she had been ill'.[2]

The nineteenth-century scholar that discovered and translated this letter treated it with typical Victorian moral outrage. This proves, he argued, that Katherine was not the bastion of purity that other sources present her as. She was clearly infatuated with the confessor and allowed him far too much power over her. Katherine, like so many others, could not 'bear close examination without their characters being more or less lowered in our estimation.'[3]

We, of course, would see it rather differently. Was Katherine irresponsible for letting her affections get the better of her? Or was she a vulnerable girl, desperate for friendship, ruthlessly taken advantage of by a man she believed she could trust?

If this letter can be taken as truth – and we must also maintain a degree of caution when Spanish officials are trying to undermine one another – then the confessor's behaviour was that of an abuser. He made Katherine feel bad about herself. He made it clear that going against his wishes would cost her his affections. He even cut her off from other sources of support.

What Arthur and Katherine's marriage would have been like we will never know. There is no real evidence that during their time together they formed a particular bond, but nor is there anything to suggest that they wouldn't. What we can be clear on, is that if Arthur had not perished in 1502, Katherine would not have endured years in the political and dynastic wilderness. A wilderness that left her on the brink of poverty and vulnerable to the clutches of an abusive power relationship.

Epilogue

The Shadow of a Prince

When a grief-stricken Elizabeth of York had comforted her husband and offered him another child to replace the one painfully torn from them, she knew full well that she was taking a monumental risk. The Queen's pregnancies had never been easy, and it is likely that, mindful of the risk to her health, the King and Queen had deliberately avoided a pregnancy for the past five years. True to her word, Elizabeth fell pregnant quickly. On 2 February 1503, she gave birth to a baby girl, named Katherine. Just nine days later the Queen was dead. Her new-born child quickly followed her to the grave. Henry VII had never enjoyed an easy life. But the demise of his wife caused him greater pain than anything he had endured before. Coming less than a year after Arthur's death, the King was finally overwhelmed by grief. He took to his chamber, and none were admitted.

The loss of Elizabeth, Henry's love, friend, and partner in the building of a dynasty, marked a tragic turning point in his reign. Though he had long been austere and spend-thrift, his tendency toward avarice would now flow unchecked. Even his 'official' historian, Polydore Vergil says that all Henry's considerable virtues were 'obscured latterly by avarice. In a monarch indeed it may be considered the worst vice since it is harmful to everyone.'

Arthur's death had led not only to the breaking of his father's heart, but to a series of policy decisions that forever damaged Henry VII's reputation. It is only now that historians are starting to seriously reassess the first Tudor king and rescue him from the reputation of a tyrannous miser.

Prince Henry had been devastated by the loss of his mother. We have no way of knowing whether he felt similarly dismayed by the death of his brother, but it was Arthur's death in 1502 that truly changed the course of the 11-year-old prince's life.

No longer was Henry the carefree younger son, indulged by his mother and spoilt by his father. He was now heir to the throne and the sole hope of Tudor succession. But despite losing his easier-going lifestyle and sheltered existence, the young Henry was never to enjoy Arthur's independent status as heir to the throne. He was created Prince of Wales shortly after his brother's death, but there seems to have been no great ceremony to mark the occasion. While he was titular head of the council of Wales and the Marches, as Arthur had been, he was never dispatched to Ludlow to head a household and government of his own. Henry VII almost certainly felt Arthur's isolation from his family had contributed to his early demise. His surviving son was staying close.

Arthur's death left his widow Katherine in the political wilderness. As we saw in the previous chapter, she was quickly engaged to Prince Henry. But the youth of the prince meant it would be some years before they could feasibly marry. In that time, the death of Katherine's mother and shifting continental allegiances consigned the princess to the political wilderness and left her at the mercy of her unscrupulous confessor. Katherine's fortunes changed dramatically in 1509. Henry VIII ascended the throne in the immediate wake of his father's death and decided to take Katherine for his queen. The princess, now aged 23, married the 18-year-old king almost immediately.

To start with, it seemed like a match made in heaven. But it wasn't long before cracks started to appear. Henry quickly took mistresses and, after an early period of influence, the queen's voice on matters of politics and global affairs was gradually silenced. None of this would have greatly mattered to either member of the couple if the marriage had been fruitful. But by 1526 and after seventeen years of marriage, it had become clear that Katherine would never give Henry the son he so desperately believed he needed.

Arthur's name had been largely absent from the Tudor records following his death. His affairs were wrapped up quickly and there was little merit in reminding his heart-broken father of the treasured son he had so tragically lost. Nor was there any great desire, once Henry VIII had ascended, to draw attention to the fact that it was the spare, rather than the heir who was wearing the crown of England.

But in Henry VIII's attempts to divorce Katherine of Aragon, Arthurs ghost was hastily resurrected. The prince's former servants were assembled to testify that he had been a lusty and vigorous teenager that had taken great delight in boasting about his sexual exploits. Former servants of the princess came together in Spain to denounce him as a weak and frail boy who could never have been much good as a husband. What Katherine thought of Arthur, all these years later, remains a mystery. Did she inwardly curse the reckless child who had bragged about a sexual exploit that she knew full well to have been a fiction? Did she secretly pine for her tender prince, who would surely never have treated her as savagely as his younger brother?

Sadly, it is far more likely that Katherine scarcely thought of Arthur at all. Their marriage had been brief, and almost everything she would have associated with him would have reminded her of lonely and isolating experiences which led to little but years in the wilderness. Henry, despite his cruelty, was the man she had grown to love. Perhaps she even reflected to herself, that had it not been for the inconvenience of her pitiful first marriage, she and Henry could truly have been happy.

*

The Shadow of a Prince

On 30 September 1553, Queen Mary I was led in glorious victory from the Tower of London to Westminster Abbey. Riding in an adorned open litter with a small crown on her head, she was followed by coaches of the great lords and ladies of the realm. It was a crucial moment in history. Mary was about to become the first woman to be crowned Queen of England.

The streets were hung with tapestry, decorated with triumphal arches and the procession was a memorable one. In the days that followed Mary would take an oath to her people, create new knights of the Bath, and come into her power as ruler of the realm. It was a moment to face the future. But first, Mary had to make her peace with the past.

Among her first acts was to contact her cousin, Charles V. She pleaded with him to send any documentation in his keeping that signified the Pope's judgement that her parents, Henry VIII and Katherine of Aragon had been legally married and that her mother's first marriage to Prince Arthur, the uncle she had never known, had not been consummated. With it, she could remove the stain of bastardy from herself and walk into her new role with her head held high. This is one of the last mentions of Arthur in Tudor records. When he was born in 1486, he represented the great hope of the Tudor dynasty. An end to the Wars of the Roses and an era of England's triumph on the European stage. Now, just 67 years later, he had been reduced to an administrative inconvenience that his niece could quickly solve. He had once been the centre of the Tudor story. Now he was being written out of it.

Too often, conversations about Arthur revolve around what he did or didn't do during a five-month marriage that represents just a tiny fraction of his days on earth. His life, like all our lives, had far more meaning than that. Young though he was, he had witnessed some of the most tumultuous events in England's history. Through his own determination he grew to take a leading role in his own affairs and came close to shaping his destiny. It is my great hope that this book makes some small contribution to telling Arthur's story: a story that deserves to be heard. Arthur Tudor was more than the prince that died. He was a boy that really lived.

Notes

Chapter one

1. Geoffrey of Monmouth
2. André
3. Memoir
4. Memoir
5. Griffiths, Ralph A., and Thomas, Roger S. "The Making of the Tudor Dynasty" pp 7-8
6. Griffiths and Thomas pp 26-29
7. Bayani p 16
8. Bayani p 18
9. Griffiths and Thomas p 40
10. André
11. Vergil
12. Vergil
13. Vergil
14. Croyland

Chapter two

1. Calendar of State Papers: Spain
2. Parliamentary Rolls of Medieval England, available at www.british-history.ac.uk
3. Francis Bacon
4. Materials for a History for the Reign of Henry VII
5. André, Bernard, *The Life of Henry VII*
6. A history of the country of Hampshire, available at www.british-history.ac.uk
7. Materials
8. André
9. Anglo, Sydney, "Spectacle Pageantry and Early Tudor Policy", Clarendon Press, Oxford.
10. https://www.british-history.ac.uk/vch/hants/vol2/pp108-115
11. Weir, Alison, "Elizabeth of York"

12. Leland, John, *Antiquarii de Rebus Britannicis Collectanea*
13. Ordinances
14. Beaufort book of hours

Chapter 3

1. Leland
2. Orme, Nicholas, *From Childhood to Chivalry*
3. Leland
4. Leland
5. License, Amy, *Edward IV and Elizabeth Woodville*
6. License
7. Vergil
8. Jones and Underwood, *The King's Mother*
9. R.S. Thomas, Oxford Dictionary of National Biography
10. ODNB
11. Leland
12. https://zenodo.org/record/1431417#.YXrRG57MI2w
13. Materials
14. Leland
15. Sean Cunningham, Oxford Dictionary of National Biography
16. Leland
17. Leland

Chapter 4

1. Hobbins, Daniel, "*Bernard André, The Life of Henry VII*"
2. Leland
3. Vergil
4. Vergil
5. Leland
6. Vergil
7. Vergil
8. Hall
9. Vergil
10. Rosemary Horrox, Oxford Dictionary of National Biography
11. Horrox
12. Michael Jones, Oxford Dictionary of National Biography
13. Vergil
14. Vergil
15. Vergil

16. Hall
17. Original letters, illustrative of English history: 1418-1529
18. David Starkey, Henry, Virtuous Prince
19. Starkey
20. Vergil
21. Vergil
22. Vergil
23. Vergil
24. Vergil
25. Vergil
26. Vergil
27. Nathen Amine, Henry VII and the Tudor pretenders
28. Vergil
29. Hall
30. Hall
31. Vergil, Hall
32. Bacon
33. Find reference
34. Matthew Lewis, The Survival of the Princes in the Tower
35. André
36. Wier
37. Materials v2
38. Vergil

Chapter 5

1. Ordinances
2. Orme
3. CPR
4. CPR
5. https://www.farnham-castle.com/
6. CSP: Spain
7. Materials
8. Orme
9. Materials
10. Ordinances
11. Ordinances
12. Orme
13. Orme
14. Materials
15. Materials

16. Ordinances
17. Materials
18. André
19. André
20. Orme
21. Orme
22. Materials
23. CSP: Spain
24. CSP: Spain
25. CSP: Spain, Ian Arthurson
26. CSP: Spain
27. CSP: Spain
28. CSP: Spain
29. CSP: Spain
30. CSP: Spain
31. Materials
32. CSP: Spain
33. CSP: Spain
34. CSP: Spain
35. CSP: Spain
36. Arthurson
37. Parliamentary Rolls
38. Memoir – but check
39. Memoir

Chapter 6

1. Leland
2. Leland
3. Leland
4. Leland
5. Risk, James C. The History of the Order of the Bath and its Insignia
6. Leland
7. Starkey
8. Starkey
9. Leland
10. Starkey
11. Leland
12. Leland
13. Leland

Chapter 7

1. CPR
2. Given-Wilson, Chris, *The English Nobility in the Late Middle Ages*
3. BL Add MS 7099 f2
4. CPR
5. CPR
6. Ian Arthurson, *The Perkin Warbeck Conspiracy 1491-1499*
7. Arthurson
8. Arthurson
9. Arthurson
10. CPR
11. CPR

Chapter 8

1. CPR
2. CPR
3. Shoesmith, Ron, *Ludlow Castle,* Logaston Press (2006)
4. CSP: Spain
5. The Tudor Travel Guide, https://thetudortravelguide.com/2019/03/23/tickenhill-house/
6. Given-Wilson
7. Oxford NDB
8. Orme
9. NDB
10. CPR
11. Vergil
12. Vergil
13. Arthurson
14. Stanley
15. Vergil
16. Vergil

Chapter 9

1. Carlson, David, *Royal Tutors in the Reign of Henry VII*
2. E101/413/2/2 folio 32r
3. Carlson

4. Carlson
5. André
6. ODNB
7. André
8. Carlson
9. Carlson
10. Morgan-Guy, John, *Arthur, Harri Tudor and the Iconography of Loyalty in Wales*, in *Arthur Tudor, Prince of Wales*
11. CSP: Spain
12. Anglo
13. Gunn
14. Boffey, Julia, *Henry VII's London in the Great Chronicle*

Chapter 10

1. Cunningham, Sean, Prince Arthur: the Tudor King who never was
2. CSP: Milan
3. CSP: Milan
4. CSP: Venice
5. CSP: Venice
6. E101/414/6 folio 87r
7. E101/414/6 folio 87r
8. André
9. Weir, *Elizabeth of York*
10. Starkey, *Henry: virtuous Prince*
11. Bowker, Margaret, *Oxford Dictionary of National Biography*
12. Gunn, Steven
13. Cunningham, Sean
14. André

Chapter 11

1. CSP: Spain
2. CSP: Spain
3. CSP: Spain
4. CSP: Spain
5. CSP: Spain
6. CSP: Spain
7. CSP: Spain
8. CSP: Spain

9. E101/414/6 folio 37r
10. CSP: Venice
11. CSP: Spain

Chapter 12

1. Autograph letter by Prince Arthur, to Katherine of Aragon, in Clarke, Andrea, *Tudor Monarchs Lives in Letters*
2. CSP Spain
3. CSP: Spain
4. CSP: Venice
5. CSP: Spain
6. CSP: Spain
7. CSP: Spain
8. CSP: Spain
9. CSP: Spain
10. CSP: Spain

Chapter 13

1. Unless otherwise stated, all quotes and references in this chapter are sourced from Kipling, Gordon, *The Receyt of the Ladie Kateryne*
2. BL Add MS 7099 folio 73
3. CSP: Spain
4. CSP: Spain
5. Cunningham
6. Anglo

Chapter 14

1. This section is based on "The portraiture of Prince Arthur and Katherine of Aragon" by Frederick Hepburn in Gunn & Monckton's *Arthur Tudor, Prince of Wales*
2. CSP: Spain
3. Starkey, *Six Wives*
4. Hepburn
5. CSP: Spain
6. Williams, Patrick, Katherine of Aragon

7. CSP: Spain
8. CSP: Spain
9. Williams
10. Manchester, Duke of, *Court and Society from Elizabeth to Anne: edited from the papers at Kimbolton by the Duke of Manchester*
11. Tremlett, Giles, *Katherine of Aragon*

Chapter 15

1. Letters and Papers, Foreign and Domestic, Henry VIII, Volume 4 1524-1530
2. Tremlett
3. CSP: Spain
4. Thurston, Herbert, *The Divorce of Henry VIII,* in *An Irish Quarterly Review, March 1932 Vol 21*
5. CSP: Spain

Chapter 16

1. CSP: Spain
2. CSP: Spain
3. CSP: Spain
4. CSP: Spain
5. Court and society
6. Cunningham
7. Gunn, Steven,
8. Morgan-Guy, John, *Arthur, Harri Tudor and the Iconography of Loyalty in Wales,* in *Arthur Tudor, Prince of Wales: Life, Death and Commemoration*

Chapter 17

1. Kipling
2. Cunningham
3. Kipling
4. CSP
5. Cunningham
6. Houlbrooke, Ralph, *Prince Arthur's Funeral,* in *Arthur Tudor Prince of Wales,* ed. Gunn & Monckton
7. Kipling
8. Cunningham

9. Kipling
10. Kipling

Chapter 18
1. Bacon
2. CSP: Spain
3. CSP: Spain

Selected Bibliography

Online sources

British History Online – https://www.british-history.ac.uk/ (providing access to the Calendar of State Papers, Calendar of Closed Roll, Parliamentary Rolls of Medieval England and many other essential sources)
Calendar of Patent Rolls, preserved in the Public Record office, available at – https://babel.hathitrust.org/
Farnham Castle Website – https://www.farnham-castle.com/
Oxford Dictionary of National Biography - https://www.oxforddnb.com/
Polydore Vergil, Anglica Historia (1555 version) - http://www.philological.bham.ac.uk/polverg/
Tudor Travel Guide – https://thetudortravelguide.com/

Primary sources

André, Bernard, *The Life of Henry VII,* translated and introduced by Daniel Hobbins, (Italica Press, 2011)
Boffey, Julia, *Henry VII's London in the Great Chronicle,* (Medieval Institute Publications, 2019)
Campbell, William, *Materials for a History for the Reign of Henry VII* (Eyre and Spottiswoode, 1877)
Clarke, Andrea, *Tudor Monarchs: Lives in Letters* (The British Library, 2017)
Ellis, Henry, *Original letters illustrative of English history,* (ULAN Press, 1923)
Hall, Edward, *The union of the two noble and illustre families of Lancastre & Yorke,* printed by (Paternoster, 1809)
Kipling, Gordon, *The Receyt of the Ladie Kateryne,* (Oxford University Press, 1990)
Leland, John, *Antiquarii de Rebus Britannicis Collectanea* ed. Thomas Hearne (London, 1770)

Manchester, Duke of, *Court and society from Elizabeth to Anne, edited from the papers at Kimbolton,* (Hurst and Blackett, 1864)

Nichols, John, *A collection of Ordinances and Regulations for the Government of the Royal Household made in divers reigns from King Edward III to King William and Queen Mary* (The Society of Antiquaries, 1787).

Secondary sources

Amine, Nathen, *Henry VII and the Tudor Pretenders* (Amberley Publishing, 2021)

Arthurson, Ian, *The Perkin Warbeck Conspiracy 1491-1499* (The History Press (2009)

Anglo, Sydney, "Spectacle Pageantry and Early Tudor Policy" (Clarendon Press, 1997)

Bacon, Francis, *The History of the Reign of King Henry VII* ed. Brian Vickers (Cambridge University Press, 1998)

Bayani, Debra, *Jasper Tudor: Godfather of the Tudor Dynasty* (Made Global Publishing, 2015)

Carlson, David, *Royal Tutors in the Reign of Henry VII,* in "The Sixteenth Century Journal, Summer, 1991, Vol.22 (Summer, 1991)

Chrimes, S. B. *Henry VII* (Yale University Press,1999)

Clegg, Melanie, *Margaret Tudor: The Life of Henry VIII's Sister* (Pen and Sword, 2018)

Cunningham, Sean, *Prince Arthur: The Tudor King Who Never Was* (Amberley Publishing, 2016)

Given-Wilson, Chris, *The English Nobility in the Late Middle Ages* (Routledge, 2002)

Griffiths, Ralph A., and Thomas, Roger S. *The Making of the Tudor dynasty* (The History Press, 2013)

Gunn, Steven & Monckton, Linda eds. *Arthur Tudor, Prince of Wales: Life, Death and Commemoration* (The Boydell Press, 2009)

Jones, Michael and Underwood, Malcolm, *The King's Mother* (Cambridge University Press, 1992)

Jones, Michael, *Bosworth: Psychology of a Battle* (John Murray, 2002)

Lewis, Matthew, *The Survival of the Princes in the Tower* (The History Press, 2018)

License, Amy, *Edward IV and Elizabeth Woodville* (Amberley Publishing, 2016)

Orme, Nicholas, *From Childhood to Chivalry* (University Press Cambridge, 1984)

Risk, James C. *The History of the Order of the Bath and its Insignia* (Spink & Son Ltd, 1972)

Shoesmith, Ron, *Ludlow Castle* (Logaston Press, 2006)

Starkey, David, *Henry, Virtuous Prince* (Harper Press, 2008)

Starkey, David, *Six Wives: The Queens of Henry VIII* (Vintage, 2004)

Selected Bibliography

Thurston, Herbert, *The Divorce of Henry VIII,* in *An Irish Quarterly Review, March 1932 Vol 21*

Tremlett, Giles, *Katherine of Aragon, Katherine of Aragon: Henry's Spanish Queen* (Faber and Faber, 2011)

Weir, Alison, *Elizabeth of York* (Vintage Books, 2013).

Williams, Patrick, *Katherine of Aragon* (Amberley Publishing, 2014)

Index

Alcock, John, Bishop, 31, 159
Alfonso, Earl of Chester, 60
Almor, John, 69
Ambassadors:
   Italian, 94–5, 98
   Spanish, 14, 49, 53–5, 91–2, 106, 113 (*see also* Puebla, Dr Gonzalvo de; Ayala, Don Pedro de)
André, Bernard, 8, 16, 33–4, 43–5, 52, 85–7, 96
Anjou, Queen Margaret of, 4, 6, 8, 27
Aragon, Katherine of, 54–7, 62, 105–14
   delays travel to England, 122–4
   arrives in England, 125–7
   eventually meets Arthur, 127–8
   marries Arthur, 131–3
   moves to Ludlow with Arthur, 155–61
   after Arthur's death, 180–5
   and Henry VIII, 145–6, 153, 184
   see also Arthur, Prince; Monarchs of Spain, Catholic
Arthur (Pendragon), King, 1–2, 17–18, 179
Arthur, Prince:
   conceived, 16
   birth, 2, 20
   choice of name, 17–18
   christening, 21–2, 28
   godparents, 22–32
   infant years, 48–53
   household, 51–2, 68–70, 159–60
   education, 52–3, 85–7, 96–7
   marriage to Katherine of Aragon, 54–7, 106–14, 131–3
   created Prince of Wales, 59–67
   and principality of Wales, 70, 75–81
   admitted to Order of the Bath, 62–4
   acts as regent, 73–5
   council, 78–81, 159
   and execution of Warwick and Warbeck, 118–21
   writes to Katherine, 115–16
   eventually meets Katherine, 127–8
   returns to Ludlow with Katherine, 155–61
   determination of character, 137–8
   health, 138–44, 152, 162–5
   musicians, 95–7
   portraiture, 134–6
   relationship with father, 95–7
   relationship with mother, 97–9
   relationship with siblings, 101–104
   and young companions, 87–8
   compared to Henry VIII, 172–7
   death, 147, 162–71
   see also Aragon, Katherine of
Arundel, Sir John, 30, 65, 79, 81
Atwater, John, Mayor of Cork, 71
Audley, Lord, 91
Austria, Margaret of, 121

Index

Ayala, Don Pedro de, 120–1, 140, 155–7
   see also Ambassadors: Spanish

Bacon, Francis, 43, 172
Barge, Royal, 61
Barnet, Battle of, 9, 27
Bath, Order of the, 62–4
Baynard's Castle, 156
Beaufort, John, Duke of Somerset, 23
Beaufort, Lady Margaret, 4–5, 10, 12, 20, 29, 38–9, 78
   and Arthur's christening, 22–6
   influence on Arthur, 99–102, 159
Bedford, Jasper Tudor, Duke of see Tudor, Jasper, Duke of Bedford
Bedford, John of Lancaster, Duke of, 22
Bereworth, Dr Stephen, 53
Berkely, Marquess of, 65
Bermondsey Abbey, 42, 99
Bewdley Manor, 77, 168–9
Blackheath, Battle of, 91
Blore Heath, Battle of, 28–9
Blount, Sir Thomas, 167
Bluet, Robert, 51
Boleyn, Anne, 15, 177–8, 180
Bosworth, Battle of, 13, 27, 29, 36, 41–2, 46, 83
Boteler, Eleanor, 11
Bray, Sir Reginald, 12, 32, 135
Brittany, 10, 12–13, 58, 71
Broke, Lord Willoughby de, 58
Buckingham, Edward (Stafford), Duke of, 128–9
Buckingham, Henry (Stafford), Duke of, 11–12, 24
Burgundy, Duchess of see York, Margaret of
Butler, Agnes, 51
Bywymble, Alice, 51

Cadwaladr, King, 17
Calais, 92
The Calendar of State Papers: Spain, 139, 142
Cambria, Countess of, 133
Camelot, 1–2, 17–18
Cancer, testicular, 162–71
Carlson, David, 86
Catalina, Infanta, of Spain see Aragon, Katherine of
Celestial code, 130
Charles V, King of Spain, 177, 185
Charles VIII, King of France, 58, 70–2, 74, 81, 106
Cheney, John, 40
Church law, 15–16
Civitas Dei (St Augustine), 86
Clarence, George, Duke of, 8, 10–11, 35
Cleves, Anne of, 180
Clifford, Sir Robert, 83
Collection, Royal, 135
Consummation, Arthur and Katherine's, 133, 145–50
Cork, 71–2
Cornwall, 89–91
Courtenay, Peter, Bishop, 31, 39
Coventry, 38, 40, 92
Cradles, 48
Croft, Sir Richard, 79, 159, 167
Cromwell, Thomas, 179
Cuero, Johan de, 155
Cunningham, Sean, 164

Damys, William, 16
Darcy, Lady Elizabeth, 49–50, 67, 78–9
Daubeney, Giles, 55
Davies, Piers, 135
Death of Arthur, 162–71

Derby, Lord Thomas Stanley, Earl of *see* Stanley, Thomas, Earl of Derby
De Vere, John, Earl of Oxford, 27–8, 30–2, 37–8, 40, 65, 133
Devon, Earl of, 91
Digby, Benjamin, 16–17
Disease, 163–4
Dorset, Marquess of, 37–8, 176
Dowry, Katherine of Aragon's, 56–7
Dudley, Thomas, 167
Duwes, Giles, 85

Edenham, Dr, 168
Edward II, 60
Edward IV, 7–8, 10, 23, 26
Edward, Prince, of Middleham, 61
Edward, Prince, of Westminster, 60–1
Edward V, 10–11
   see also Princes in the Tower
Elizabeth of York, Queen *see* York, Queen Elizabeth of
Essex, Earl of, 30, 65
Estrada, Ferdinand, Duke of, 147–8

Farnham Castle, 34, 39–40, 48–9
Ferdinand II of Aragon *see* Monarchs of Spain, Catholic
Fernandez, Fray Diego, 180
Fisher, Thomas, 69
FitzGerald, Gerald, 88
Fitzwalter, John, Lord, 83
Flamank, Thomas, 91
Foxe, Richard, Bishop, 55, 86
France, 13, 26, 70–4, 108–10
French-Brittany wars, 58
Frost, Robert, 80–1
Fuensalida, Gutierre Gomez de, 123, 142, 180

Games, 52–3
Gaunt, John of, Duke of Lancaster, 23
Gerard, Lord, 88, 167, 170
Gibbs, Katherine, 50, 69
Gillespie, Simon, 135
Giraldini, Alessandro, 148
Gloucester, Richard, Duke of, 10–11
   see also Richard III
Gof, Michael Joseph an, 91
Great Malvern, 134–5
Grey, Sir John, of Groby, 22, 167
Guildford, Lady, 128
Guildford, Sir Richard, 30

Hall, Edward, 36, 42–3
Health, Arthur's, 138–42
Henry V, 3
Henry VI, 3–9, 22, 26, 60
Henry VII:
   born, 5
   belief in King Arthur (Pendragon), 1–2, 12–13, 17–18, 34
   taken to Brittany, 10, 26
   marries Elizabeth of York, 14–15
   and Edward, Earl of Warwick, 35–42
   banishes Elizabeth Woodville, 42–7
   commissions treaties with Catholic monarchs, 54–7, 109–23
   and Perkin Warbeck, 71–4, 81–4
   leads force against France, 72–3
   visits Katherine, 127
   commits Prince Henry to marry Katherine, 148–9
   relationship with Arthur, 95–7
   and question of consummation, 147–53
   hears of Arthur's death, 165–6
Henry VIII, 101–104, 134
   born, 65

Index

meets Katherine of Aragon for first time, 129
disputes Arthur and Katherine's consumation, 145–6
after Arthur's death, 172–84
Herbert, William, 9
Hever Castle, 135
Historia Regum Britanniae (Geoffrey of Monmouth), 18
Hobbes, Evilyn, 51
Hoo, John, 51
Howard, Edward, 167
Howard, Katheryn, 179–80
Howard, Thomas, 175
Howell, Richard, 68–9
Humanism, 85–6
Hungerford, Edward, 167

Ireland, 35–6, 38, 43, 45, 71–2
Isabella I of Castille *see* Monarchs of Spain, Catholic
Isabella, Princess of Aragon, 116, 122

Jacquetta of Luxembourg, 22
James IV of Scotland, 90, 101–102, 109–14
Jewels and ornaments, Katherine's, 57, 123, 155–8
John, King, 77, 168
Juan, Prince, 106, 116, 121–2, 151

Kenilworth Castle, 38–9
Kent, Earl of, 167
Kingston upon Thames, 128–9

Lancaster, John of, 22
Langton, Thomas, Bishop, 31
League, Holy, against France, 108–10
Le Morte d'Arthur (Thomas Malory), 18

Lewis, Matthew, 43–4
Lewis of Caerleon, Dr, 12, 24
Lincoln, John de la Pole, Earl of *see* Pole, John de la, Earl of Lincoln
Lisle, Viscountess, 74
London, 92–3
Louis XI of France, 26
Lovell, Francis, Viscount, 36
Lovell, Thomas, 37
Ludlow, 10–11
Ludlow Castle, 76–81, 155–60
Luther, Martin, 177–8

Malory, Thomas, 18, 138–9
Maltravers, Lord, 28, 31
Manuel, Donna Elvira, 148
March, Earldom of, 76
March, Edmund, Earl of *see* Edward IV
Margaret Tudor, Princess, 16
Maria, Princess of Aragon, 147–8
Marriage portion paid by Catholic monarchs, 55–7, 111, 155
Marriage validity, 15–16
Mary I, Queen, 185
Maximilian, King of the Romans, 82–4, 107
Mechelen, 81–2
Medina del Campo treaty, 54–7, 105, 155
Mercenaries, German, 38, 40
Mistresses, lady, 49–50
Monarchs of Spain, Catholic, 54, 77, 101, 105–14
 doubt consummation, 147–53
 negotiate Katherine and Arthur's marriage, 54–7, 116–23
 see also Aragon, Katherine of
Monmouth, Geoffrey of, 18
Moorish rebellion in Spain, 122

201

Mortimer's Cross, Battle of, 7
Morton, John, Archbishop, 74
Mould, Philip, 135
Mourdant, John, 159
Musicians, Arthur's, 95–7

Nele, John, 52
Neville, Eleanor, 29
Neville, Richard, 16th Earl of Warwick, 7–9, 27, 29
Norfolk, Duchess of, 125–6, 133
Northampton, Battle of, 6
Northumberland, Earl of, 58
Nurses, Arthur's, 49–51

Ormond, Sir James, 71–2
Owen, Sir David, 32
Oxford, John de Vere, Earl of *see* De Vere, John, Earl of Oxford

Pageants welcoming Katherine of Aragon, 131
Papal dispensations, 149–50
Parliament, 14–15
Parr, Katherine, 179
Philpp, David, 80
Plague, 5
Plantagenet, Arthur, 18
Plantagenet, Edward, 17th Earl of Warwick, 35–42, 117–20
Plantagenet, Margaret, 80
Plantagenet, Richard *see* York, Richard, Duke of
Plymouth, 125
Pole, Cardinal Reginald, 118–19
Pole, John de la, Duke of Suffolk, 3–4, 23
Pole, John de la, Earl of Lincoln, 30, 36–41
Pole, Katherine de la, 3–4

Pole, Sir Richard, 79–80, 100, 114, 159, 167, 171
Portraiture of Arthur, 134–6
Powis, Lord, 167
Poyntz, Thomas, 52
Princes in the Tower, 11–12
   see also Edward V; York, Richard, Duke of
Privy chamber, 73
Proxy weddings, 114
Puebla, Dr Gonzalvo de, 54–5, 108–14, 118–20, 155–6
   see also Ambassadors: Spanish

Radcliffe, Robert, 167
Rede, John, 85
Rhys, Sir Gruffydd ap, 88–9, 137, 167
Richard III, 11–13, 24–5, 29, 103
   see also Gloucester, Richard, Duke of
Richmond, Edmund Tudor, Earl of, 3–5, 23
Rivers, Anthony (Woodville), Earl of, 11
Romsey Abbey, 39
Royal Chapel, 28
Ruthin, Lord Grey, 167

St Albans, Battle of, 6, 22
St Augustine of Hippo, 178–9
St George's Field, 129
St John, Maurice, 88, 100, 146, 167
St Laurence church, Ludlow, 167
St Paul's Cathedral, 131–3
St Swithun, Priory of, 19
Salaries, Royal household, 50, 53
Schwartz, Martin, 40
Sepulveda, Juan de, 54–7
Servants, Arthur's, 51–2
Sex between Arthur and Katherine *see* Consummation, Arthur and Katherine's

Index

Seymour, Jane, 180
Sheen palace, 36, 61
Shrewsbury, Earl of, 40, 167
Simnel, Lambert, 41–7
Simons, Richard, 41
Smith, William, Bishop, 78, 100, 159
Somerset, Edmund, Duke of, 4–5
Somerset, Sir Charles, 32
Stafford, Lord Henry, 23–4, 128–9
Stanley, Sir William, 13, 28–9, 83–4
Stanley, Thomas, Earl of Derby, 10, 13, 24, 28–9, 31, 83
Stannaries, 89–91
Stoke Field, Battle of, 40–2
Stoner, Sir William, 32
Strange, Lord, 29, 40
Surrey, Earl of, 167
The Survival of the Princes in the Tower (Matthew Lewis), 43
Sweating sickness, 164
Swynford, Katherine, 23

Taylor, John, 71–2
Tewkesbury, Battle of, 9
Tickenhill House *see* Bewdley Manor
Tower of London, 11
Towton, Battle of, 7
Tremlett, Giles, 142
Troys, Thomas, 167
Tuberculosis, 164
Tudor, Arthur *see* Arthur, Prince
Tudor, Henry *see* Henry VII
Tudor, Jasper, Duke of Bedford, 3–4, 9–10, 26–7, 47, 159
Tudor, Margaret, 65, 68, 101–102
Tudor, Mary, 101
Tudor, Owen, 3
Tudors, history of, 2–3
Tudur, Owain ap Maredudd ap, 3
Turburvill, Sir John, 30

Uvedale, Sir William, 80, 159, 167, 171

Valois, Katherine of, 3, 10, 26
Vergil, Polydore, 10, 41–3
Vernon, Sir Henry, 80, 159

Wakefield, Battle of, 6
Wales, 2–3
  Prince of, 60–7
  Council of, 75–9
Wangham, William, 51
Warbeck, Perkin, 45, 71–4, 81–4, 90–1, 107–109, 116–20
  see also York, Richard, Duke of
La Warre, Lord, 30
Wars of the Roses, 2
Warwick, Edward Plantagenet, Earl of *see* Plantagenet, Edward, 17th Earl of Warwick
Warwick, Richard Neville, Earl of *see* Neville, Richard, 16th Earl of Warwick
Waynflete, William, Bishop, 49
Wedding of Arthur and Katherine of Aragon, 54–7, 109–14, 131–3
Weir, Alison, 19
Westminster, Palace of, 73
Whytyng, John, 52, 69
Wilford, Ralph, 116
Williams, Professor Patrick, 139, 142
Willoughby, Sir Anthony, 88, 146, 167
Winchester, 16–21
Wolsey, Thomas, 149, 151, 176, 179
Woodville, Anthony, 80
Woodville, Edward, 30
Woodville, Elizabeth, 7–13, 26, 99–102
  chosen as Arthur's godmother, 22–3
  banished to Bermondsey Abbey, 42–7

Woodville, Katherine, 26
Woodville, Richard, 22
Worcester Cathedral, 77, 168–70
Worsley, William, Dean, 83

York, Anne of, 30
York, Cecily of, 30
York, Margaret of, 37–40, 74, 115–16
York, Princess Katherine of, 183
York, Queen Elizabeth of, 2, 4, 7–8, 38–9, 113
    marries Henry VII, 14–15
    pregnancies, 15–16, 59
    confinement and birth of Arthur, 18–23
    moves to Farnham Castle, 34
    gives birth to Margaret Tudor, 65
    relationship with her children, 97–9
    hears of Arthur's death, 165–6
    death, 183
York, Richard, Duke of, 5–6, 11
    see also Princes in the Tower; Warbeck, Perkin